Teaching and Researching Speaking

Teaching and Researching Speaking provides an overview of the main approaches to researching spoken language and their practical application to teaching, classroom materials, and assessment. The history and current practices of teaching and researching speaking are presented through the lens of bigger theoretical issues about the object of study in linguistics, social attitudes to the spoken form, and the relationships between spoken and written language. A unique feature of the book is the way it clearly explains the nature of speaking and how it is researched and puts it into the context of a readable and holistic overview of language theory. This new edition is fully updated and revised to reflect the latest developments on classroom materials and oral assessment, as well as innovations in conversation analysis. The resources section is brought up-to-date with new media and currently available networks, online corpora, and mobile applications. This is a key resource for applied linguistics students, English language teachers, teacher trainers, and novice researchers.

Rebecca Hughes is Director of Education at the British Council and Honorary Chair of Applied Linguistics and International Education at the University of Nottingham, Malaysia Campus.

Beatrice Szczepek Reed is Reader in Education at the University of York, UK.

Applied Linguistics in Action
Series Editor: Christopher N. Candlin

Applied Linguistics in Action is a series which focuses on the issues and challenges to teachers and researchers in a range of fields in Applied Linguistics and provides readers and users with the tools they need to carry out their own practice-based research.

Teaching and Researching Lexicography
R.R.K. Hartmann

Teaching and Researching Computer-Assisted Language Learning, 2nd Edition
Ken Beatty

Teaching and Researching Motivation, 2nd Edition
Zoltán Dörnyei and Ema Ushioda

Teaching and Researching Autonomy in Language Learning, 2nd Edition
Phil Benson

Teaching and Researching Reading, 2nd Edition
William Peter Grabe and Fredricka L. Stoller

Teaching and Researching Language and Culture, 2nd Edition
Joan Kelly Hall

Teaching and Researching Translation, 2nd Edition
Basil A. Hatim

Teaching and Researching Listening, 3rd Edition
Michael Rost

Teaching and Researching Writing, 3rd Edition
Ken Hyland

Teaching and Researching Speaking

Rebecca Hughes

with Beatrice Szczepek Reed

Third Edition

Routledge
Taylor & Francis Group

NEW YORK AND LONDON

Third edition published 2017
by Routledge
711 Third Avenue, New York, NY 10017

and by Routledge
2 Park Square, Milton Park, Abingdon, Oxon, OX14 4RN

Routledge is an imprint of the Taylor & Francis Group, an informa business

First edition published 2002 by Pearson Education Limited

Second edition published 2011 by Pearson Education Limited

Library of Congress Cataloging in Publication Data
Names: Hughes, Rebecca, 1962– author. | Szczepek Reed,
    Beatrice, 1973– author.
Title: Teaching and researching speaking / Rebecca Hughes,
    Beatrice Szczepek Reed.
Description: Third Edition. | New York, NY : Routledge, [2017] |
    "Second edition published 2011 by Pearson Education Limited."
Identifiers: LCCN 2016024160 | ISBN 9781138911741 (Hardback) |
    ISBN 9781138911758 (Paperback) | ISBN 9781315692395
    (Master) | ISBN 9781317432999 (Web PDF) | ISBN
    9781317432982 (ePub) | ISBN 9781317432975 (Mobipocket/
    Kindle)
Subjects: LCSH: Oral communication—Study and teaching. | Oral
    communication—Study and teaching—Research.
Classification: LCC P95.3 .H84 2017 | DDC 302.2/242—dc23
LC record available at https://lccn.loc.gov/2016024160

ISBN: 978-1-138-91174-1 (hbk)
ISBN: 978-1-138-91175-8 (pbk)
ISBN: 978-1-315-69239-5 (ebk)

Typeset in Goudy
by Apex CoVantage, LLC

Printed and bound in Great Britain by
TJ International Ltd, Padstow, Cornwall

To my mother, Alyna Hughes, 1918–2009.

Contents

List of Figures   x
List of Tables   xi
Series Editor Preface   xii
Acknowledgements   xiv
Publisher Acknowledgements   xv

SECTION I

Issues in Teaching and Researching Speaking   1

1   **Conceptual and Historical Background**   3
   1.1   Introduction 3
   1.2   The Skill of Speaking 3
   1.3   The Nature of Speech in Contrast to Writing 7
   1.4   Where Does Speech Fit in Language Studies? 13
   1.5   Summary 25

2   **The Research Space: Paradigms and Issues**   26
   2.1   Introduction 26
   2.2   Classical Research Paradigms in Relation to Researching
       Speaking 26
   2.3   Attitudes to Speech Data 30
   2.4   The Applicability of Research Approaches and Frameworks
       to the Study of Speech 34
   2.5   Levels of Analysis 35
   2.6   Summary 45

SECTION II

Issues for Teaching and Assessing Speaking   47

3   **Approaches, Materials, and the Issue of 'Real' Speech**   49
   3.1   Introduction 49

3.2 *What Are Our Models and Standards When*
      We Teach Speaking? 49
3.3 *The Evolution of Materials to Teach Speaking 65*
3.4 *The Current Scene in Materials to Teach Speaking 73*
3.5 *Bringing the Skills Together 83*
3.6 *Summary 85*

4   Issues in Assessing Speaking   86
4.1 *Introduction 86*
4.2 *Why the Nature of Speaking Is a Challenge for Test*
      Designers 92
4.3 *Oral Assessment in Three High-Stakes Tests 106*
4.4 *Summary 121*

5   Approaches to Researching Speech   123
5.1 *Introduction 123*
5.2 *Quantitative and Qualitative Approaches Towards*
      Researching Speaking 125
5.3 *Theory-Driven, Positional, or Ideas-Based Approaches to*
      Researching Speaking 129
5.4 *Examples of Contrasting Approaches in Researching*
      Speaking 132
5.5 *New Directions 150*

SECTION III
Researching Speaking   155

6   Spoken Language and the Classroom   157
6.1 *Introduction 157*
6.2 *The Status of Speaking in Classrooms 158*
6.3 *The Role of Spoken Interaction in Communicative*
      Language Teaching Classrooms 162
6.4 *Drawing on Classroom Practice for Research and Vice*
      Versa 167
6.5 *Summary 171*

7   Research Project Ideas and Frameworks   173
7.1 *Introduction 173*
7.2 *A Project on Spoken Language Found in Textbooks Versus*
      a Corpus 173

7.3 A Project on the Effects of Speech Rate in the Context of English as Lingua Franca Presentations 178

7.4 An Exploration of Intercultural Expectations in Conversation 181

7.5 A Project That Analyses a Professional Speaking Genre So It Can Be Handled in the Classroom 185

7.6 A Project on Speaking Assessment With Low Education Immigrant Test Takers 189

7.7 A Project Investigating the Relationship Between Gesture and Speech Processing Using fMRI Scanning Techniques 193

SECTION IV
Resources and Further Information 197

8 Research Borders and Boundaries 199
8.1 Introduction 199
8.2 Speaking and Ethnographic or Cross-Cultural Studies 200
8.3 Speaking and Psycholinguistics 201
8.4 Speaking and Neurolinguistic Studies 201
8.5 Speaking and Corpus Linguistics 202
8.6 Speaking and New Technologies 203

9 Research Resources 204
9.1 Journals and E-Journals 204
9.2 Societies and Organisations 206
9.3 Online Resources 207
9.4 Speech Corpora 208
9.5 Speech Recognition and Text-to-Speech 209
9.6 Online Pronunciation and Intonation Resources 209
9.7 Miscellaneous Sites for the Applied Linguist With an Interest in Spoken Discourse 210
9.8 Moving Towards Your Own Project on Spoken Discourse 210
9.9 Sources of Inspiration for Research 212
9.10 Research Skills Summaries 216

References 219
Index 234

Figures

1.1   Levels and Fields of Research Into Speech and Conversation   5
1.2   Aspects of Production   8
1.3   Social Aspects of Spoken and Written Discourse   8
3.1   Spoken Data in Theoretically Orientated Models of Grammar   51
3.2   Spoken Data in Descriptively Orientated Models of Grammar   52
3.3   Word Cloud of Teachers' Responses to What They Enjoy About Teaching Speaking   74
3.4   Word Cloud of Teachers' Responses to What They Find Challenging About Teaching Speaking   75
4.1   End Points of a Continuum of Oral Test Types   105
4.2   Categories Underlying the Speaking Construct   108
5.1   Action Graph Showing Gesture Timings in Relation to Spoken Directions   150
9.1   Information Exchanges Between Academe and Classrooms   211
9.2   A Possible Cycle of Information Exchange Between Teachers, Researchers, and Publishers   211

Tables

1.1 Comparison of Prevalence of 'Writing' and 'Speaking' in
    Scholarly Articles as Indicated by Key Word Search   12
2.1 Branches of Linguistics in Relation to Data and the
    Relevance of Mode   29
2.2 Extract From National Institute of Education Singapore
    Corpus of Spoken Singaporean English   36
4.1 Based on TOEFL Test ETS Independent Speaking Rubrics   109
4.2 Top and Bottom Criteria for the IELTS Speaking Test   114
4.3 Summary of Perceived Negative Features in Oral Discourse
    Represented in iBT Speaking and IELTS Speaking   115
4.4 Summary of Perceived Positive Features in Oral Discourse
    Represented in iBT Speaking and IELTS Speaking   115
9.1 Broad Research Questions Growing Out of Previous Work   216
9.2 The Cycle of Research   217
9.3 Examples of Data Commentary and Diverse Functions   217
9.4 Features of Conclusions   218

Series Editor Preface

Applied Linguistics in Action, as its name suggests, is a series which focuses on the issues and challenges to teachers and researchers in a range of fields in applied linguistics and provides readers and users with the tools they need to carry out their own practice-related research.

The books in the series provide the reader with clear, up-to-date, accessible, and authoritative accounts of their chosen field within applied linguistics. Starting from a map of the landscape of the field, each book provides information on its main ideas and concepts, competing issues and unsolved questions. From there, readers can explore a range of practical applications of research into those issues and questions and then take up the challenge of undertaking their own research, guided by the detailed and explicit research guides provided. Finally, each book has a section which provides a rich array of resources, information sources, and further reading, as well as a key to the principal concepts of the field.

Questions the books in this innovative series ask are those familiar to all teachers and researchers, whether very experienced, or new to the fields of applied linguistics.

- What does research tell us, what doesn't it tell us, and what should it tell us about the field? How is the field mapped and landscaped? What is its geography?
- How has research been applied, and what interesting research possibilities does practice raise? What are the issues we need to explore and explain?
- What are the key researchable topics that practitioners can undertake? How can the research be turned into practical action?
- Where are the important resources that teachers and researchers need? Who has the information? How can it be accessed?

Each book in the series has been carefully designed to be as accessible as possible, with built-in features to enable readers to find what they want quickly and to home in on the key issues and themes that concern them. The structure is to move from practice to theory and back to practice in a cycle of development of understanding of the field in question.

Each of the authors of books in the series is an acknowledged authority, able to bring broad knowledge and experience to engage teachers and researchers in following up their own ideas, working with them to build further on *their* own experience.

The first editions of books in this series have attracted widespread praise for their authorship, their design, and their content, and have been widely used to support practice and research. The success of the series and the realisation that it needs to stay relevant in a world where new research is being conducted and published at a rapid rate have prompted the commissioning of this third edition. This new edition has been thoroughly updated, with accounts of research that has appeared since the previous edition and with the addition of other relevant material. We trust that students, teachers, and researchers will continue to discover inspiration in these pages to underpin their own investigations.

Chris Candlin
David Hall

Acknowledgements

I would like to thank all those who have helped me in the process of writing this book including my co-author, Beatrice Szczepek Reed. Beatrice and I have highly complementary areas of research interest in relation to spoken mode, and I was delighted when she accepted my suggestion that she become a collaborator on this third edition of my book, which was first published in 2002. It has been a huge pleasure to work with her on this, and my thanks to her for input, particularly in Chapters 1 and 5. Second, I would like to thank British Council researcher in international education Heather Lonsdale for editorial support to a very high standard and complex work on permissions and copyright for this edition. Heather has been patient, professional, and good humoured throughout and kept the two busy authors on track and to deadline (which was not always an inevitable outcome). I would also like to thank colleagues at British Council, particularly Dr Jo Beall, for the support given me in finishing this edition alongside other commitments.

British Council English teachers in eight countries gave invaluable input to the book, and I would like to thank the following in this respect: Lesley Ashcroft, Rachael Burnham, Riadh Chelly, Katarzyna Chodzko, Ana Garcia-Stone, Yvonne Leonard, Carolyn Leslie, Katy Simpson, Sheona Smith, and Lisa Warner.

Rebecca Hughes, November 2016

Publisher Acknowledgements

We are grateful to the following for permission to reproduce copyright material:

Figures

Figure 2.1 is provided with the kind permission of the National Institute of Education, Singapore. The use of Figure 4.2, 'Categories underlying the speaking construct' (Xi et al., 2008), is granted by John Wiley and Sons on behalf of Educational Testing Service. Figure 5.1 (Clark and Krych, 2004), is taken from 'Speaking while monitoring addressees for understanding', *Journal of memory and language*, 50(1), pp. 62–81, and is used with the kind permission of Elsevier.

Tables

Table 4.1 is adapted from http://www.ets.org/Media/Tests/TEOFL/pdf/Independent_Speaking_Rubrics_2008.pdf (Copyright © 2014 Educational Testing Service. All rights reserved), and its use has been granted by the Educational Testing Service. Table 4.2, Top and bottom criteria for the IELTS speaking test, is adapted from http://www.ielts.org/PDF/OUBDs_SpeakingFinal.pdf (IELTS, 2009), and is supplied with the kind permission of Cambridge English.

Text

Permission for Quotes 1.4 (Biber, D. and Barbieri, F., 2007) and 2.4 (Auer, 2009) is granted by Elsevier.

The use of Quote 3.1 (Yungzhong, 1985) is approved by the Shanghai Foreign Language Education Press. Quotes 3.2 (Carter and McCarthy, 1997), 3.3 (Wallwork, 1997), 3.4 (Carter and McCarthy, 1998), and 3.17 (Anderson and Lynch, 1992) are all used with the permission of Cambridge University Press. Permission for use of Quote 3.8 (Lennon, 1990) is supplied by Wiley. Efforts have been made to trace the owners of the copyright for Quote 3.13 (Hargreaves and Fletcher, 1979), since the original publisher liquidated in 2012, having previously authorised use of this material in earlier editions of this book. Use of Quote 3.18 is kindly permitted by Barron's Educational Services, Inc.

Use of Quote 4.5 (Ginther, 2012) is granted by Wiley. Quotes 4.9 (Taylor, 2006) and 4.11 (Gan et al., 2009) are used with the permission of Oxford University Press. Quote 4.13 (Fulcher, 2003), is kindly permitted by Taylor and Francis. Quote 4.19 is from http://www.ets.org/toefl/ibt/scores/improve/speaking_familiar_fai (ETS, 2016b) and is used with the kind permission of the Educational Testing Service (Copyright © 2008 Educational Testing Service. All rights reserved). Quote 4.20 (IELTS, 2016a) is from https://www.ielts.org/about-the-test/test-format-in-detail and is used by kind permission of Cambridge English. Quotes 4.21 and 4.22 are kindly permitted by Trinity College London.

Quotes 5.1 and 5.2 (Mushin and Gardner, 2009), 5.9 (Morton, 2009), 5.10 (Blake, 2009), 5.11 (Wolf, 2008), and 5.12 and 5.13 (Clark and Krych, 2004) are all used with the kind permission of Elsevier. Use of Quote 5.3 (Liberman, 1998) is permitted by Springer, and Quotes 5.4 (Uppstad and Tonnessen, 2007) and 5.6 (Speer and Ito, 2009) by Wiley. For Quote 5.5 (Gussenhoven, 2002), the author assumes copyright and grants permission for its use here. Permission for the use of quote in Chapter 5 from Ohala (1994) is kindly permitted by Cambridge University Press.

The use of Quotes 6.2 (Walsh, 2006) and 6.3 (Widdowson, 1972) has been granted by the kind permission of Oxford University Press and has been endorsed by the works' own authors. Permission to use Quotes 6.5 (Ellis et al., 2002), 7.3 (Hincks, 2010), 7.4 and 7.5 (Cheng and Tsui, 2009), 7.6 and 7.7 (Burns and Moore, 2008), 7.8 (Simpson, 2006), and 7.9 (Straube et al., 2010) are all granted with the kind permission of Elsevier. Permission to use Quotes 7.1 and 7.2 (Lam, 2010) are granted by the kind permission of Oxford University Press.

Permission for the use of Quote 9.1 (Tyler, Jeffries, and Davies, 1988) is granted by Wiley. Efforts have been made to establish permission for Quote 9.5 (Haynes, 1992).

In some instances we have been unable to trace the owners of copyright material, and we would appreciate any information that would enable us to do so.

Section I

Issues in Teaching and Researching Speaking

1 Conceptual and Historical Background

This chapter will . . .

- describe some of the defining features of spoken discourse;
- provide a historical context for the attitudes to teaching and researching speech;
- begin to highlight some of the issues in teaching and researching speaking arising from attitudes to speech that have tended to prevail in linguistic theory.

1.1 Introduction

This chapter discusses the status of speech in society at different points in time and in linguistic theory and practice in particular. A significant issue which I will be addressing throughout this book is the fact that the spoken form gained primacy of status in language studies in the twentieth century to the point where there was, and there remains, a merging in applied linguistic and wider research circles of the concept of 'speaking' with 'language'. This convergence has had an impact on how the form is assessed, taught, and researched, as later chapters will show.

The chapter explains this process, why it is significant, and why, paradoxically, it has led to a lack of explicit attention within linguistic theory to the faculty of speech in its own right. The conceptual and historical overviews in this chapter are intended to provide an analysis of some of the implications of this issue for the practice and theory of language teaching that the later chapters deal with in detail.

1.2 The Skill of Speaking

Quote 1.1 sets out an early statement of the difficulty societies have in focusing on the skill of speaking in its own right when it comes to pedagogy. The factors that lead to this are dealt with in the following sections.

Quote 1.1   An early plea for the teaching of speaking in its own right

With regard indeed to the pronunciation of our tongue, the obstacles are great; and in the present state of things almost insuperable. But all this apparent difficulty arises from our utter neglect of examining and regulating our speech; as nothing has hitherto been done, either by individuals, or societies, towards a right method of teaching it.

(Sheridan, 1781: v–vi)

1.2.1   Speaking Is Not a Discrete Skill

One of the central difficulties inherent in the study of speaking is that it overlaps with a considerable number of other areas and disciplines. How far, for instance, is the structure of conversation culturally determined (also dealt with in pragmatics and ethnography)? How far is the grammar and vocabulary of speech different from other sorts of grammar (which is related also to the fields of syntax and semantics)? How is language represented and processed in the brain, and how does this make human speech production possible (neurolinguistics, psycholinguistics)? In addition to these there are two core disciplines that directly address speaking. The first is the combined fields of phonetics and phonology, which cover the physical nature of sound production and the way it relates to the meanings conveyed by language. The second is the related areas of (spoken) discourse analysis and conversation analysis, where the social behaviours that humans engage in through speaking are explored. The way in which these areas of interest broadly relate to areas of activity in linguistics can be seen in Figure 1.1.

This book attempts to carve out a niche for speaking in its own right whilst relating it from time to time for clarity to three distinct areas that are commonly used in linguistic descriptions: the global or discourse level, the structural level, and the level of speech production.

1.2.2   Core Skills for Speaking in the Real World

In order to speak, humans need to be able to articulate the sounds of language. Articulation is one of the main concerns of the discipline of phonetics. Each language sound is produced through the interplay of a number of speech organs, or 'articulators', such as the vocal folds, the lips, and the tongue. In the second language-learning classroom, pronunciation teaching often focuses on how individual sounds are produced in the new language, especially if they do not exist in the learners' first language. A related but often neglected area is

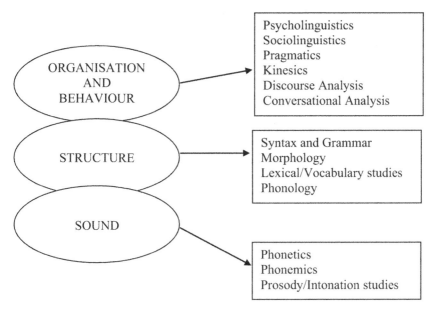

Figure 1.1 Levels and Fields of Research Into Speech and Conversation.

how the more 'musical' elements of speech production, such as intonation and speech rhythm, influence the meaning of words and sentences. These elements are often referred to as the prosodic aspects of speech. Both the pronunciation of sounds and the prosodic delivery of utterances are core skills for speaking.

In order to speak *meaningfully* in real-world conversations, humans not only need to be able to pronounce sounds, words, and sentences correctly according to the comparatively static rules of a given language, but they need to be able to do so in the socially appropriate manner at the time of speaking. This skill is referred to as communicative, or interactional, competence. In the fields of spoken discourse analysis and conversation analysis researchers have investigated natural conversation for many decades. Their results show that everyday talk has its own rules and systematics, which are very different from written language use (see also Section 1.3). Speaking successfully requires the mastery of interactional patterns and customs, such as how to show that one has finished speaking, how to demonstrate to others that one is listening to them, and when precisely to ask for clarification.

1.2.3   *Teaching Speaking Is Not Easily Separated From Other Objectives*

When the spoken language is the focus of classroom activity there are often other aims which the teacher might have. For instance, a task may be carried out to help the student gain awareness of, or to practise, some aspect of linguistic knowledge (whether a grammatical rule or application of a phonemic regularity to which they have been introduced), or to develop pragmatic skills (e.g. how to respond to a compliment appropriately or show that one agrees or disagrees), or to raise awareness of some sociolinguistic point (e.g. how to use the correct style and register in a given context).

1.2.4   Teaching Speaking or Using Speaking to Teach?

A key question to ask, therefore, is whether a teacher is engaged in 'teaching the spoken form of a language' or 'teaching a language through speaking'. This distinction is important although it may seem trivial at first sight. Spoken forms of language have been underresearched, whether at the level of grammar or in broader genre-based studies. I will be arguing that this is due, in part, to attitudes towards language data in linguistic theory. A teacher or materials writer may feel some confidence in dealing with stable written forms and genres—the essay, the business letter, or the laboratory report—and have a genuine understanding of the language appropriate to newer discourses, such as e-mail, texts, or social media etiquette. However, the notion of how spoken genres are structured and what forms are most typical of them is difficult to establish. I will also be suggesting at various points in this book that there is a great deal of speaking going on in classrooms but that this may be different from the effective teaching of speaking as a holistic skill. In particular, in Chapter 6, I will suggest that there has been too great a separation of form (grammar and vocabulary) and delivery (pronunciation and fluency). This has had the effect of dislocating the fundamental fabric of spoken mode—fluent intelligibility across a sophisticated range of styles and discourses—from other linguistic features. These are too often taught in isolation from the speaking skills needed to deliver them. A simple example to illustrate this would be the teaching of idioms, for which timing, accurate and fluent delivery, and cultural knowledge of how to place them in a conversation are all key requirements. They are presented as instances of informal conversational linguistic features, but learners are generally taught them when they have a level of productive speech that is too low for them to ever achieve delivery without causing confusion. Far preferable would be to teach simple conversational strategies, such as showing understanding with a response token such as 'mm', with the appropriate timing of delivery and intonation.

1.2.5   Bringing the Facets of Speaking Together

The human voice and the faculty of speech are inherently bound up with the projection of the self into the world. As a second language learner acquires a living language, a large number of aspects other than grammar and vocabulary also need to be acquired for successful communication to take place. These relate to culture, social interaction, and the politeness norms that exist in the target language. To learn to communicate expertly in another language a speaker must change and expand identity as he or she learns the cultural, social, and even political factors which go into language choices and are needed to speak appropriately with a new 'voice'. Therefore, while this book often treats the different 'layers' of speaking—discourse, grammar, and phonology—separately, for the purposes of analysis, an underlying theme is that the teacher will ultimately need to help the student bring all these elements together into a new, unified, and appropriate means of communication on the journey from beginner to fluent speaker of another language.

Quote 1.2   The authors of the *Cambridge Advanced Grammar of English* on what speech data can tell us about a word which is generally described as a preposition

Like can be placed in end position in order to qualify a preceding statement. It also indicates that the words chosen may not be appropriate:

> *Then she got out of the car all of a sudden **like**, and this bike hit her right in the back.*
> *It was a shattering, frightening experience **like**.*

Like is very commonly used (particularly among younger speakers) as a marker of reported speech, especially where the report involves a dramatic representation of someone's response or reaction:

> *So this bloke came up to me and **I'm like** 'Go away, I don't want to dance'.*
> *And my **mum's like** nonstop three or four times 'Come and tell your Grandma about your holiday'.*

(Carter and McCarthy, 2006: 101–2)

1.3   The Nature of Speech in Contrast to Writing

Figures 1.2 and 1.3 provide a visual summary of some of the major, very general contrasts between the spoken and the written forms of language. Further information about the written form aimed at a similar audience to this book can be found in *Teaching and Researching Writing* (Hyland, 2015). Figure 1.2, 'Aspects of Productions', represents aspects that relate to how the two forms are generated, and Figure 1.3, 'Social Aspects', deals with tendencies in attitudes to the two forms.

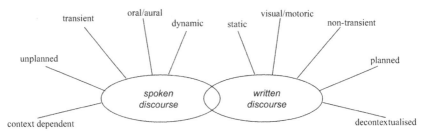

Figure 1.2 Aspects of Production.

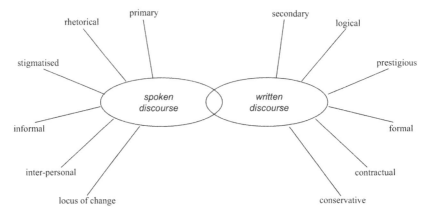

Figure 1.3 Social Aspects of Spoken and Written Discourse.

1.3.1   How Speech Reaches the World

When speech is considered in opposition to writing, several distinctive features become evident, particularly if the way it is produced is taken as the starting point (see Figure 1.2). Many of these features also affect the skill of listening, dealt with more fully in *Teaching and Researching Listening* (Rost, 2015).

Most important and generally least considered in a linguistic discipline dominated by texts and recording of texts is the fact that the spoken form of any language is fundamentally transient. When a word is spoken, this event happens within the 'co-ordinates' of a particular place and moment, and these can never be reduplicated, although we can now record the word via several different media.

A second, related, factor underpinning the nature of speech and affecting the type of language choices that can be made is its delivery via the oral/aural channel.

Concept 1.1   Channel

A term used to describe the physical means by which communication takes place. In terms of speaking there is the aural/oral channel and in terms of writing the visual/motoric channel. Discourse can be studied in terms of the effects of channel on the language. These include the constraints of speech processing in real time versus the capacity to reflect and edit what the written channel allows.

Whether in face-to-face situations or via televisual or other media, language which is spoken spontaneously in a way that is easy to comprehend is quite different from texts created to be read. One of the most common problems in oral presentations is information overload for listeners as they try to process densely informative language that has been prepared via a written text. Several studies over a number of years have shown that speakers 'package' their information differently from writers, whether at the level of the clause or through vocabulary choices (Chafe and Danielewicz, 1987; Biber, 2006), and subsequent chapters will look at these features in more detail.

Quotes 1.3 and 1.4   Language choices in speech as opposed to writing

Choosing lexical items is partly a matter of choosing aptly and explicitly, and partly a matter of choosing the appropriate level. In the first case, the deliberateness and editability inherent in writing lead to a more richly varied, less hedged, and more explicit use of words. Speakers are so strongly constrained by their need to produce language rapidly and by their inability to edit, that they are unable to imitate the lexical richness and explicitness of writing even when, as in lecturing, such qualities would be especially valued. In the second case, although the separate histories of spoken and written language have led to partially divergent vocabularies, it is not as hard for speakers to borrow liberally from the written lexicon, or conversely for writers to borrow from the spoken. Thus lectures that are more literary than conversations, and letters more conversational than academic papers. The constraints are not imposed by cognitive limitations, but by judgements of appropriateness.

(Chafe and Danielewicz, 1987: 94)

In contrast, previous research on university registers has found that mode differences are by far the most important in accounting for linguistic variation: spoken university registers are consistently different from written university registers in the use of a wide range of lexical and grammatical features (see, e.g. Biber, 2006, chap. 8). For example, verbal and clausal features are common in all spoken university registers and relatively rare in all written registers. In contrast, complex noun phrase features are common in all written university registers and relatively rare in all spoken registers. The results of previous 'multi-dimensional' analyses similarly show a fundamental divide between the spoken and written university registers (see, e.g. Biber, Conrad, Reppen, Byrd, and Helt, 2002): all spoken university registers, regardless of purpose, are 'involved', 'situated in reference', and characterized by the absence of 'impersonal' styles; in contrast, all written university registers, again regardless of purpose, are highly 'informational', 'elaborated in reference', and marked for 'impersonal' styles.

(Biber and Barbieri, 2007: 282)

Further salient aspects of the way speech is produced again relate to the transient and situated nature of the spoken channel. The vast bulk of spoken material is spontaneous, face-to-face, informal conversation. This kind of discourse is generally unplanned, dynamic, and context dependent. A conversation may be led by one speaker or another who wishes to deal with a particular topic; however, the vagaries of real-time contexts mean that most speech takes the form of a give and take, not only between speakers but also between the discourse and the context. The type of interesting study which can arise from this is how topics and topic changes are managed by speakers, how speakers accommodate themselves to one another, how misunderstandings between speakers are 'repaired', how activity affects language produced, or how reference is made to new/old information within a conversation.

1.3.2   How Speech Is Regarded

Figure 1.3 summarises some of the typical attitudes to speech, particularly as it is regarded in literate societies where the function of spoken and written forms are generally clearly demarcated.

Although some theorists, for example Vachek (1973), have argued that the written form of language should be regarded as a separate and wholly independent language system, the spoken form has generally been regarded as the primary form of language upon which the written form is essentially dependent.

One of the reasons for this is that, in the absence of a pathological reason to prevent it, all humans develop the capacity for speech, and it is only later in literate societies (and in the history of humankind) that the skill of writing develops. Hence, in Figure 1.3 the indication 'primary' versus 'secondary' for the spoken and written forms.

Quotes 1.5 and 1.6   Two different views of the 'transferability' of speech into writing

It may sometimes happen that an utterance primarily intended for listening needs reading, and vice versa . . . In such cases . . . transposition from the one into the other material is not done with the intention of expressing the given content by means of the other material; if it were so, the only possible accomplishment of the task would be to replace the spoken utterance with the written one or vice versa.

(Vachek, 1966: 154)

If a text is unintelligible when read aloud, it will also be unintelligible in writing, since the writing merely symbolises the spoken expression.

(Halliday, 1989: 44)

The spoken form is very highly valued in linguistics and applied linguistics, where it is regarded as the primary form of a language and the source of innovation and language change. In the realm of second language teaching there is also a high degree of attention paid to the skill of speaking. Indeed, to be a fluent *speaker* in a language is often the layperson's goal. The source of input in highly influential 'communicative approaches' is largely the spoken form, and, as I have previously noted, there has been a conflation in linguistics of the term 'language' with 'speech', as if the two are entirely interchangeable.

This is due, in part, to the dominance of theories of first language acquisition that influenced theories of second language acquisition throughout the twentieth century. The spoken form is the basis for investigations in first language acquisition. Since no child learns to write before he or she learns to speak, the spoken mode is the only mode available for consideration and, therefore, in first language acquisition studies the issue of distinguishing 'language' from 'speech' is irrelevant. However, paradoxically, there is very little attention paid to the spoken skill in its own right to be judged by its own criteria in the world of linguistics, or of language teaching. A survey of respected international journals in the field will find many more articles dealing explicitly with the written form than with the spoken. An Internet search of scholarly activity using the key terms 'writing' and 'speaking' in the social sciences, arts, and humanities suggests that there may be a growing attention to spoken mode but that the balance of attention given to each form remains strongly in favour of the written:

Table 1.1 Comparison of Prevalence of 'Writing' and 'Speaking' in Scholarly Articles as Indicated by Key Word Search

Key word	1995–2005	2006–2016
Writing	192,050	176,822
Speaking	34,228	78,263

Source: *Web of Science* (2016); accessed 15 April 2016.

There is a similar 'invisibility' factor at work in the teaching and researching of the skill of listening (see also Rost, 2015, in this series for further discussion of listening as a discrete skill).

This is not the place to debate at length the issue of the relative positions of the two forms—speech and writing—in the discipline of linguistics; however, it is important to understand that the innate, universal human capacity for speech has led to its being regarded as the central form of interest to linguists. Therefore, even when theorists appear to pay no attention to actual instances of speech, fundamentally they are pursuing questions related to the primary language faculty. This faculty is the universal linguistic form: speech.

Ironically, however, although the spoken form takes pride of place in linguistic theory, its status is more ambiguous in society in general. The nature of and, therefore, the functions to which written language is put (most significantly its use as the medium of the binding contract and other legal functions) mean that it is generally held in higher esteem in literate society than the spoken form.

Speech is also quintessentially the form in which the interpersonal functions of language are carried out, and the form is subject to the benefits and disadvantages that stem from the way it is produced, as detailed earlier and summarised in Figure 1.3. Therefore, whereas the tangible, nonephemeral nature of writing lends it to logical and contractual functions in society, for example record keeping and legal tasks, the spoken form, being essentially more dependent on the time and place it is produced, is used for more informal or rhetorically based tasks. A powerful political speaker can sway an audience by oratorical devices in debate, but it is the written act of Parliament that can be scrutinised and redrafted which eventually becomes law. Moreover, while you can be known to all your friends and work colleagues by a first name quite different from the name on your passport, to change your name so that it becomes accepted on this legally recognised written document you must engage in an extensive legal process.

A final point to consider, but one of very great importance in terms of language change, is that the spoken form of a language tends to be the laboratory for linguistic innovation. New linguistic items, words and, less quickly, grammatical features tend to be generated in the spoken, rather than the written, form of a language as speakers accommodate their language behaviour to one another and fashions of speaking come and go. As new media such as text messaging on mobile phones, Internet chat rooms, e-mail, and other electronically delivered forms of writing emerge, this distinction between the speed of innovation in the aural/oral and the visual/motoric channels has become increasingly blurred. However, it is in the deeply interactive forms of language, where people affect one another's language judgements as they communicate in ways that are less restricted by stable, widely accepted conventions, that rapid alterations to language can take place. Despite new media (and in fact because of them in the case of the influences of the Internet and other electronic media), speech remains the most important locus of change in a language.

To sum up, when speech is looked at both in terms of how it is produced and how it is regarded, some of the paradoxes and unique challenges involved in studying it come to the fore. This is particularly true when the form is looked at in comparison with the written. For the teacher and for the researcher the dynamic, ever-changing, interpersonally oriented and contextually defined nature of speech can be both a benefit and a drawback.

1.4   Where Does Speech Fit in Language Studies?

I suggested earlier that there has tended to be a collapsing together in the discipline of linguistics of the concepts 'language faculty' and the 'faculty of speech'. This in turn has clear repercussions on what comes under the scope of 'research into speaking' at the current time. For if language and speech are seen as indistinguishable, one kind of research will be carried out, and if they are regarded as distinct areas for investigation, then different kinds of research—ones that attend to channel, mode, and context—will be seen as appropriate.

One of the cornerstones underlying this issue is the paradigm set out by Noam Chomsky in the 1960s and which in turn has underpinned the greater part of second language acquisition studies, advances in grammatical models, and computer programming in which a linguistic element is required. A central aspect to the discussion of speech is the dichotomy between the language faculty (for which Chomsky and subsequent scholars use the term 'competence') and the way language is used in actual speech or writing ('performance'). Essentially, this division stemmed from Chomsky's questioning of how children can master language and master it in such a way that, eventually, any speaker of a language can create and understand an infinite amount of discourse, most of it entirely new (see Concept Box 1.2 for further information).

Concept 1.2   Competence

Human beings do not have infinite brain power, and when they produce or comprehend language, they cannot, Chomsky argued, simply recognise or process each new example of language afresh. Therefore, Chomsky suggested that there must be an underlying, more basic, language capacity which could generate infinite sentences but was itself pared down enough to be within finite human abilities. This language faculty is what is referred to as 'competence'. Competence, the innate language potential which all babies seem to be born with, contrasts with the samples of language which any individual baby might hear. Debate continues about the role of input in language acquisition, but, in terms of theory, the peculiarities of any particular speaker, sample of speech, or actual instantiation of a phoneme are categorised as 'performance'. Performance, it is argued, since it is open to the vagaries of individuals, is not really very useful to language theorists. Therefore, in this highly influential distinction, speech data have no place in 'pure' language science, which is more interested in finding out about the nature of competence.

Concept 1.3   Rationalism and empiricism in linguistics

Rationalist and empiricist schools of thought are generally described in contrast to one another. As an empirical approach to something values real-world data, a linguist of this persuasion takes it as fundamental that samples of language and 'Language' are inextricably linked. A rationalist, on the other hand, would suggest that we must look inside the brain or the mind in order to investigate 'Language' and, further, would propose the idea that examples of data from the real world are unhelpful and even misleading. The strong influence of the rationalist approach has clear implications for the study of the spoken form, as it has tended to move the debate towards idealised and decontextualised examples which in turn fit better with the norms of writing than of speech.

The notion that humans have an innate, more recently articulated as a biological or genetic, language ability, which provides the basis for all language use no matter how seemingly diverse, developed in the twentieth century in opposition to earlier behaviourist models. These two opposing camps, one based on the notion of an innate cognitive model which sees the human child as 'preprogrammed' at birth to learn to speak, the other seeing learning as wholly dependent on an external stimulus, have a strong bearing on both the status of speech data in linguistic science and on theories of teaching language. The second half of the twentieth century saw the rationalist camp win the theoretical battle (see also Concept Boxes 1.2, 1.3., and 1.4).

The rationalist model grew from dissatisfaction with the highly situated nature of earlier behaviourist explanations of language that relied entirely upon tangible, quantifiable data for input. The rationalist paradigm placed greater store on the logic of the underlying abstract system than on data, and particularly speech data.

Concept 1.4 Behaviourism

This concept is strongly associated with the American psychologist B. F. Skinner (1904–1990). The philosophy behind behaviourist models is that learning takes place through interaction with the world— through exposure to examples, through positive and negative stimuli, and trial and error—rather than from any inner faculty.

A great number of the important current issues in linguistics, therefore, relate to how much a researcher believes that the language system can usefully be abstracted away from the situatedness of speech described in previous sections. For example, in universal grammar studies or second language acquisition work a fundamental assumption is that it is not only acceptable but also necessary to ignore most of the vagaries of real speech data (performance) in order to investigate more significant underlying inherent language faculties (competence). A language learner's speech in the target language may be analysed for patterns of grammatical use and misuse, but this will be investigated to provide evidence as to the state of their underlying linguistic knowledge.

At the other end of the spectrum, researchers in the fields of conversation or discourse analysis deal in the actual texture and dynamics of speech. They look at how language is delivered and how linguistic and paralinguistic mechanisms, for example, eye contact, pausing, or laughter, affect communication. Again, the findings of a particular study will be related to generalisations beyond the limitations of the data analysed, but scholars on this side of the discipline do not in general attempt to link their conclusions to an inherent mental capacity. In these fields there can be seen a swing of the pendulum in recent decades back towards a greater faith in data and against rationalist models (see also Concept Boxes 1.5 and 1.6 for further information about conversation and discourse analysis).

It can be seen from the brief description of rationally versus empirically based approaches to language study (of which Chomskian rationalism and empirically grounded methods such as discourse and conversation analysis have been presented at each end of the spectrum) that the latter will have more direct and immediate relevance to studies of speech than the former. If researchers do not believe that actual examples of speech (or writing) provide a sound basis for reaching conclusions about language, they will not give very much consideration to spoken data for their own sake.

Concept 1.5 Discourse analysis

Many influential ways of looking at language, for example, syntax, regard it as made up of sentences or clauses and investigate the relations between words inside these elements. Discourse analysis, however, is not interested in the relations between items at this level. Rather, it looks beyond the sentence or the clause to see what patterns exist between longer sections of conversation or text. For instance, the pair of sentences, 'Good morning, it's a lovely day!' and 'Goodbye, see you later!' are individually well formed but said one after the other would be rather strange as an opening remark by one person and a response by another. Discourse analysts are interested in what constraints there may be on pairs of exchanges, in the typical patterns of initiation and response, or the organisation of talk more generally. Whereas conversation analysis (see Concept 1.6) only engages with spoken data, discourse analysis deals with both written and spoken mode. When written examples are the basis for the research, the term 'text analysis' will be used as synonymous with 'discourse analysis'.

Concept 1.6 Conversation analysis (CA)

Conversation analysis is a branch of social sciences which investigates the structure and social significance of patterns within conversational data. Conversation analysis shares many features with discourse analysis in that both are interested in structures beyond sentence level and the way stretches of language cohere and relate to one another. However, whereas discourse analysis, in its early forms at least, is concerned with 'rule-like' constraints on patterns of turns in conversation, conversation analysis tends to be more purely descriptive in nature and sociolinguistic in orientation.

Many individual studies have from time to time questioned the scope and role of performance data. For example, Berg (1997) took production errors in speech and in writing as the basis for an investigation of underlying regularities in the language system and in so doing moved from data towards theory. Equally, in the realm of data-driven linguistic research the growth of large corpora of the spoken word together with advances in the technology of storing and analysing corpora of speech data mean that there is a growing potential for generalisable conclusions to be made about patterns of speech and speech behaviour. In time, and with a growth of coherent research projects being carried out on them, these corpus-based generalisations may come to match the theoretically elegant conclusions of rationalist frameworks. Finally, cognitive and neurolinguistic approaches are pointing up fascinating insights about the processing demands of the spoken and written forms of a language. These emerging approaches are dealt with in Chapters 6 and 7.

1.4.1   *Historical Perspectives on Speaking*

The divisions between researchers who rely more heavily on data and those who treat them with some suspicion did not spring into being in the middle of the twentieth century. Attitudes to the spoken form of language and its position in the curriculum have varied considerably through time and in different cultures. The germ of the debate can be seen in classical philosophy and attitudes to rhetoric described here.

Furthermore, the status which is given to the faculty of speech in a particular society or at a particular point in its history is reflected in the position and emphasis placed on teaching the skill of speaking in the curriculum—something which is as true today as it was in earlier centuries. By looking at how the teaching and study of speech has varied through time, a clearer perspective can be gained on how present attitudes fit into a bigger picture and may point to the ways in which attitudes will change in the future.

Attitudes to the spoken form of language have waxed and waned since the earliest available records of how and why speaking was taught. These attitudes are usually linked to the ephemeral nature of speech production and the fact that, until very recently in the history of humanity, spoken language was directed at a present audience by a physically present speaker. In these key facts lie the strengths and weaknesses of the spoken form. On the one hand, its nature permits a speaker to convince, persuade, argue, or cajole using all the benefits of being physically in view of the listener through gesture, intonation, eye contact, and so on. On the other, unless captured and recorded in some form, the spoken word is fundamentally transient in nature and cannot be checked or scrutinised after the event.

Whereas today the pedagogy of the spoken form tends to be overlooked in favour of the more stable and generally manageable written form, the following brief survey shows that at various times great emphasis has been placed on the teaching of speech.

1.4.2   *Early Attitudes to Speech*

As far back as Ancient Egypt, the art of speaking has been connected to the skill of persuasion, and the ability to influence others by means of rhetoric. One of the earliest extended examples of written language is a five-thousand-year-old papyrus containing advice on the topic of public speaking and disputation for an up-and-coming Egyptian politico: *The Instruction of Ptah-ho-tep and the Instruction of Kegemni* (Gunn, 1906).

Quote 1.7   Attitudes to speaking in ancient Egypt

1. Be not proud because thou art learned; but discourse with the ignorant man, as with the sage. For no limit can be set to skill, neither is there any craftsman that possesseth full advantages. Fair speech is more rare than the emerald that is found by slave-maidens on the pebbles.

2. If thou find an arguer talking, one that is well disposed and wiser than thou, let thine arms fall, bend thy back, be not angry with him if he agree (?) not with thee. Refrain from speaking evilly; oppose him not at any time when he speaketh. If he address thee as one ignorant of the matter, thine humbleness shall bear away his contentions.

3. If thou find an arguer talking, thy fellow, one that is within thy reach, keep not silence when he saith aught that is evil; so shalt thou be wiser than he. Great will be the applause on the part of the listeners, and thy name shall be good in the knowledge of princes.

4. If thou find an arguer talking, a poor man, that is to say not thine equal, be not scornful toward him because he is lowly. Let him alone; then shall he confound himself. Question him not to please thine heart, neither pour out thy wrath upon him that is before thee; it is shameful to confuse a mean mind. If thou be about to do that which is in thine heart, overcome it as a thing rejected of princes.

(Gunn, 1906: 42–3)

With the ancient Greeks the systematisation of argument through speech began with Zeno of Elea (early in the fifth century BC) and reached its height in the teachings of Corax of Syracuse (around 460 BC) and the Sophists. Again, rather than learning the skill of speaking for its own sake, to improve one's own language or for any high-minded pedagogic objective, the impetus for this formalisation was practical and, in particular at this time, related to the need to argue a case at law.

Given the strong link between the spoken form and the Sophists, it is perhaps interesting that the word 'sophistry' has come to have the negative meaning it now has. The modern meaning of a deliberate use of false or misleading reasoning arose from the attack on the successful teaching of speaking techniques (or rhetorical tricks and devices) by higher-minded philosophers, most notably Plato. In the history of ideas, Plato has strong links with arguments based on idealised abstraction that in turn link up with a great deal of modern linguistic theory-driven approaches.

Yet away from the arena of law and individuals' disputation, the art of speaking continued to influence the history of the Greeks in major ways as central players in political life (most famously Demosthenes, who remained synonymous with oratory and on the curriculum through to the Renaissance) combined powerful speech-making with influential positions in public life. The most extensive 'textbook' to come down to us on the art of speaking at this time is Aristotle's *Rhetoric*, in which the teaching of speaking is divided into notions of the speaker, the audience, and the matter of the speech. A great strength of this text was that it managed to synthesise theory and application and, to some extent, bring together the two sides in the controversies about style versus content, and tricks of delivery versus serious seeking after truth, that had raged since Plato's attack on the Sophists.

The early Greek teachers of the art of speaking introduced key concepts that still underpin Western modes of disputation, such as the persuasive device of arguing from probability, the systematic structuring of speeches, and the art of swaying an audience through emotional appeal. However, the backlash against the spoken form as superficial, transient, and open to the ability of individuals to twist listeners' opinions through rhetorical devices reflects the denigration that the spoken form has tended to suffer from. This is particularly seen where the mode exists side by side with a more prestigious written discourse.

With the rise of Roman civilisation and scholars, for example, Cicero (106–43 BC) and, later, Quintilian (AD 35–post 96), the theories of oratory of the Greeks were put to consistent, practical use in law and the political arena. However, the debate between the critics of empty rhetoric and proponents of oratory continued. Cicero did much to bridge the gap by emphasising the need for appeal to the emotions, the sense of humour, and the ear of the listener, together with a deep and detailed understanding of the content being delivered. On the pragmatic side, he preferred to speak last in any debate so that his could be the final appeal to the emotions of the listeners, and he studied what particular combinations of phrases, rhythms, and cadences were most effective in swaying the audience. However, in *De Oratore* he noted that the truly persuasive speaker needs to have an exceptional grasp of the topic and that a good general education is the best starting point for a good speaker. Quintilian continued this tradition and was famous as an educator. His *Institutio Oratoria* provides a coherent teaching manual, placing great emphasis on the needs of the individual student.

Quote 1.8 Quintilian on pronunciation

Let him in the first place correct faults of pronunciation, if there be any, so that the words of the learner may be fully expressed and that every letter may be uttered with its proper sound. For we find inconvenience from the too great weakness or too great fullness of the sound of some letters. Some, as if too harsh for us, we utter but imperfectly or change them for others not altogether dissimilar, but, as it were, smoother.

(Quintilian, 1856/2006, I.11,4)

Interestingly, in Rome the need for individuals to plead their own case at law declined. With the work of Quintilian, the emphasis shifted from the use of speech education to meet social and legal needs towards the teaching of rhetoric as an end in itself and a valuable educational tool to allow individuals to reach their full potential.

Much of the subsequent influence of the classical tradition in Europe can be seen in this change of emphasis from the teaching of speech to underpin the use of rhetorical devices, towards speech as an educational adjunct. The legacy of classical attitudes to speech in the Middle Ages and beyond was largely felt within the educational and, initially, religious context. An early solution to the 'style-versus-content' issue was the splitting up of the teaching programme into different areas, such as grammar (looking at the history and structure of language), logic (the arrangement of thoughts), and rhetoric, which at this later stage came to be limited to the delivery of the thoughts. This, in turn, led, in Elizabethan England and wider Renaissance Europe, to an emphasis on language ornamentation for its own sake, quite divorced from any other educational or social need.

In classical attitudes to teaching speech, several issues that remain pertinent today have their roots—for example:

- the relationship between speech delivery and style versus structure or content,
- the role of training versus the natural acquisition of speech,
- the position of speech in the curriculum, and in society,
- the influence of differences between individuals on speaking ability and how this affects the way they are regarded by others.

1.4.3 *The Eighteenth Century and Beyond*

The following sections continue the historical thread, but look at some of these issues in the narrower context of language teaching as opposed to rhetoric or oratory. The history of language teaching in relation to speaking is developed further in Chapter 3.

Quote 1.9 Howatt on the teaching of speech and social status in eighteenth-century Britain

While the emphasis on correct grammar was even more pronounced in the eighteenth century, the promotion of 'good speech' was another expression of the same passion for accuracy of expression and stylistic elegance. There was considerable popular enthusiasm for instruction in the arts of 'polite conversation', public speaking, and elocution. Out-of-work actors and others with similar gifts had a field-day among the socially ambitious upper-middle classes, particularly in cities anxious to impress the metropolis with their accomplishments. . . .

In spite of this interest in spoken language, it remained essentially 'extra-curricular' and made little impact on the basic education system.

(Howatt, 1985: 76–7)

The beginning and end of the nineteenth century show a marked change in the status of speech in the language teaching process. This was brought about in the transition from 'grammar translation' methods which dominated language teaching in the early parts of the century in Europe to what came to be termed the 'Reform Movement' which arose around the 1880s.

Concept 1.7 Grammar translation methods

Although initially intended to simplify the language learning process and widen it from classical Greek and Latin, which had dominated the curriculum, these methods have come to be associated with all that current theories of language teaching abhor: a strong focus on isolated sentences, mechanical translation of sentences in and out of mother tongue, arcane and overly complex grammatical explanation, and no place for real (spoken or written) communication.

In the situational (and later functional) and audio-lingual methods developed later in the twentieth century, aided by the improvements in both colour publishing and digital technology, the emphasis on teaching and learning a language through the medium of speech remained at the heart of most teaching methodologies. However, it should be noted that although speech was used

---

Concept 1.8 'Natural' or 'direct' methods

Partly as a reaction to the 'grammar translation' approach, language teaching reformers at the end of the nineteenth and beginning of the twentieth century argued for a more natural approach to the teaching process. Critically in terms of the interest of this book, they placed the spoken form at the forefront of their pedagogy, generally insisting on monolingual speech-based interactions between student and teacher and focusing on matters arising from prompts in the learning context. At its most extreme the 'natural' or 'direct' methods led to 'total physical response' or 'TPR' approaches. In this the student responds through action to instructions given by the teacher in the target language. Fundamental to all the approaches is the primacy of speech, together with a move away from isolated sentences towards meaningful whole texts or interactions.

---

in these 'naturally' oriented teaching processes, the actual forms used were very far from naturally occurring speech or indeed natural spoken communication. Typically, the interactions were highly constrained so that particular grammatical structures could be practised. Such structures were derived from standard formal grammars that were grounded in the norms of 'literate' writing.

Therefore, speech held a paradoxical status in language teaching through the first half of the twentieth century. The notion of 'speaking well' had dominated attitudes to the form from the very earliest teaching traditions associated with it, as noted in previous sections. The grammar translation methods which held sway through much of the nineteenth century were strongly associated with the written form, and it was partly as a reaction to this that later movements adopted the oral medium with such enthusiasm. Nonetheless, the return to speech as the primary medium of instruction began a process that remains largely unresolved, that is to say, the simultaneous high regard for the spoken form and the lack of precise attention to the structure and peculiarities of this form in its own right.

The 1960s, with the influence of the work of Noam Chomsky, and the 1970s and 1980s, with the growth of 'communicative' approaches, marked two distinct sea changes in the field of language teaching, both of which did much to underpin present attitudes to the spoken form. While these two threads are brought into commonality by research in the field of second language acquisition, they have marked differences in the emphasis they placed on speech in their thinking. On the one hand, the transformational grammar movement internalised and made abstract the language system to such an extent that actual speech became something of an irrelevance. On the other, the tenets of the communicative movement held that language was acquired by meaningful and interesting communication in contexts which mimicked real communicative settings as closely as possible. Thus, for the latter school of thought, to conceptualise speech as either simply the medium of instruction (as was the case with natural or direct methods) or as something largely irrelevant to the process of language study (as in the competence/performance distinction) was anathema. At its most extreme, the communicative approach sees the struggle to make and share meaning through the dynamic spoken form as the very engine of language acquisition. Nonetheless, the role of mode and the status of speech in language acquisition paradigms have been remarkably undertheorised.

Concept 1.9   Communicative approaches

Due to its wide and deep influence on the field of English language teaching, one often hears about the 'communicative approach'. However, it is perhaps useful to think of a variety of approaches which have changed and developed since the late 1970s in the UK and the USA, but all of which share common ground and ideology. Communicative approaches have been strongly associated with the work of Stephen Krashen in the USA on second language acquisition and, among others, Henry Widdowson in the UK. In particular communicative approaches:

- place high value on language in use (as opposed to abstract, isolated examples);
- assert that effective language acquisition (often opposed to language learning) only takes place through language use;
- aim to foster and develop the learner's communicative competence (as opposed to the more abstract concept of linguistic competence);
- regard errors as a natural part of the progression towards a greater understanding of the target language;
- link teaching methodologies to appropriate communicative tasks (rather than seeing classroom tasks as a means of practising a particular grammatical feature);
- tend to favour inductive, student-centred routes to understanding (rather than explicit, teacher-led explanations);
- place the learner at the centre of the learning process and assess progress in relation to factors affecting the individual (e.g. levels of motivation).

The basic methods (e.g. pair and group work) and beliefs (e.g. that teachers should be facilitators of communication tasks rather than dominant 'lecturers' to students) of communicative language teaching have become the backbone of modern English language teaching since the 1970s. Task-based learning, the language awareness movement in the UK, and the focus on form movement in America are all later responses to these fundamental tenets.

1.4.4   *Insights From Speech Corpora and Digital Technologies*

The objectives in the speaking classroom may well change quite radically over the next few years. Insights emerging from corpora of natural speech and language processing are being combined with new ways for teachers and students to access examples of speech data, helping us understand what speaking is actually like and to find relevant and engaging examples with ease. Quotes 1.2 and 1.10 provide examples of this. In the first, the authentic use of a word in a corpus of speech ('like') that is generally presented to the learner as a preposition is shown in contexts where it is used as a discourse marker to lead in to reported speech or to show focus. In the second, the prevalence of modal verbs in spoken academic discourse over written is highlighted as a finding from a corpus study. Chapter 3 discusses the complex relationships between research findings such as these and the commercial publication of classroom materials.

Concept 1.10   Corpus/corpora (pl.)/corpus linguistics

At its most simple, a corpus (in linguistic contexts) is a collection of language samples. As such, a teacher's collection of photocopies of student essays might be regarded as a corpus. However, the term is strongly associated with the computer-aided analysis of language, and, in corpus linguistics, with the statistical analysis of word (and less often) structural frequencies. Just as the teacher might look through a collection of learners' essays before planning a class to see what common problems they were encountering, a corpus linguist can find patterns and frequencies in many million word samples of language. The collection of speech data for corpus design is a particular problem, as large amounts of naturally occurring speech need to be both recorded and transcribed for the computer. This is a time-consuming (and difficult to automate) process and means that there has been a tendency for corpora to be biased in favour of the written mode.

Quote 1.10   The authors of the *Longman Grammar of Spoken and Written English* (LGSWE) on findings about speech that run counter to expectations

In many respects, the patterns of use described in the LGSWE will be surprising to materials writers, since they run directly counter to the patterns often found in ESL/EFL coursebooks. For example, progressive aspect verbs are the norm in most books that teach English conversation, in marked contrast to the language produced by speakers in actual conversation, where simple aspect verbs are more than 20 times more common than progressive aspect verbs. Similarly, most ESP/EAP instructors will be surprised to learn that modal verbs are much more common in conversation than in academic prose: in fact, only the modal *may* is used much more commonly in academic prose.

(Biber et al., 1999: 46)

1.5   Summary

To sum up, this chapter aimed to place the teaching and research of speaking into a conceptual and historical context. In so doing, it drew attention to a fundamental issue in dealing with speech data: the status of instances of real speech within current theories of language, and in particular in the dominant research paradigm behind second language acquisition. The tendency to split off 'pure' linguistic theory from more descriptively or pedagogically oriented studies was discussed. I argued that this is because, generally speaking, linguistic theory gives little weight to the activity of speaking itself.

In this chapter, the threads of today's issues for teaching and researching speaking were also traced back to classical concerns with the division of form and content in the teaching of speech, and the long shadow cast by these ideas was described. In the concluding section, the issue of the status of speech in dominant second language teaching paradigms was noted. Within this section, I argued that there has been a tendency for speech to be both highly valued in the modern language teaching contexts and at the same time under-theorised and underinvestigated as a faculty in its own right.

Further Reading

Candlin, C. (2000). *English Language Teaching in Its Social Context: A Reader*. London and New York: Routledge.

Chapman, S. and Routledge, C. (Eds) (2009). *Key Ideas in Linguistics and the Philosophy of Language*. Edinburgh: Edinburgh University Press.

Cornbleet, S. and Carter, R. (2001). *The Language of Speech and Writing*. London: Routledge.

Howatt, A.P.R. and Widdowson, H. G. (2004). *History of English Language Teaching ELT* (2nd edn). Oxford: Oxford University Press.

Hughes, R. (1996). *English in Speech and Writing: Investigating Language and Literature*. London: Routledge.

Long, M. H. and Doughty, C. J. (2011). *The Handbook of Language Teaching* (Vol. 63). Hoboken, NJ: John Wiley & Sons.

McCarthy, M. (1998). *Spoken Language and Applied Linguistics*. Cambridge: Cambridge University Press.

2   The Research Space
Paradigms and Issues

This chapter will . . .

- describe some classical research paradigms as they relate to spoken mode and to analysing spoken data;
- discuss particular issues surrounding research into speaking;
- discuss the role and status of spoken data in language theory.

2.1   Introduction

This chapter begins with a brief introduction to research paradigms in general and then discusses their usefulness and applicability in relation to researching speaking. In this chapter, I also address the question of the nature of spoken data and how this relates to the kind of research that is undertaken in spoken mode.

2.2   Classical Research Paradigms in Relation to Researching Speaking

The research approaches dealt with in this book are, in general, empirically based. That is to say, they deal in real-world data of some kind—systematically recorded observations of classroom behaviour, transcripts of conversation, and recordings of learners' utterances analysed for the occurrence of particular phonemes, and so on. These data are gathered to investigate a central research question, often posed as a hypothesis, and are used as the basis of either a quantitative analysis (most often) or a qualitative analysis (less frequent apart from areas such as critical linguistics, sociolinguistics, and ethnographically based work).

A second type of approach is a more theoretically oriented one. Here, rather than taking data as the starting point of an investigation, the researcher is primarily interested in theories, models, high-level concepts, and, crucially, the relationships between previous theories and ones that may emerge from a current investigation. In the context of extremely theoretically oriented work, for example, philosophical logic (a discipline with a surprising amount of influence on linguistics), any real-world data are, if they are considered at all, seen as 'messy', subject to the vagaries of individual circumstances and irrelevant.

Different research approaches are often called 'paradigms' (see Concept 2.1), and these strongly influence how research is carried out. A paradigm functions as a framework or point of reference for both researchers and users of research output. It gives coherence to a study and links it to the work of others, providing a shorthand by which it can be prepared and judged. If the researcher positions a study in, for example, an experimental paradigm, he or she creates a set of expectations in his or her audience about the way the research will be conducted. These expectations might, for instance, be that there will be a 'control group' to compare changes in patients' blood pressure in a drug trial who do not receive the drug. These considerations affect how research is received and what is regarded as 'good research'.

Concept 2.1 What is a paradigm?

A paradigm is a framework for ideas which includes definitions of key terms and the relationships between them. The framework is coherent because the researcher assumes certain things as a starting point and new knowledge is absorbed into this mental 'map'. During the 1960s in the USA Noam Chomsky created a major shift in what people assumed about language when he conceptualised it as an inherent rule-governed system for which the human mind is hard-wired from birth and also set up key concepts such as performance and competence. This was in sharp contrast to pre-existing paradigms in American linguistics. These had been strongly data oriented/ethnographic in nature, and Chomsky's new thinking also contrasted to the European structuralist paradigms that had emerged after the work of Ferdinand de Saussure. This kind of change is referred to as a 'paradigm shift'.

Different disciplines work within different paradigms, and even within the same academic department several paradigms can compete with one another. Research outcomes normally make only small changes to the paradigm rather than altering it fundamentally—this is the nature of research findings generally. These small changes in the state of knowledge do not amount to a new paradigm. Paradigm shifts can and do occur when either a brilliant individual or a team compel others to change their entire mental map of a particular topic due to the strength of their findings or arguments.

All paradigms orient towards a theory and towards data, but the balance between these will differ according to the tradition in which the academic is working. Academic research is meaningless if it is not embedded in the context of the work of others. This work is in turn framed within a paradigm that has a particular orientation towards data and theory. Different disciplines will also place different emphasis on the role of theory versus data. In linguistics,

---

Concept 2.2 Empirical versus nonempirical approaches

An empirical approach to a research project begins from situated questions and facts rather than decontextualised issues or questions of theory. Both kinds of approach can be used to deal with the same topic. The clearest differences between them lie in the methods used and what is regarded as a coherent approach and reliable evidence. The less empirically motivated researcher in linguistics has traditionally been concerned with intuitions about language and the fit between new data and existing theory. The empirically oriented researcher will be more open to seeing patterns emerging from data and drawing conclusions from these that may challenge pre-existing ideas or intuitions. Both approaches will draw on theory and a pre-existing paradigm, so the contrast is not so much between empirical and theoretical work but between the emphases placed on data in terms of conclusions reached. All research needs to abstract away from particular instances of data in order to reach some coherent conclusion, but empirically grounded work will retain stronger links to concrete examples and give these greater weight than nonempirically oriented research.

---

and particularly in the realm of spoken discourse, the relationship is quite complex and the locus of ongoing debate. At one end of the spectrum, an academic working in the field of syntax will aim to achieve an elegant, comprehensive, and convincing description of a language feature such as negation in a particular language and relate this to current theories of negation generally. Kamp and Reyle (2013), for instance, work on the idea of negation not from real-world transcribed examples but in the context of language intuition and semantics and in contrast to assertion. To be convincing the work will need to orient towards all previous work on negation and, in the case of this study, would tend to do this within a theoretically oriented paradigm. While examples will be used, the work is not 'data driven' in the way that the work of a text or corpus linguist will be. At the other end of the spectrum, in computational linguistics there are academics developing models of grammar via automatic 'parsers' purely from massive numbers of examples in ways that allow syntactic categories and patterns in language to be described in a bottom-up fashion, for instance, Morante and Sporleder (2012). In a similarly data-driven study Eskildsen (2012) looks at the development of negation in a longitudinal study of two adult language learners. The literature review sections of the three studies on negation cited here and the references cited throughout would not cover the same studies, although the topic they are researching is the same. This is because they are all working in different paradigms and regard the role of data in their frameworks very differently.

Table 2.1 Branches of Linguistics in Relation to Data and the Relevance of Mode

Group 1	Data driven or highly data informed
Computational linguistics Discourse and conversational analysis Text and corpus linguistics Phonetics Sociolinguistics	
Group 2	Less data driven, but data and mode relevant to the analysis
Historical linguistics Lexicography Neurolinguistics Phonology Pragmatics Psycholinguistics Second language acquisition	
Group 3	Theory driven, and mode generally not relevant
Morphology Philosophy of language Semantics Syntax	

Table 2.1 gives an indication of how far, in general, some of the major branches of linguistics deal with situated data, whether they regard mode as relevant or in contrast deal primarily with abstractions.

The groupings shown in Table 2.1 should be regarded as broadly indicative, and they are there to help situate a debate about the role of spoken data in language theory and, in turn, address the question of why there are so few holistic theories of speech available. By holistic I mean theories that can incorporate and integrate the range of resources that speakers draw on: grammatical, semantic, phonetic, pragmatic, as well as the demands and influence of speech processing and production, memory, and psycho-social factors. As an example, sociolinguistic research frequently draws its data from the spoken mode (for example, on the social marking carried by a particular phoneme or the speaking strategies of a particular racial group) but does not relate the findings to any broader theory of speech. It is important therefore to distinguish between research into speaking and research that uses speech data for a different research purpose.

There are reasons for the different status of data, and particularly speech data, in various branches of language studies. Linguistics as we know it today has a surprisingly short history and, since the 1960s, has been developing and positioning itself among several disciplines newer and older than it. In the early part of the twentieth century, what we call linguistics was termed the 'science of language'. It was primarily interested in concrete examples of language. Scholars studied the history of the development of a language or the comparison of different languages (the area known as philology and its branches). There was then a transition in linguistic science from what was a largely descriptive analytical discipline (and one that in its attention to detailed contrasts and taxonomies was akin to botanical science and related disciplines that mapped and categorised the natural world) to one that set great store on the need to theorise away from the messy, real-world data, to universal regularities or competencies. This process has led to particularly interesting and complex issues surrounding the attitude to speech data in language theory generally, and the next sections will deal with this further.

Concept 2.3   The powerful influence of a compelling and coherent theory

An interesting example to flesh out the differences between empirically oriented studies and those that take theory as a starting point is research on rhythm in spoken language. The classical paradigm set up and developed by among others Pike (1945) and Abercrombie (1967) proposes that languages should be categorised in terms of two different rhythmic systems: syllable timing and stress timing. In the former kind of language every syllable has the same duration, and in the latter syllable length varies so that a regular 'beat' is created by the words and phrases of the language. Spanish and French are, traditionally, categorised as syllable timed and English and Russian as stress-timed languages. This very compelling idea of a binary contrast (nicely described as 'machine gun' [syllable timing] versus 'Morse code' [stress timing]; Lloyd James, 1940) has held sway, with variations, for nearly 70 years. This is despite the fact that researchers admit that when they measure and time samples of languages it is difficult to find data that consistently fit the theory. Very complex systems of metrics have been created (Low and Grabe, 1995; Grabe and Low, 2002) to investigate speech rhythm, most of which begin from this binary contrast or refer back to it. More recently the idea of stress/syllable timing being less clear-cut categories towards which individual languages tend, rather than having them as their defining rhythmic characteristics, has emerged, but the paradigm remains largely unshifted or at least still has currency.

2.3   Attitudes to Speech Data

Even the most theoretically oriented work engages with data at some level. At its most basic the research is grounded in some real-world concepts, if not 'hard' data. When researchers think of empirical approaches in opposition to more theoretically oriented ones, it is a matter of what role the data are seen to have in the research process. In 'classical' theoretically oriented, scientific methods, the model or theory on which a study is based is not going to be fundamentally redefined by the outcomes of the research. Data which challenge the prevailing theory are likely to be set aside as 'blips', and more generally the phenomena being investigated will be selected in such a way that they will tend to fit in with the existing paradigm. Examples of scholars who see the world from this perspective are given in Quotes 2.1 and 2.2 (see also Concept 2.3 for a further example of this perspective).

Quote 2.1   Goodwin on attitudes towards speech data in linguistics in the early 1980s

Methodologically, most contemporary linguists do not use actual speech as a source of data for the analysis of linguistic structure. They base this position in part on the argument that the phrasal breaks, such as restarts, found in actual speech give evidence of such defective performance that the data are useless for the study of competence.

(Goodwin, 1981: 12)

Quote 2.2   Noam Chomsky on the status and usefulness of natural speech in linguistic analysis

A record of natural speech will show numerous false starts, deviations from rules, changes of plan in mid-course, and so on. The problem for the linguist, as well as for the child learning the language, is to determine from the data of performance the underlying system of rules that has been mastered by the speaker–hearer and that he puts to use in actual performance.

(Chomsky, 1965: 5)

The role of data is a particularly pressing issue for the researcher into speech for three reasons. First, unlike the written form, the building blocks of speech do not come to us in a clearly demarcated set of units. Our literate view of language means that it is a surprise to realise that the stream of speech is exactly that: there are no gaps between individual words in normally uttered speech. This lack of the spaces between words we see in writing in the spoken form has come as a surprise to every student I have taught when it is pointed out to them. The process of understanding speech, therefore, is highly dependent on an interpretive capacity on the part of the listener at a fundamental level during speech comprehension. The discipline of speech processing deals with this, and the complexity of the demands on the listener are reflected in the algorithms created to allow nonhumans to process human speech (e.g. in automated responses to telephone enquiries). This interpretive role is not one that the researcher can completely stand apart from when handling authentic speech data. Second, capturing and analysing speech depends largely on the written form, and careful attention is needed to the relationship between the original data and its visual representation—which by its nature is always secondary data. Finally, as noted earlier in the influential binary of syllable-timed and stress-timed languages, neat and clearly defined categories and patterns are extremely compelling. There can be a tendency to 'retrofit' speech data to predesignated categories better suited to the written form due to this natural human bias. Research into spoken grammar shows this particularly clearly, where the terminology of traditional pedagogic or prescriptive grammars struggles to describe the norms of the spoken mode (see also Concept 2.4).

Concept 2.4 Finding words to describe the grammar of speech

Traditional and/or pedagogic grammar provides a fairly consistent set of constructs, definitions, and structural relations. A grammatical construct like 'relative clause' or 'noun phrase' is relatively stable and clearly defined—a researcher will find several hundred articles on the topics with ease.

Research into the grammar of spoken discourse has suggested that there are a number of constructions regularly used by speakers (e.g. subject–verb ellipsis—'Nice day' as opposed to 'It is a nice day'; Nariyama, 2004) which do not fit into the norms of traditional grammar models. There are also items which have a high occurrence in spoken language (e.g. semi-modal verbs such as 'tend to'; Moore, 2007) but which are presented as 'unusual' in standard grammars. Structures such as these that fall outside the standard definitions are less easy to handle for two reasons. First, by their nature they do not fall into the neat categories of the existing grammar model. Second, there will be no accepted terminology for the elements being described. Thus, a construction typical of spoken English such as the following, 'where he went wrong my mate Tony was not getting the car taxed before he went on his holiday', might be defined as a 'cleft' sentence, 'preposed', containing a 'left-shifted head' or other terms which may or may not mean exactly the same thing to everyone or overlap with one another exactly.

In the first decades of the twentieth century, speech as a primary data source was difficult to capture. Even the advent of the tape recorder meant that gathering large samples of data and analysing them was a hugely laborious process. The ability to record speech and the comparatively recent growth in the power of the personal computer have brought the possibility of large corpus studies to the office of the applied linguistics researcher. However, the complexities of capturing large quantities of spontaneous spoken data have meant that most corpora still depend for their input on the written mode. Insights from corpora that combine a balance of both spoken and written material are beginning to filter into the public domain in forms that can be used by the teaching community (see, e.g. Biber et al., 1999, *Longman Grammar of Spoken and Written English*; or Carter and McCarthy, 2006, *Cambridge Advanced Grammar of English*).

Quote 2.3   The *Longman Grammar of Spoken and Written English* on surprises from corpus-based approaches to grammar

[E]ven basic word classes—such as nouns, adjectives, verb, and adverbs— are far from evenly distributed across registers. Nouns and prepositional phrases are much more common in news than in conversation, whereas verbs and adverbs are much more common in conversation. These distributional patterns reflect differing functional priorities. For example, news texts have an informational focus, frequently using nouns to refer to people and things in the world. . . . In contrast, the interpersonal focus of conversation results in frequent use of verbs to narrate events and to present personal attitudes, while the online production and context dependent circumstances of conversation make it more appropriate to use pronouns instead of nouns.

(Biber et al., 1999: 11)

It is noticeable, however, that despite advances in the capturing and the analysis of speech data, research questions continue to be oriented towards areas other than finding out more about the nature of speech, *per se*. Considering the universality of the ability to speak across humankind there has been little attempt to draw together a unified theory of the process. Many disciplines value real speech data and place them at the heart of their theories. However, these approaches have tended to incorporate the spoken language into a theory that aims to describe or explain something else. For instance, second language acquisition (SLA) gives high importance to the effect of spoken input on the learner, but the elements under discussion have tended to be the learners' inherent capacity for language learning, the closeness or distance between a target language and current utterances, how their first language affects their second, and so on.

Notable exceptions such as Levelt's seminal work *Speaking: From Intention to Articulation* (Levelt, 1989) fall outside what is considered core work in applied linguistics, coming under the umbrella of psycholinguistics. Even here work stops largely at the point of utterance and does not pursue the important issues of interaction, the influence of intonation and prosody, turn-taking, and so on, nor how these features might relate to one another in a process of communication that is unique to spoken mode. In language acquisition, research with an interest in bridging some of these gaps began to emerge in the early years of this century (see, e.g. Judit Kormos' [2014] readable *Speech Production and Second Language Acquisition*).

2.4   The Applicability of Research Approaches and Frameworks to the Study of Speech

The previous sections have argued that care is needed in researching speaking due to three aspects. These were the strong influence of a literate view of the form, the tendency to tidy speech data and to abstract away from the messiness of real-world, situated talk in context, and the tendency to use speech data as the basis for research into some aspect of language other than spoken mode in its own right. Here we look at the implications of these points and what research into speaking *per se* may, in due course, emerge as.

Hand in hand with a removal of the object of study to the theoretical, unsituated, or abstract level is a convenient merging of the construct 'speech' with 'language'. It is convenient because it permits the models and theories being developed to use isolated examples as the basis of analysis that are closer to the norms of formal, published written mode and ignore deviant, ill-formed and difficult-to-parse forms which might come under debate if real-world examples of speech (and, indeed, writing) were the basis for the model. Secondly, such abstract approaches permit the theorist to ignore sound-based meaning-bearing elements of language, such as intonation, which are again less easy to formalise than text-based elements.

Much of a person's identity and communicative force is carried by the vocal pattern that we associate with him or her, and many of the affective aspects of language reach the world via the slightest changes in voice quality. In teaching spoken language one might imagine these aspects would be seen as of highest importance. However, since most abstract language paradigms do not take into account or try to account for aspects of the dynamic, interpersonally oriented mode that is speech, the focus tends to fall on structural input, disengaged both from its discourse context and from its meaning-bearing 'music'. In contrast to this, work that has emerged in computer science and human-computer interaction aimed at better understanding and incorporating findings about the links between communicative impact, affect, and prosody (e.g. Partala and Surakka, 2004; Davletcharova et al., 2015). It will be interesting, with the growth of multimodal corpora and new techniques for searching these, how far the findings of computer science, corpus linguistics, and the language classroom can be combined to provide insights that are eventually applicable to the spoken language curriculum.

Functional magnetic resonance imaging 'fMRI' technology used for linguistic research developed in the early years of this century and has had an interesting effect on the study of spoken language. The capacity to link brain function to particular spoken stimuli has meant researchers can now build hypotheses to investigate questions about links between oral/aural input and events in the brain. The reason that this is a step change in the field is that earlier neurolinguistic work depended on making links between spoken events in the outside world and possible brain activity. This was often done by contrasting brain-damaged and nonbrain-damaged speech performance. While this approach remains valid, the capacity to map and link spoken events and normal brain activity is an exciting new development for linguistics.

Concept 2.5 Functional magnetic resonance imaging (fMRI) and language

fMRI is a method by which activity in different parts of the brain can be shown as an image. The process is noninvasive, as it scans and analyses differences in blood flow from outside the body. Changes in blood flow cause measurable fluctuations in oxygen levels and in turn its magnetic properties. The scanner translates these into data that are mapped onto particular areas in the brain. The assumption is that blood flow and neural activity happen hand in hand, and therefore these images represent the physical location of the brain's response to particular stimuli.

Work in this field on language developed rapidly from around 2000, and the process has been used for a wide variety of studies ranging from vocabulary (Ellis et al., 2006) to emotional responses to language (Beaucousin et al., 2007) to understanding the links between spoken language and dyslexia (Kovelman et al., 2012).

2.5   Levels of Analysis

The study of language is traditionally based on the study of categories of language features that are described in terms of different levels. The simplest day-to-day example is the written word in formal settings. A word is made up of discrete symbols, words can often be broken down into a root word and affixes (LOAD + ED; UN + DO), words in turn create phrases and sentences, these sentences form paragraphs, and the paragraph fits into a higher genre or text category such as a newspaper column or a chapter in a novel.

One of the difficulties in researching speech is the fact that, unlike written texts, the notion of a freestanding genre or clearly delimited sample to be investigated does not readily lend itself to speech. Whereas researchers into writing can start, if they wish, from a relatively well-defined set of texts that clearly fit into a category (newspaper language, popular fiction, advertising texts, academic writing, and so on) the researcher into speech will generally find no such helpful categories to hand. Writing presents itself in front of the researcher through the materiality of its visual medium. The researchers into speech must usually look beyond the discourse to the context in order to delimit the data under investigation and to ensure they are, for instance, comparing like with like.

The issue can be best understood by looking at a stretch of talk and thinking about the different levels and perspectives through which it could be investigated.

Table 2.2 shows a brief extract from interviews conducted to create a corpus of Singaporean English. The corpus was created by researchers at the National Institute of Education in Singapore primarily for the purposes of research into prosodic features. It presents a readily accessible set of transcripts alongside digital audio files of the original speech data. This leads to a preliminary, overarching comment that the transcript and the spoken data are not the same thing and should not be conflated. Researchers into speaking all need to reach a carefully thought-out position in relation to the visible recording of their data in the written form, as this is rarely a neutral process. This can be understood in terms of a metaphor of degrees of magnification. This sample captures a number of aspects of talk: socio-pragmatic relationships (interviewer/subject,

Table 2.2 Extract From National Institute of Education Singapore Corpus of Spoken Singaporean English

secs	speaker	
00	I	Where do they live in America?
01	S	Los Angeles and erm San Francisco.
04	I	Do you like it there?
06	S	Yeah . . . well not as much as Australia, because like you know in the States
10		it's more like erm a place to visit . . .
13		not so much a place to stay . . . yeah and to live in.
16	I	You don't think that you [could live in Los Angeles.
17	S	[No.
19		No no no definitely not.

Available online with digital audio file at: http://videoweb.nie.edu.sg/phonetic/niecsse/f15/f15-f-tr.htm

lecturer/student), structural features (turns, questions/answers, clauses) and acoustic data relating to the stream of speech (temporal information in seconds, onset of overlapping talk). However, these are only a small subset of features that may interest the researcher. At a level of higher 'magnification', a researcher investigating talk between different sexes or different ways that people interrupt one another might wish to represent relative loudness or pitch movement in individual words. The greater the acoustic information being captured, the greater the efforts involved in transcription. There is therefore always a relationship between the 'magnification' (level of detail captured in a transcription of speech) and the research focus. Researchers may make a very simple initial transcript showing no data, such as overlapping talk or pauses, if they are primarily interested in finding instances of a particular type of interaction (e.g. jokes) and then increase the level of detail for those extracts. Taken seriously, transcription is a powerful research tool and can reflect the perspectives and needs of the researcher. As it is never an entirely neutral process, it is good practice for the individual transcriber to cross-refer with other researchers when difficulties of interpretation arise or when new categories of talk are being investigated. Edwards (2003) gives a full overview of the decision process with clear examples; O'Connell and Kowal (2009) provide a thoughtful summary of the development of transcription systems and issues to be considered. The most commonly used system is often referred to as the 'Jefferson method' after the linguist Gail Jefferson, who developed it. A definitive overview can be seen in Jefferson (2004). Setting on one side this methodological preliminary issue, the extract shown in Table 2.2 could be the object of study at many levels, and the following sections deal with each of these.

2.5.1 Analysing Speaking Skills at the Level of Discourse and Social Interaction

Discourse-level studies are interested in questions of how speakers interact with one another (e.g. how they know when it is their turn to speak) and how talk is organised in particular kinds of patterns over long stretches of language (e.g. how speakers structure their talk for listeners so that they can follow changes in topic easily). At a wider level, researchers are often also interested in how, through talk, social features are expressed, such as identity, shared knowledge, or power relations. In the extract in Table 2.2, the speakers are a lecturer (male) and a student (female). Their interaction takes place in a semi-formal interview setting. Their relationships, gender, and the interview context influence how they behave to one another conversationally. For instance, it is more likely that the lecturer/interviewer will initiate talk in this setting, and it is likely that more of his discourse will be in the form of questions. Many disciplines outside linguistics are becoming increasingly interested in discourse analysis because of the insights it can give about how participants in a spoken interaction behave. For instance, researchers in the medical sciences may be interested in how to understand patient and practitioner relationships better in order to enhance training in communication for professionals and therefore the efficacy of treatment (see Salter et al., 2007, for an example of this work). Similarly, a wide-ranging recent summary of applications of linguistic analysis in the realm of business studies can be found in Bargiela-Chiappini et al. (2007).

During the 1970s and 1980s the main concern in the field was to consider where the discourse level of language fitted in with current views of language and to what extent regularities or even 'rules' of interaction could be uncovered. This focus on rule-based paradigms reflected the dominant model for language that had grown up in the USA. Seminal work was carried out in America by conversational analysts, who developed highly sophisticated systems for representing language features which had previously been studied very little, for example laughter or pauses or apparently trivial utterances, such as 'uh-huh' or 'oh' (e.g. Schegloff, 1981). This detailed investigation into the mechanics of conversation led to concepts such as 'openings', 'closings', 'pair parts', 'formulaic exchanges', or the 'transition-relevance point' (TRP).

Concept 2.6 Transition-relevance point (TRP)

This is a moment in speaking when several linguistic features combine to signal to an interlocutor that they could take over the speaker role. In Anglophone cultures these tend to be the ends of clauses and are signalled by pitch, intonation, pace, and micro-pausing as well as extra-linguistic features such as gaze. Next time you are in a free-flowing conversation you might like to stand back (or better still record a conversation) and see how speakers know that they can begin to speak without seeming to interrupt one another. For many learners of a language, ability to speak words and sentences is not the factor which isolates them in a conversation. Rather it is the inability to 'read' the moments when they might be able to begin to speak. Work in this area is therefore an enabler for learners which should be incorporated into the spoken language teaching curriculum.

In the UK discourse analysis took a different turn from the USA: key features of the structuring of discourse were investigated, and notions such as 'discourse markers', 'transactions', and 'exchanges' were developed.

Both discourse analysis and conversation analysis have links to sociolinguistics in that they prefer not to deal with samples of language in isolation, and conversation analysis in particular is interested in the relations between interlocutors. Discourse analysis, however, has traditionally tended to concentrate

---

Concept 2.7 Discourse markers

These are words 'outside' clauses which carry little or no meaning in their own right but signal something to the listener about the structure or organisation of the talk, for example 'right' or 'ok' in English. As well as logical relations, discourse markers can signal more subtle aspects of talk: 'well' can indicate reservation or hesitation; 'now' can indicate a change in topic; 'actually' can mean many things including difference of opinion or correction or even defensiveness (cf. English cooking is very good. English cooking is very good, actually). Because learners are usually taught a form of the language which is strongly influenced by written mode, spoken discourse markers are not given high prominence in a syllabus, if they are taught explicitly at all. This can leave a learner floundering both in terms of listening to conversation and taking part.

---

on longer sections of language and focused on interrelations between different sections of text. Within this, the discourse analyst is interested in how speakers carry out functions of language and the choices made by them in different contexts.

In terms of the application of some of the main ideas of conversation and discourse analysis, but with a stronger focus on the former, Brown and Yule (1983), in *Teaching the Spoken Language: An Approach Based on the Analysis of Conversational English*, provided something of a bridge between the schools of thought outlined earlier and more practically classroom-oriented applications. Interestingly, despite the crucial aspects of speech that discourse-level studies have uncovered, they have, overall, been very slow to trickle through into classroom teaching and published teaching materials in general. There have been books for teachers on the topic (e.g. McCarthy's [1991] *Discourse Analysis for Language Teachers* or Evelyn Hatch's [1992] very different *Discourse and Language Education*). Carter, Hughes, and McCarthy (2000) attempt to bring some of the complexities of spoken grammar in discourse to the classroom via grammar materials. Chapter 3 deals with this more fully.

Discourse analysis in the UK does have strong incidental links to the classroom, however, in that much of the most influential early work (e.g. Sinclair and Coulthard, 1975) was carried out on classroom interaction. These classic studies, which generated some of the fundamental categories of discourse analysis, were based on teacher–pupil talk.

During the 1990s and beyond there was increasing interest in the telecommunications and computing world that discourse analysis would solve problems of automation of human-computer understanding. This area took time to fulfil the early promise, and even so humans are generally still constrained to limited lexical choices and clear talk in these contexts rather than the system being able to adjust to spontaneous talk. Nevertheless, it will be interesting to see what twenty-first-century discourse and conversation analysis can offer other disciplines and users wanting to apply the insights of linguistics to real-world applications.

The relationship between psychology and speech behaviour is another thread to research into global aspects of speech, and one which again links in with the bigger questions of how spoken language data relate to underlying linguistic systems, whether neurological, biological, or genetic. Whereas discourse or conversation analysts will describe patterns of speech behaviour in order to uncover regularities in the organisation of spoken discourse and will see these patterns of interest in themselves, the psychologist will generally regard utterances as a source of evidence of mental or behavioural processes. So, for example, whereas discourse or conversation analysts may look at a feature such as patterns of repetition in speech and see how far they can generalise about lexical repetition in its own right, the psychologist would investigate how such repetitions relate to how humans process complex utterances or the timing and levels of preplanning. For example, Clark and Wasow (1998) investigated a typical pattern of repetition, either PRONOUN + PAUSE/ FILLER + PRONOUN (I uh I (think). . .) or ARTICLE + PAUSE/FILLER + ARTICLE (The uh the (problem). . .), and suggested that the different stages in this pattern related to the way in which speakers committed themselves to an utterance. They proposed that these items were an integral part of the underlying psychological processes by which utterances reach the world.

In terms of teaching languages, the fields of higher-level studies into speech described here open up several questions and ways forward, particularly in relation to uncovering differences between cultures with respect to how conversation is organised. This in turn can help learners and teachers understand potential pitfalls in language interaction that are not due to any grammatical or lexical mistake but different pragmatic and cultural expectations.

2.5.2   The Research Space at the Level of Language Choices: Grammar and Vocabulary

A prominent strand of work on grammar and lexis that takes into account spoken mode has been developed through corpus studies. Douglas Biber's work, most notably his influential *Variation Across Speech and Writing* (Biber, 1988), gives a strongly data-oriented analysis of a wide variety of spoken and written sources, concluding that certain grammatical features cluster together to make up the distinctive style of a spoken or written genre. These features in turn map onto dimensions of contrast, such as whether the language is concerned with conveying information or is more interpersonally oriented. Rather than suggesting a simple binary division between speech and writing, Biber broke new ground in suggesting that there were patterns of probability among language features that show statistical regularity in how they co-occur in spoken and written genres.

There have been two major strands of work that have developed from this approach: applications of the register analysis in discrete fields and genres and more theoretical and detailed insights about general language features. In terms of the former, this has been taken forward in, for instance, Douglas Biber's own work on English for special purposes, including university writing and speaking (Biber, 2006), and, with colleagues on English language assessment (Biber et al., 2004), the large body of work around the Michigan Corpus of Spoken Academic English (MICASE). In terms of the latter there has been, for instance, some work on language change as a feature capable of being investigated through corpora (see Concept 2.8 describing the process known as 'grammaticalisation').

Concept 2.8 Grammaticalisation

This is a concept associated with the study of language change. It is based on an underlying idea that words in a language can be categorised as primarily carrying semantic meaning or as primarily carrying out syntactic functions. The verb 'walk' would be in the first category and the verb 'have' would be in both categories. It has a lexical meaning when used in the sentence 'I have a brother' and carries different semantic load when used in its auxiliary functions, as in 'I have broken my arm'. At different phases in the evolution of a language, words can change from lexical to grammatical functions, and this process is called grammaticalisation. An example that is often given is the expansion of the lexical word 'back' as part of the body into an adverbial to indicate past time, as in 'Back then . . .'. Lindquist and Mair (2004) provide a collection of research papers on what is also termed 'historical corpus linguistics'.

Early corpus-based work helped to inform research into speech on detailed aspects such as tenses (Aarts and Meyer, 1995), vocabulary (Stenström, 1990), clauses (Nelson, 1997), and ellipsis (Meyer, 1995). Later work has involved broader questions of the extent of generalisability and applicability of findings (e.g. Conrad, 2000; Mindt, 2002; Baldwin et al., 2005). Academics also began working on bridging the gap between corpus findings and the classroom (e.g. Johns, 1991; Tribble and Jones, 1990; Knowles, 1990; and most relevantly for the spoken mode, Svartvik, 1991) as soon as large corpora of speech became readily available. Scholars have also focused attention on the interrelations between second language acquisition theories or approaches to teaching and the grammatical frequencies found in corpora (e.g. Biber and Reppen, 2002; Anderson, 2007; Barbieri and Eckhardt, 2007). However, while these can provide some interesting ideas for classroom activities, there is still a gap between findings on the realities of grammatical and lexical choices in spontaneous talk and what is presented in published material.

On the other hand, for the teacher or researcher starting out in research into spoken mode, gaining access to spoken corpora has become relatively straightforward in recent years. These resources range from sampling a larger corpus online (e.g. the British National Corpus at: http://sara.natcorp.ox.ac. uk/) to ordering a corpus or a sample on a CD-ROM (e.g. via ICAME at http:// clu.uni.no/icame/lanspeks.html) to gaining full access for scholarly work either via the corpus designers or publishers associated with the project (for further details, see Chapter 9). The power of open access to large collections of language resources and networked platforms is also growing. The CLARIN project allows users to search multiple resources, including speech corpora, across the European Union, for instance (http://clarin.eu/guest-portal).

Another area of work on spoken grammar looks at the interface between prosody and syntax. In the latter decades of the twentieth century, there were some notable attempts to set aside descriptive and prescriptive grammars and to incorporate prosodic elements into the analysis of the form. David Brazil's (1995) *A Grammar of Speech* was particularly unusual because the linear nature of speech production is taken seriously and talk is described in terms of having 'purpose'. It is interesting to note that, although Brazil's book is highly regarded, the teaching profession as a whole has found it difficult to assimilate many of the principles that underpin the work. The class text on pronunciation for advanced learners of English, also by David Brazil (Brazil, 1994), presents a similar unification of discourse level and other meaning-bearing language features. Hence, in many ways Brazil's work represents one of the most consistent attempts to look at the spoken form on its own terms.

Klein and Purdue's (1992) *Utterance Structure: Developing Grammars Again* was another exception to the rule. In this deliberately provocative and stimulating work, the authors take issue with many of the assumptions of second language acquisition and base their analysis on the notion that learner utterances are a language to be studied in their own right (rather than in relation to a 'target' language). The book is of particular interest to the researcher into speech because it takes a strongly empirical (data-oriented) stand and builds the discussion on real utterances. However, the researcher new to speech research studies, reading either of these books, should realise that while both of them are fascinating, neither of them has succeeded in becoming centrally accepted into the inner circle of applied linguistics, partly due to their (intentional) lack of overlap with the theories underlying the field more generally. They have not produced a paradigm shift of the kind described at the beginning of this chapter.

During the last decade of the twentieth century and first decade of the following one, a growing trend in the research into spoken grammar has been the field known as interactional linguistics. This is a highly relevant area for the researcher interested in approaching spoken data in terms of the dynamic and 'real-time' aspects that tend to be lost when the spoken form is examined entirely through the lens of the written mode (see also Quote 2.4).

Quote 2.4 Peter Auer on the linearity of speech and how grammar is conceptualised

One fundamental difference between spoken and written language has to do with the 'linearity' of speaking in time, in that the temporal structure of speaking is inherently the outcome of an interactive process between speaker and listener. But despite the status of 'linearity' as one of Saussure's fundamental principles, in practice little more than lip-service is paid to the temporality of spoken language, which is treated as having few if any consequences for syntactic analysis. It is trivial to point out that a structuralist definition of the sentence is incompatible with an on-line model of syntax processing. A structuralist analysis, even of ostensibly spoken language, is carried out not from a real-time emergence perspective but as if it were—like a written text—a finished product.

(Auer, 2009)

Concept 2.9 Interactional linguistics (IL)

This is a branch of linguistics that is closely related to conversation analysis. Whereas CA analyses speech data to better understand patterns of talk and the social aspects of talk that are revealed by interactions between participants, IL uses many of the same methods of analysis, but the emphasis is on insights about language itself that can be gained from examining talk in interaction.

Work in IL has a strong connection with the Santa Barbara Corpus of Spoken English, and the development of this by John Du Bois and colleagues was something of a catalyst for work at the interface between discourse and grammar. A bibliography of work in the area can be found at http://www.linguistics.ucsb.edu/faculty/sathomps/ILbib.html, and the approach has been used to allow better understanding of grammatical variation that appears sensitive to interactional context (e.g. how talk is organised around repetition [Bybee, 2006], syntactic constraints on offers of assistance [Curl, 2006], and so on).

Interactional linguistics is closely related to conversation analysis and approaches the emergent nature of grammatical elements from that perspective. Some scholars have begun to argue that syntax itself should be looked at through the lens of interaction, a change that would signal the start of a real paradigm shift (Du Bois, 2014). There is also work on the interface between prosody and syntax that is aligned towards the experimental paradigm: for example, Grosjean (1983) and Grosjean and Hirt (1996), who looked at the issue of how listeners predict the end of a clause from acoustic information earlier in the clause; or Marsi et al. (2002), who carried out work on this area in text-to-speech recognition; and Degand and Simon (2009), who analysed their own corpus of speech genres to look at the interaction between prosodic and syntactic units.

2.5.3   The Research Space at the Level of Speech Production: Fluency and Pronunciation

Traditionally, in the mid- to late twentieth century, a great deal of research into phonology was undertaken to find evidence of an underlying system. This was generally carried out in relation to the model of language that tended to dominate at that time and, to an extent, still does: the transformational or the universal grammar paradigm (see, e.g. Nestor and Vogel, 2007, *Prosodic Phonology*). Within this paradigm, some consideration has continued to be given to the interplay between the different levels and the direction of influence between them (Anttila, 2016). However, the aim of the work has generally been to find evidence of internal language knowledge rather than to describe the system for any applied purpose. For example, Berg and Hassan (1996) examined speaker errors in three languages but were less interested in classifying or explaining the errors than in gaining insight into the 'mapping' or hierarchical conceptualisation of speakers' linguistic knowledge in the three cases.

In contrast to this approach, work into pedagogically related phonology has been carried out within a much less theoretically oriented, and generally an experimentally based, framework. Experimental-style research into the teaching of pronunciation is an area that can provide clearly relevant results for the classroom, and Derwing and Monro (2015) provide a good summary of the research and teaching interface in this area. Keeping up to date with these kinds of results can help teachers plan the balance of the speaking syllabus and can also account for contrasts between student progress in and outside the classroom, for example if a student appears to be making good progress in pronunciation in controlled circumstances but remains difficult to understand when producing longer sections of speech.

Around the start of the twenty-first century there was a rise in the interest in describing and drawing inferences from forms of English spoken as a lingua franca (Concept 2.10). This work emerged during the early years of this century and is an area that provides lively debate about standards, ownership of the language, and the balance between intelligibility versus a native speaker model in teaching speaking. Work such as Jenkins (2000) crystallised some of these ideas, and a readable summary of the issues can be found in Pickering (2006). Chapter 6 returns to this topic in detail.

Concept 2.10 Lingua franca, intelligibility, and common core features

A lingua franca is a form of language used as a common one between speakers of different languages. It is, by its nature, associated with particular domains and language registers where people need to use language to talk to people they are unfamiliar with and to carry out functions beyond the family and day-to-day tasks. Latin was a dominant lingua franca in mediaeval Europe, where it was used for religious and scholarly purposes alongside local 'mother tongue' languages. Today, English is often used as a common language for business, academic, and other purposes, and a branch of applied linguistics research is on 'ELF' or English as a lingua franca (Seidlhoffer, 2001). This work relates to discussions surrounding the importance of intelligibility over accuracy (as defined by an Anglophone speaker's norms) and what 'common core' of grammar and vocabulary is required for users to carry out communicative functions in what is their second or third language.

2.6   Summary

This chapter reviewed some classical approaches to the research process and addressed the particular constraints and issues for the researcher working with spoken forms of language. Beside the issue of the lack of extensive work on the spoken form in its own right, I raised the question of the role of speech data in language theory generally and of the attitude to situated spoken discourse as the basis for generalisations about language. In relation to research based around teaching the spoken form, the further issue of the cultural and pragmatic problems raised by real speech data was aired.

Further Reading

Bloom, R. L., Obler, L. K., De Santi, S. and Ehrlich, J. S. (2013). *Discourse Analysis and Applications: Studies in Adult Clinical Populations*. Hove, UK: Psychology Press.

Derwing, T. M. and Munro, M. J. (2015). *Pronunciation Fundamentals: Evidence-Based Perspectives for L2 Teaching and Research* (Vol. 42). Amsterdam: John Benjamins Publishing Company.

Kormos, J. (2014). *Speech Production and Second Language Acquisition*. London: Routledge.

Paltridge, B. and Phakiti, A. (Eds) (2015). *Research Methods in Applied Linguistics: A Practical Resource*. London: Bloomsbury Publishing.

Price, C. J. (2012). A review and synthesis of the first 20 years of PET and fMRI studies of heard speech, spoken language and reading. *Neuroimage*. 62(2), 816–847.

Szczepek Reed, B. (2007). *Prosodic Orientation in English Conversation*. Basingstoke: Palgrave-Macmillan.

ten Have, P. (2007). *Doing Conversation Analysis*. London: Sage Publications.

Waring, H. Z. (2015). *Theorizing Pedagogical Interaction: Insights from Conversation Analysis*. London: Routledge.

Section II

Issues for Teaching and Assessing Speaking

3   Approaches, Materials, and the Issue of 'Real' Speech

This chapter will . . .

- look at the issues involved in dealing with authentic speech in the class-room, particularly in the context of materials development and attitudes to the spoken form;
- give an overview of the development of approaches seen in published materials over the last few decades and relate these to some of the changes in the approaches to language teaching generally;
- present some examples of more recent approaches, with commentary in relation to the influence of international tests of speaking and balancing authenticity against the practicalities of the classroom.

3.1   Introduction

What is the overriding objective of a speaking component in a language teach-ing syllabus? It seems a tautology to suggest that it is to enable the student to speak the target language. However, that simple objective is actually quite com-plex when authentic speech in context is given a central role, as I am arguing in this book it should be. These complexities about what is being taught work at many levels. As teachers and researchers, we have preconceptions about the spoken form that influence our attitudes to it. These affect how we think about speech at the level of interaction, at the level of language choices, and in what we think it means to be a 'fluent' speaker. Speaking is 'primary', as noted in Chapter 1, but messy and difficult to define; it is fundamental to language learn-ing but open to the vagaries of individual use and context. The production of teaching materials and the handling of speaking in the language classroom show these tensions about how we define the norms of speaking particularly clearly.

3.2   What Are Our Models and Standards When We Teach Speaking?

The attitudes to the spoken form of language expressed in Quotes 3.1 and 3.2 represent two widely differing schools of thought on the topic of speech. Both recognise the distinctive features of spoken discourse but contain markedly different value judgements about the implications of those distinctive characteristics. In the case of Quote 3.1 there is a sense of 'high' and 'low' register being the main distinguishing feature between the spoken and written forms of language. The writer has a notion of a minimal level of structure and vocabulary, 'slurred' and elliptical forms, and commonplace or everyday discourse being the norm for speech as opposed to high-flown or literary style being the norm for writing. This means that the spoken form is not something to be taken as a model for correct, acceptable language use in all circumstances. In this view, therefore, although the spoken form is unique, the features that go to make up that uniqueness may not be entirely desirable for the learner to emulate or for the teacher to introduce into the classroom. While this is an extreme view of the spoken form, it is not that far from what we will see underlies many assessments of spoken language.

Quotes 3.1 and 3.2   Two different perspectives on spoken grammar

In spoken language grammar and vocabulary are reduced to a minimum. The words used often have special or hidden meaning born of some shared experience which an outsider would fail to grasp. The speaker makes much use of elided and slurred forms in the familiar patter of their ordinary everyday speech. Utterances are typically short and often elliptical. . . . Short and rugged homespun words are usually more powerful and expressive than elaborate and high-flown words. Constructions that occur commonly in speech are not necessarily acceptable in formal and dignified writing.

(Yunzhong, 1985: 15)

. . . [S]poken grammars have uniquely special qualities that distinguish them from written ones, wherever we look in our corpus, at whatever level of grammatical category. In our work, too, we have expressed the view that language pedagogy that claims to support the teaching and learning of speaking skills does itself a disservice if it ignores what we know about the spoken language. Whatever else may be the result of imaginative methodologies for eliciting spoken language in the second-language classroom, there can be little hope for a natural spoken output on the part of language learners if the input is stubbornly rooted in models that owe their origin and shape to the written languages. Even much corpus-based grammatical insight . . . has been heavily biased towards evidence gleaned from written sources.

(Carter and McCarthy, 1997)

In the case of the second quotation, the term 'uniquely special qualities' of speech and the plea for more investigation of the form in its own right imply that it is to be viewed as at least on a par with the traditionally more prestigious written form. Moreover, far from being a rather reduced and 'low' form of language, the spoken form is presented as having a rich and diverse grammar of its own. In this school of thought, then, the spoken form is a neglected source of subtle language choices for the learner and a form needing to be brought closer to the heart of language descriptions and into the 'menu' of language choices made available to learners (see also Figures 3.1 and 3.2).

The two different approaches outlined here represent the end points of a continuum of attitudes about the spoken form. On the one hand, teaching forms that are unique to the spoken mode are seen as a marginal activity, rather as idioms or colloquialisms are often introduced into the syllabus— something to enliven a lesson but not regarded as an essential part of a student's structural knowledge. On the other hand, the spoken form is seen as a neglected source of richly diverse language choices that should be central to the teacher's repertoire of vocabulary and grammar structures to teach.

In the debates surrounding models for teaching spoken grammar or pronunciation, the role of authentic speech data is fundamental. Two books which can be used to exemplify the implications of deciding how far to incorporate real and contextualised data were published in the same year: Adrian Wallwork's (1997) resource book for speaking activities, *Discussions A–Z*, and Carter and McCarthy's (1997) *Exploring Spoken English*. Wallwork's book is

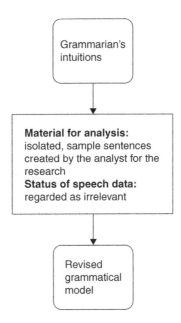

Figure 3.1 Spoken Data in Theoretically Orientated Models of Grammar.

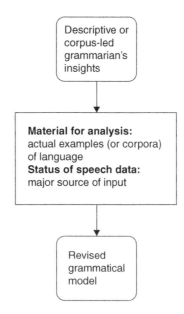

Figure 3.2 Spoken Data in Descriptively Orientated Models of Grammar.

an extremely teacher-friendly, photocopiable resource book (see Quote 3.3) with a better than usual range of diverse, engaging, and often witty topics and visual stimuli for discussion work. Its aim is to engender discussion, and it meets this aim extremely well. These are materials to be handled by a teacher experienced in group work, as there is little guidance for the novice, but they will almost inevitably get students talking.

The nature of discussion is dealt with briefly in the introduction, but beyond that the material is there to function as a prompt rather than to raise awareness about matters such as the nature of interactions during discussion, cultural differences between discussions in different contexts, or any sociolinguistic issues underlying debate or argument. In this sense, the book is solidly in the tradition of the past several decades in language teaching, which holds that it is imperative for the student to engage in activities that generate speech and that such activities will promote language acquisition through processes similar to first language development.

In contrast, a book such as *Exploring Spoken English* focuses on the processes of talk and uses these as starting points for discussion (see Quote 3.4). As a classroom text it will be less easily incorporated into the standard language learning context, since it requires advanced competence on the part of students and a high degree of confidence in handling language awareness raising tasks on the part of the teacher. On the other hand, it provides an excellent set of resources, with accompanying audio material, of the realities of spoken interaction.

These two books are interesting examples at the two extremes of distinctive perspectives on the role of speech in the classroom context. The former represents a classroom tool that will encourage lively and engaging speaking events to emerge and be sustained. These spoken interactions are in themselves the object of the classroom event. In assessing the success or failure of the section of a lesson based on these materials, a significant aspect would be the quantity of speech generated and the balance of the speech events between different class members. Conversely, the awareness-raising nature of material based on analysing actual speaker interactions will be judged not so much by the quantity of speech the student produces when engaging with the tasks and examples but the depth of their understanding of why speakers use the language they do in particular generic and social context.

These two extracts usefully epitomise several factors that have influenced how spoken language is taught. In the late 1990s and the early years of this century three trends were affecting spoken language teaching. First, in the preceding decades there had been what was termed the 'communicative revolution' in language acquisition circles. This amounted to a set of new principles underpinning language teaching that gave more emphasis to the function, appropriateness, and fluency of speech than its grammatical accuracy. Whereas language teaching syllabi in the 1950s and early 1960s would have been organised around the grammatical structures of the language, after the persuasive insights of Dell Hymes in the USA and Christopher Brumfit, Peter Skehan, and other proponents in the UK, the focus changed to functions, tasks, situations, and, crucially for this chapter, the quantity of talk produced by the learner in the classroom. Canale and Swain (1980) provide a useful flavour of the debates at that time and a clear explanation of the relationship between this drive for 'communicative competence' and the dominant paradigm of the time: Chomskyian linguistics. Second, in some influential critiques of the communicative approach (e.g. in the work of Henry Widdowson, 1972, 1978), who was both a proponent and critic of the approach for many years, or later through Nina Spada (1987) looking at different methods and outcomes) scholars began to call for a balance between a focus on fluency and accuracy and on correct use of form and a more discourse-based understanding of competence. This led to a tension between the free flow of the task or the functional-based curriculum and the need to build in grammatical accuracy. The grammar norms that were prevalent were those of written mode, and the third major trend that influenced the status of spoken language in the classroom came from the insights of corpus and discourse linguists working in the 1990s and beyond. This work began to open up the possibility that the norms of writing and the norms of speaking led to different models of correctness. Therefore the two examples of materials to teach speaking skills shown in Quotes 3.3 and 3.4 echo these trends. *Discussions A–Z* was primarily designed with the communicative approach in mind, with its requirement on the teacher to facilitate engaging and stimulating tasks that generate good amounts of student talk. It remained a well-received title and was published in several editions, including a 2013 edition with CD-ROM (Wallwork, 2013). In contrast, *Exploring Spoken English* was a product of the deepening understanding of the distinctiveness of spoken language that began around the late 1990s and reached a high point in the *Cambridge Grammar of English* in 2006 (Carter and McCarthy, 2006), which drew extensively actual examples of spoken language in a range of settings.

Quote 3.3   Are you a good lover?

1. *Love* is an art which needs to be learned if it is to be practised well.
2. You can *love* someone too much.
3. A man and woman can be really good friends without being in *love*.
4. Women have deeper relationships with same-sex friends than men.
5. Men are more attracted to women who are hard to get.
6. Women should never make the first move.
7. You cannot be truly in *love* with two people at the same time.
8. You should only have eyes for your *lover*.
9. It is impossible to *love* and be wise.
10. *Love* can never be forever.

A kiss is just a kiss?

While the language of love-making may be universal when two people are from the same culture, the act of kissing can mean very different things in different parts of the world.

In China, for example, kissing someone in public is seen as unhygienic and repulsive. In Japan, it may be tolerated, but only if the couple stand with bodies well apart and lips shut tight. And the Inuits of Alaska wouldn't dream of doing anything more oral than rubbing noses—not out of any moral scruples but because Inuit women tend to use their mouths for more everyday tasks such as cleaning oil lamps and chewing animal hides to soften them up.

Even if your intentions aren't amorous, you can still run into trouble. Many a foreigner has come unstuck when greeting a friend who is Dutch (mandatory three cheek-pecks) or French (two only).

1. Men kissing each other is disgusting.
2. Shaking hands is the best way to greet someone.
3. Kissing relatives is always embarrassing.

4. Scenes from films which show lovers kissing should be cut.
5. Couples should not be allowed to kiss in the street, on the bus, at the cinema, at school, at work.

(A. Wallwork, *Discussions A–Z Intermediate*, Cambridge University Press, 1997)

Quote 3.4   Cooking rice

Activity

The text examined in this unit was recorded in the kitchen of a family home; all the participants are members of the same family. Here are some brief conversational exchanges. Would you expect to find conversations such as this in a family kitchen?:

A: Would you like a biscuit?
B: I beg your pardon.
A: Would you like a biscuit?
B: Oh, yes please. Thank you very much.
A: I didn't know you used boiling water to make rice.
B: You don't have to use boiling water but it is reckoned to be quicker.

Write short notes explaining why you would or would not expect to find such styles of conversational exchange in the text examined in this unit.

Speakers and setting

<S 01>	female (45)
<S 02>	male (19)
<S 03>	male (46)
<S 04>	male (49)
<S 02>	is <S 01> and <S 04>'s son
<S 03>	is <S 04>'s brother

This extract takes place in <S 01>, <S 02> and <S 04>'s house. <S 03> is visiting them.

3 [4 secs]
4 <S 02> Will it all fit in the one?
5 <S 01> No you'll have to do two separate ones
6 <S 03> Right . . . what next?
7 [17 secs]
8 <S 03> Foreign body in there
9 <S 02> It's the raisins
10 <S 03> Oh is it oh it's rice with raisins is it?
11 <S 02> No no no it's not supposed to be
12 [laughs] erm
13 <S 03> There must be a raisin for it being in there
14 <S 02> D'you want a biscuit?
15 <S 03> Erm
16 <S 02> Biscuit?
17 <S 03> Er yeah
18 [9 secs]
19 <S 04> All right
20 <S 03> Yeah
21 [10 secs]
22 <S 04> Didn't know you used boiling water
23 <S 02> Pardon
24 <S 04> Didn't know you used boiling water
25 <S 02> Don't have to but it's erm . . . they reckon it's erm quicker
26 [5 secs]
27 <S 04> Tony was saying they should have the heating on by about
Wed
28 <S 02> Just gonna put the er butter on
29 <S 04> What you making Ian?
30 <S 02> Mm
31 <S 04> What's that?
32 <S 02> Oh er just gonna do some rice
33 <S 04> Mm
34 <S 02> Doing some rice in the micro
35 <S 03> So you put margarine with it
36 <S 02> Pardon yeah little bit don't know why cos otherwise it'll
37 <S 03> Separate it

(Carter and McCarthy, 1997)

As soon as real speakers in real interactions and in socially and culturally diverse situations are taken into account in models of language, some kind of assessment is required as to how far the features found are universal in the spoken form and to what extent they are particular to that speaker or that context. In this sense, descriptive linguistics meets up rather interestingly with conventional language theories. This is an area that remained under-researched during a phase of rapid improvement in the descriptions of spoken forms and greater emphasis on its importance in the curriculum, and to this day the norms of speech are underrepresented in descriptive grammars. There remains a great deal of opportunity for fruitful research projects in the area of both descriptive studies of spoken forms and more theoretically informed work on how far one can generalise from specific instances to patterns and norms.

These debates lead us to a more practical question for the classroom practitioner, which is how far one would want actually to incorporate any generalisations about spoken forms into the syllabus, whether as an individual teacher or into course components at an institutional level. In general, the tendency to see the grammatical faculty at such an abstract level has permitted the majority of us to continue to teach via models of grammar that are extremely traditional and strongly influenced by historically 'high-prestige' standard forms. These forms, as noted by McCarthy and Carter in the quotation given at the start of this section, tend to be closer to the norms of published writing than of casual speech. However, with the growing body of evidence about the grammar of speech, individual teachers or teacher trainers can quite easily examine what these norms look like and begin to decide where they stand on the issue of how, and how far, to incorporate descriptive linguistics into their teaching.

The issues of target language are of particular interest in relation to the present section. The questions that are particularly relevant in thinking about the structure and vocabulary of spoken forms are outlined here:

- What dialect form or target accent shall I teach?
- What model of correctness, if any, will I use?
- What model of pragmatic or cultural behaviour will I use?

There is little difficulty in taking real speech data as the material for listening classes or using actual examples of interaction (e.g. in student seminars) as indicative models for awareness raising of pragmatic issues among learners. More contentious, and ideologically charged, issues arise when real instances of the spoken form are taken seriously as grammatical models for the target language.

Would you, for example, teach the following to your students if they were learning English? If you were learning a language, would you want to learn similar expressions in the target language?

1. 'ain't'
2. 'bloomin' thing'

3. 't'window' (instead of 'the window')
4. 'the man I told you about, his brother's wife's bought my car'
5. 'good job you told me'
6. 'he's a nice man, Harry is'.

Each of the examples given here is more typically found in the spoken form than the written. However, they also exemplify different types of features, some of which are traditionally excluded from the standard language teaching syllabus, for instance, forms that are felt to mark uneducated or colloquial speech such as 'ain't'. Equally, informal or archaic expressions such as 'bloomin' thing', while recognised as existing, have not normally been felt appropriate for extensive teaching, other than as fairly minor adjuncts to standard grammar and vocabulary or needing to be glossed over in a listening comprehension. Finally, forms which cluster together to form the dialects of geographically distinct regions, such as the use of 't' in place of 'the' in parts of the north of England, are again well known but generally excluded from all but specialist courses. These decisions to marginalise or exclude certain forms have developed over the years in the teaching profession mainly along practical lines, where the fundamental model of grammar is standard (written) English and regional, idiomatic, or historical usage can be dipped into as deemed necessary for a particular class. The argument for this is particularly strong where English is being taught to students who will in all likelihood never use the language in situ in an English speaking country. The argument goes that teaching them a very standardised form will stand them in good stead in globalised settings and regional or other forms can be introduced to the syllabus for learners such as international students who may need to live in the UK and deal with local accents and usage. This position is, however, rooted in a view of spoken language that has been challenged by more detailed understanding of what has been called the grammar of speech.

The final three items in the list are examples of the type of feature described by Carter and McCarthy (1995) in 'Grammar and the spoken language', in which the authors suggest a number of forms which are very common in speech but underdescribed in previous grammatical models. Cullen and Chun (2007) surveyed 24 ELT adult course books published between 2000 and 2007 to examine the extent to which the insights of corpus and discourse findings were being picked up in commercially published materials. Their findings were that a little over half the books had no evidence of these insights being cascaded to the general ELT market. Where they were seen, the items tended to be easily assimilated lexical chunks such as common discourse markers ('you know') and vagueness expressions ('and stuff'). It was much less common for the textbooks to incorporate less superficial grammatical elements (such as items 4, 5, and 6, listed earlier), and the bulk of the spoken grammar items were excluded from lower intermediate and earlier levels. It could be argued that the form of a language that is taught has rarely, if ever, reflected the full range of native speaker forms and registers, but a balance does seem to need to be struck between emergent models of spoken grammar and the norms of classrooms and published materials.

Quote 3.5   Reflecting on research output for teaching

Worthwhile training needs to be informed by mature understanding of research and not by the latest news from the PhD and the research project.

(Davies, 2008: 343)

Overall, in the first few years of the twenty-first century, the field of applied linguistics is in an interesting state of flux over its attitudes to the spoken form and, in particular, spoken grammar. It will take some time for the teaching profession and materials developers to evaluate the multitude of novel ideas about speech that the work of corpus linguists and discourse analysts is throwing up. As I implied earlier, the fact that a structure is commonly found in the spoken form of a language has never made it automatically a target for language topics in classrooms and materials. Davies (2008) expresses this pithily in Quote 3.5 in a discussion of the translation of research insights into the assessment domain. Time is always required to reflect on the output of research in applied and theoretical linguistics and then translate this into the knowledge base for sound pedagogy. The rest of the chapter deals with the flow of insights about spoken language into classrooms and the issues surrounding commercial materials developed for teaching speaking.

The 'gap' between research output and the teachers' knowledge base and requirements is particularly evident when cutting-edge research into a dynamic and socially influenced medium such as speech is being carried out, as the applied linguistic community needs time to absorb information and judge the status of the insights before incorporating them into a syllabus. The teaching community in general will in due course need to reach a view on whether structures such as 'he's a nice man, Harry is' or 'good job you told me' (examples of a structural 'tail' and subject + verb ellipsis, respectively) have the status of core grammatical features or of less central or simply less widely useful forms such as 'ain't' or 'bloomin' thing'.

In addition to the issues surrounding spoken grammar, a significant area where standards and targets of the spoken norm are an issue is the teaching of pronunciation. This is a multifaceted set of arguments, as fluency is often seen as being at odds with accuracy, while at the same time giving the learner plenty of opportunity for unfettered and unself-conscious talk is a key goal of many practitioners. The issue was raised vigorously by Hector Hammerly (1991) in his book *Fluency* and [sic] *Accuracy* (his use of 'sic' indicating an ironic note that, at the time, the bulk of the readership may have felt there was too much tension between these two to combine them with a co-ordinating conjunction). An indicative extract showing his position is given in Quote 3.6.

Quote 3.6   Hammerly on the problems of the communicative approach in relation to accuracy

With its emphasis on communication, [the communicative approach] stresses early vocabulary development while largely ignoring language structure, whether it be phonological, morphological or syntactic. Most second-language-acquisition-through-classroom-communication/interaction advocates do not seem to care that students mispronounce sounds, use wrong stems or endings, or construct sentences following faulty rules—all of these problems are supposed to disappear, eventually, through communicative classroom interaction. Well, there is no reason why they should, and it is clear that most don't.

(Hammerly, 1991: 9)

Just as explicit grammar teaching has always been carried out and has been very popular with many teachers, despite being unfashionable in current language teaching methodology, the teaching of pronunciation and, more broadly, 'fluency' skills persisted largely unchanged over at least a 35-year period. Foote et al. (2011) surveyed Canadian teachers ten years apart asking a similar cohort about their approaches and materials used and found that, by and large, there had been little change in methods aside from a slight rise in teaching segmental features (individual sounds) as opposed to supra-segmental features (e.g. stress patterns). Given that research has suggested in the same period that supra-segmental features may be more important to intelligibility than mastery of individual sounds, this is not entirely positive and again points to some barriers to the flow of insights from the research domain into the classroom.

Quote 3.7   Ur on accents

It needs to be said at the outset that the aim of pronunciation improvement is not to achieve a perfect imitation of a native accent, but simply to get the learner to pronounce accurately enough to be easily and comfortably comprehensible to other (competent) speakers. 'Perfect' accents are difficult if not impossible for most of us to achieve in a foreign language anyway, and may not even be desirable. Many people—even if subconsciously—feel they wish to maintain a slight mother-tongue accent as an assertion of personal or ethnic identity.

(Ur, 1996: 52)

Quote 3.8   Lennon on impressions of fluency

There is also some evidence that learning background may affect the sort of fluency behavior a learner manifests. Shin (1989) studied two learners of Japanese at similar proficiency levels at a British university. Both were native speakers of English. Subject A had spent only a few months in Japan whereas Subject B had been born in Japan and had lived there until aged 12 years. Subject A had six years of formal study of Japanese, and Subject B only three years, however. To Shin (a native speaker of Japanese), Subject B appeared the more fluent in conversation. Analysis revealed she used more colloquial forms than did Subject A, longer sentences, fewer and more appropriate fillers and fewer repetitions. Although Subject A actually paused less than did Subject B, Subject B's pause positioning seemed more appropriate. Interestingly, Subject B actually made more mistakes than did Subject A, but corrected fewer of them. In particular, she tended to let her grammatical mistakes go quite uncorrected.

(Lennon, 1990: 398)

Approaches to teaching these overt speaking skills generally revolve around awareness-raising activities based on phonemic distinctions and practice focusing on models of correct pronunciation. This approach changed very little for at least 35 years and is still at the heart of teacher training in this field.

The social and cultural aspects of teaching pronunciation are very sensitive to changing attitudes, however. For example, while earlier teacher training manuals spoke unashamedly of the remedial work needed to correct a 'foreign accent' (original scare quotes), the work from the mid-'90s onwards became more circumspect on this topic (see Quotes 3.9 and 3.10, in contrast to Quote 3.11). More recently still the focus has shifted even further away from accepting the native speaker as the model towards which the learner is aspiring. Increasing attention has been paid to mutual intelligibility, often between speakers using English as a second or even third language that they find they have in common. In an extreme example of this, Anglophone speakers find that they are the ones who cannot understand the spoken interaction, while the lingua franca speakers comprehend one another easily (McCrum, 2006). Clearly in such a case the dominance of the native speaker as a target for spoken language performance will have been reduced, and this would, taken to its logical conclusion, affect language teaching materials.

Concept 3.1 Accent versus intelligibility?

At the start of the twenty-first century two related strands of research into pronunciation emerged that have clear implications for the classroom. The first was work based on distinguishing some of the features that second language users need to be intelligible rather than pursuing the idea of 'foreign' (i.e. to be improved) and a 'native-like' (i.e. to be aspired to) accent. Hahn (2004), for instance, looked at how the placement of primary stress in a sentence affected intelligibility of second language teaching assistants when listened to by native speakers. This work brought about some insights about certain features of speech being more significant for intelligibility than others, and a debate arose as to whether these should be the focus of the speaking curriculum. This work is closely related to a second strand of research that arose around the same time into English as a lingua franca (see Concept 2.10) which asks what a description of language used solely between nonnative speakers of English would be like and whether focusing on the language that emerges between them is preferable to attempting to attain native speaker norms. What these debates do not tend to note is that the accomplishment of an accent closer to a native speaker and becoming intelligible to listeners is not a binary choice. The former will lead to the latter. Learners will choose the level of effort they are willing to put into their language learning to bring them up to intelligibility or to an accent they identify with in the new language.

However, while the wider culture of applied linguistics shifts to reflect current mores and beliefs among influential players in the discipline, the basics of pronunciation teaching remain largely untouched and firmly at odds with much of the ideology of modern teaching theory. There can still be seen a strong focus on external models, practice, and 'getting it right'. For example,

Hewings (2004) begins with a section on awareness raising, but the core of the material is based on approaches and technical knowledge that would be familiar 20 to 30 years before. Equally, in Seidlhofer (2001) the central sections on the 'how' of teaching overlap greatly with earlier approaches despite being embedded in thought-provoking discussions of the problem of the native speaker as a problematic figure. Derwing (2008) notes that, setting aside larger issues such as motivation and amount of exposure to the language, the fundamental factor in teaching pronunciation is perceptual, i.e. whether the learner can discriminate the relevant sounds. This, again, echoes the approaches noted in the quotations from the 1970s and 1990s (Quotes 3.9 and 3.10).

Quotes 3.9 and 3.10   The fundamentals of teaching pronunciation in the final years of the twentieth century

The sounds we make are *phones*. Although the number of phones that can be produced by any individual speaker is practically unlimited, only certain sounds are recognised by the speakers and hearers of the particular language as conveying meaning. The smallest unit of significant or distinctive sound has been called a *phoneme*. A phoneme is actually an abstraction rather than a concrete description of a specific sound. Any particular phoneme comprises a group or class of sounds that are phonetically similar but whose articulations vary according to their position relative to the other sounds which precede or follow them.

(Rivers and Temperley, 1978: 149)

The first thing that needs to be done is to check that the learner can hear and identify the sounds you want to teach. The same goes for intonation, rhythm and stress: can the learner hear the difference between how a competent, or native, speaker of the language says a word, phrase or sentence and how a foreign learner says it?

This can be done by requesting imitation; or seeing if learners can distinguish between minimal pairs (such as ship/sheep, man/men, thick/tick; see Gimson, 1978); or by contrasting acceptable with unacceptable pronunciation through recordings or live demonstration.

(Ur, 1996: 53)

Quote 3.11 Social and contextual aspects of the task of teaching pronunciation

[P]honetics provides the technical underpinning of pronunciation teaching, and this is what is traditionally given prominence in introductory books and teacher education courses. However, it is probably more helpful to start with considerations of the role of pronunciation in a broader perspective: the 'macro conditions' which in combination eventually lead to specific 'micro conditions' for particular classroom settings. . . .

Starting with *pronunciation in individual and social life* . . . , it is easy to see why the notion of 'correct pronunciation' is questionable as a learning target as soon as we realize how inextricably bound up it is with social and individual identity.

(Seidlhofer, 2001: 57–8)

Quote 3.12 Correctness versus intelligibility affects the curriculum

The voluminous work on error prediction models seems to have limited pedagogical significance because advance knowledge of learner errors is unhelpful in prioritizing phonological structures in an instructional programme that aims at intelligibility.

(Munro and Derwing, 2011)

Further debate within teacher education programmes is needed on the teaching of pronunciation in novel ways and in the light of current thinking about individual motivation to acquire native-speaker-like command, common core features, and intelligibility. As with the features of spoken grammar discussed previously, there may be distinctive and useful insights in the research domain, but these may not easily or rapidly be incorporated into the pedagogic context. The nature of the target of a pronunciation class similarly relates to issues that are interesting in both theoretical and practical terms. There is some evidence that this process is underway. A guest issue of the influential journal *TESOL Quarterly*—read by many practitioners with an interest in research—addressed these issues and in particular the integration of new thinking about accent and pronunciation in relation to classroom applications and uptake by teachers (*TESOL Quarterly*, 30/3, September 2005) and considerable sections of the 2015 *Handbook of English Pronunciation* were devoted to relating research insights about discourse, intelligibility, accent, and English as an international language to the classroom (Reed and Levis, 2015).

3.3 The Evolution of Materials to Teach Speaking

This section looks at published materials on the spoken form taken from different eras in the evolution of language teaching. It provides a commentary that relates them to some of the broader changes in approaches to teaching English that have been seen. The issue underpinning many of the commentaries is that it is significantly easier to teach speaking as if it were isolated from its users, and the greater the flexibility and authenticity of the materials, the harder it can be to manage them in a structured syllabus. In addition to questions of norms of grammar or of targets for pronunciation dealt with in the first part of this chapter, authentic speech brings real people into the classroom and with them the complex matters of class, gender, race, religion, politics, and other culturally sensitive issues.

3.3.1 The Trace of Audio-Lingual and Notional-Functional Approaches

During the 1970s and into the 1980s a focus on structured practice and decontextualised tasks was the norm in materials produced to develop speaking skills. In these the long shadow of what had been a dominant paradigm in language teaching, the audio-lingual method, could still be seen. Whereas in the research domain at this time communicative approaches were emerging, and the audio-lingual approach had been largely set aside from the early 1960s, commercial materials still showed features of the older approach. Very few exercises to generate 'free' talk or allow students to negotiate meaning between themselves were evident, and pattern practice would take place through a highly structured and constrained set of exercises. In addition, as was the norm in the audio-lingual approach, there would be very little description at the meta-level, that is to say, there would be little or no attempt to explain point of language, and the focus was for the student to gain fluency and automaticity by filling in gaps and repeating patterns. In some materials, however, the influence of 'functional' approaches to language teaching—those in which a brief context/scenario and a conversational purpose/function were related to particular forms which speakers might be expected to produce—also made their way into materials produced for teaching speaking.

An example from the late 1970s combining gap-fill with some attention to functional purpose was *Making Polite Noises* by Roger Hargreaves and Mark Fletcher (1979), in which a selection of structures for language functions are introduced which the student is then required to insert into a taped dialogue (see Quote 3.13).

Quote 3.13   Starting and finishing conversations and showing interest

Sorry to interrupt but	is that a . . .?
Excuse me,	didn't we meet in . . .?
	aren't you . . .?
	I hear you're a . . .

Really? Do they? Is she? Mmmm . . .
How are you getting on with the . . .?
What was the . . . like?
What did you think of the . . .?
How interesting, but how . . .?
Tell me about the . . .
Will you excuse me, I'm

afraid I must go and	see if . . .
	say hello to . . .
	get on with . . .

It's been very interesting talking to you.
I've enjoyed hearing about . . .
I'd better go and . . .
See you again soon, I hope.

Dialogue 1

A: Fascinating. I didn't know it could be done like that.

B: Oh yes. And I've got more photos upstairs . . .

C: Really? But I'm afraid we really must be going now. Thank you for a lovely evening.

D: We've enjoyed it too. We're very glad you could come.

Dialogue 2

A: I've been looking at your brooch. It's very unusual. Where did you get it?

B: I got it in Malaysia.

A: Oh did you? How long were you there? By the way I'm John Gooch . . .

B: I'm Sylvia Martin. I was out there for three years actually.

A: Really? That must've been a fascinating experience. How did you like the people . . .?

A few minutes later

A: Good lord! How strange! Well, it's been very interesting talking to you, Sylvia. I must go and have a word with some people over by the door, so will you excuse me a moment? See you later, I hope.

Scenario

You:
A: Yes, it's American. My uncle gave it to me.
You:
A: He used to but he's retired now.
You:
A: Just for a short time—when I was a student.
You:
A: It was. Everything was so different.
You:

Situations

1. You are sitting in a café. A friend arrives with two companions and introduces you. After a short time you have to leave. What do you say?
2. You are in a colleague's office. He wants to tell you about his weekend but you are in rather a hurry. What do you say?
3. A friend has started to build a garage in his garden. Show interest.
4. A friend tells you he went to Saltwood Castle on Saturday. Show interest.
5. Your friend has been talking about Saltwood Castle for the last twenty minutes. How do you get away?

(R. Hargreaves and M. Fletcher, *Making Polite Noises*, Third Impression, 1979, London, Evans)

3.3.2   The Early Influence of the Communicative Approach

In contrast to the audio-lingual approach, many of the pair-work books which grew out of the drive for communicative materials in the ELT classroom during the 1980s and early 1990s focused less on structural input and more on scenarios to prompt 'natural' dialogue. Through such interactions the learner would be encouraged to build fluency, from which, in theory, insight about structure would be acquired. For example, *Partners 3*, by Michael Lewis (1982), contains a range of ingenious scenarios and prompts for the more advanced learner (see Quote 3.14). However, despite the difference in emphasis, it is not that far removed from the earlier materials. In particular, it asks the students to carry out their interactions in something of a void or as if the scenarios being presented were culturally universal or neutral (the British pub and drinking being a culturally loaded set of topics that not all students would appreciate or feel was inclusive).

Quote 3.14   In the pub

1. You are sitting at a table in a pub having a quiet drink on your own.

    You do not know your partner who is sitting opposite you at the same table. As your partner leaves, your drink, which was half-full, is upset all over everywhere.
    Respond naturally when your partner starts.

2. It is early evening. You have been for a drink with your partner whom you know slightly but not very well. You bought the first round and your partner has bought a round too.

    You are killing time because you are meeting a friend (not your partner) to go to the cinema in half an hour or so, so you would rather like another drink. You think your partner is rather a serious sort of person and are fairly sure that when you offer another drink he will say no. If he does, try to persuade him to have one. Insist if necessary!
    You start.

3. Last night you bought a drink for your partner who popped into the pub while you were having a quiet drink.

    It's now lunch time and a very warm day so you have popped in 'for a quick half'. Your partner is standing at the bar with a drink. Unfortunately, one of the reasons your partner is an acquaintance and not a friend is because you think he is rather mean. You're quite sure you have bought more drinks for him than he has for you.
    You start:
    Oh, hello, did you get there on time last night?

4. You are sitting in a pub talking to some friends. You left your (nearly full) drink on the table behind you.

    Respond naturally when your partner starts.

(M. Lewis, *Partners 3: More Demanding Pair Work Practices*, Language Teaching
Publications, 1982)

3.3.3   The Influence of Discourse Analytic Approaches

At the mid-point between the first two extracts, a popular text at higher levels which also balanced structural items and tasks/scenarios/prompts on each page was Keller and Warner's (1988) *Conversation Gambits* (see Quote 3.15). The influence of 1980s UK discourse analysis can be seen in the categorization of stretches of conversation (First speaker: PLAN, Second speaker: RESERVA-TION, First speaker: COUNTER-ARGUMENT). As in the previous exam-ple, the cultural norms being tapped into would perhaps be questioned by a later readership (e.g. middle-class couple with husband persuading wife to do something and taking rhetorical lead throughout).

Quote 3.15   Arguments and counter-arguments

Very often, when we have a plan, someone has an objection or a reservation. We then have to think up a counter-argument to try to persuade them.	Reservation Yes, but . . .
In this dialogue the husband is trying to persuade his wife that they need a cottage in the country.	Yes, but don't forget . . .
Him: Why don't we buy a cottage in the country—somewhere we could go at weekends and for holidays. **(Plan)**	
Her: That's a good idea, but don't you think the children will get bored—can't you hear them—not the cottage AGAIN this summer! **(Reservation)**	That would be great, except . . .
Him: That's probably true, but I think it would be nice for us, and after all, it won't be long before they'll want to go off with their own friends. **(Counter-argument)**	That's a good idea,but . . .
Work in pairs with these ideas using the phrases for reservations and counter-arguments.	Counter-arguments

1.	A:	take up skiing	Even so,
	B:	don't have the time or money	
	A:	it would be fun, good exercise	Even if that is so,
2.	A:	buy a flat	That may be so, but . . .
	B:	can't afford it	
	A:	cheaper than paying rent	That's probably true, but . . .
3.	A:	fly to Moscow	
	B:	cheaper to go by train	
	A:	we'd lose a week of holiday just travelling, plus all the money on food	Possibly, but . . .
4.	A:	buy a new car—the old one's rusty	
	B:	we haven't finished paying for the old one	
	A:	the old one's dangerous	
5.	A:	have a party	
	B:	the neighbours would object	
	A:	why not invite the neighbours	
6.	A:	your plan	
	B:	your reservation	
	A:	your counter-argument	

(Keller and Warner, 1988)

3.3.4   *Examples of Task-Based Syllabus Approaches Emerging*

Everyday Listening and Speaking by Sarah Cunningham and Peter Moor (1992) was less conversationally oriented but combined some useful language work in a variety of contexts at the intermediate level. The book contrasts with the two previous examples and shows a next stage in the evolution of materials in general in that it integrates structural items being presented into the tasks themselves (see Quote 3.16). It also reflected the changing currents of teacher training and the flow of ideas from the academic world to the classroom. In these tasks the active participation of the learner is emphasised, speaking and listening skills are integrated, and the student is asked to think about choices and solve problems reflecting moves towards the task-based syllabus and learning by doing.

Quote 3.16   Everyday listening and speaking

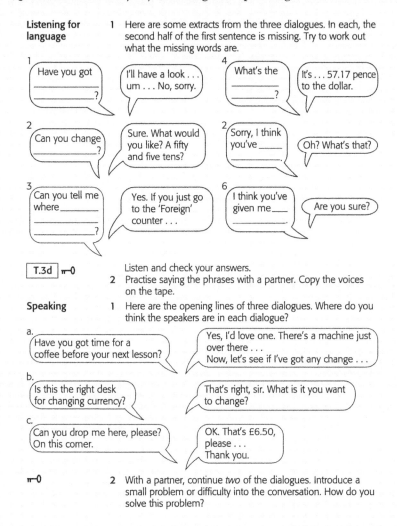

Listening for language

1   Here are some extracts from the three dialogues. In each, the second half of the first sentence is missing. Try to work out what the missing words are.

1
Have you got _____?

I'll have a look . . . um . . . No, sorry.

4
What's the _____?

It's . . . 57.17 pence to the dollar.

2
Can you change _____?

Sure. What would you like? A fifty and five tens?

2
Sorry, I think you've _____.

Oh? What's that?

3
Can you tell me where _____ _____ _____?

Yes. If you just go to the 'Foreign' counter . . .

6
I think you've given me _____ _____.

Are you sure?

T.3d   ☞–0

Listen and check your answers.

2   Practise saying the phrases with a partner. Copy the voices on the tape.

Speaking

1   Here are the opening lines of three dialogues. Where do you think the speakers are in each dialogue?

a.
Have you got time for a coffee before your next lesson?

Yes, I'd love one. There's a machine just over there . . .
Now, let's see if I've got any change . . .

b.
Is this the right desk for changing currency?

That's right, sir. What is it you want to change?

c.
Can you drop me here, please? On this corner.

OK. That's £6.50, please . . .
Thank you.

☞–0

2   With a partner, continue *two* of the dialogues. Introduce a small problem or difficulty into the conversation. How do you solve this problem?

(Reproduced by permission of Oxford University Press from *Everyday Listening and Speaking* by Sarah Cunningham and Peter Moor © Oxford University Press, 1992)

3.3.5   Task-Based Learning Materials for Teaching Speaking in the Context of English for Academic Purposes

Interestingly, in the fields of ESP and EAP the tendency to isolate speaking processes from broader contextual matters has never been as strong as in general language teaching. For example, in Lynch and Anderson's (1992) *Study Speaking* (see Quote 3.17) or Rignall and Furneaux's (1997) *Speaking* in the English for Academic Study Series, speaking skills are embedded in broader functional areas (such as disagreeing) and in turn presented within appropriate real-world contexts and genres (such as the academic seminar). This highlights the advantage of knowing the specific use to which a learner will put a target language in terms of defining the areas to be introduced into a syllabus. While these appropriacy constraints apply across all skill areas, they are more sensitive in the domain of speech.

Quote 3.17   Seminar skills: questioning

Speakers are expected to allow time at the end of their presentation for questions and discussion. Many people would say that this question-and-answer stage is at least as important as the initial presentation. However, questioning can be a problematic aspect of seminar performance. Often the speaker misunderstands a question (and not only when the questioner is a nonnative speaker), because the point is lost in an over-long sentence.

A practical solution is to keep your question short. Don't forget that the presenter may not be sure, when you start to speak, that you are asking a question—you might be wanting to disagree. So you need to make clear:

Example:

a)   that it's a question   '*I have a question . . .*

b)   what the topic is   *. . . about assessment on the course.*

c)   what the point is   *What is the overall balance between the examinations and the project work?*'

Discussion point 1

It is sometimes suggested that the speaker should repeat or summarise each question asked from the audience, before beginning to give an answer. Why is this advice given?

Discussion point 2

Questions and answers are not always straightforward. *The speaker* who is asked a question by a listener may understand the question but be unable (or unwilling) to give an answer, in which case, they may *avoid* giving a direct answer. Here are some examples. Can you think of others?

Avoiding an answer

(X) is important but it's too complex for us to deal with here.
I think we have to focus on (Y) rather than (X).
It's too early for us to say whether . . .
We don't have enough evidence to show that . . .
That's not something I've had time to deal with, but . . .

Discussion point 3

The listener may want to say that the answer they have received is inadequate:

Following up a question

That's not really what I was asking. My question was about . . .
Perhaps I didn't make my question clear. In fact what I asked was . . .
I think you've answered a slightly different question.
I've understood that but what I actually had in mind was . . .

These expressions are relatively polite and formal. What words could you omit from each example to make them more direct? What type of words are they?

(Lynch and Anderson, 1992)

3.4   The Current Scene in Materials to Teach Speaking

Developments at the end of the twentieth century and the first decades of this one continued to reflect the slow trickle of ideas from the applied linguistics research community into the classroom. Hand in hand with the greater professionalisation of the ELT community, there has been a tendency for the classroom practitioner to explore corpus, online, and task- or project-based approaches independently of published materials and/or to engage in their own materials development. A survey of British Council English language teachers based in eight countries and follow-up discussion via webinars carried out at the end of 2015 suggested that the teachers are acutely aware of the students' needs and put this at the heart of their approaches to teaching speaking. The word clouds created from their input shown in Figures 3.3 and 3.4 both have by far the greatest emphasis on the word 'students', implying their centrality

Figure 3.3 Word Cloud of Teachers' Responses to What They Enjoy About Teaching Speaking.

in the teachers' thinking when it comes to teaching speaking. Given this was their most pressing concern, they at times found the topics in generic course materials were not engaging enough or suitable for their contexts:

- 'I have found it difficult using course materials from major publishers in Malaysia, because they tend to deal with topics that students here have very little knowledge of. Students often find it difficult to contribute to discussions on topics that fall outside the areas of work and family.'
- '[Good materials use] topical things, relevant to the learners.'
- 'Learners want to talk about their own things; their own lives.'
- 'Effective materials address the students' needs and interests.'
- 'At university level, learners want to know how to get help with their major subject.'

Teachers were also aware of the students' very different needs at different levels and wanted to be able to relate this to their approach to teaching speaking.

Figure 3.4 Word Cloud of Teachers' Responses to What They Find Challenging About Teaching Speaking.

For teenagers and adults they were aware of the risk taking that speaking practice entails:

- 'Reducing the stress levels is key.'
- '[Using] creativity and humour (for young learners).'
- 'For the lower levels I tend to use the activities in the book as they are normally well structured and give students plenty of support.'
- 'Using "props" to enhance role play (for young learners).'
- 'Many teenagers have problems speaking English because of their self-consciousness in class. Teenagers also try to focus on avoiding making mistakes, which is very difficult especially at low levels.'

On the topic of authenticity there was a general feeling that this became more relevant the higher the proficiency level, where the lack of it would be more likely to be noticed. There was also a pragmatic view of the native speaker–nonnative speaker issues, whilst teachers acknowledged that for some learners the desire to acquire a native speaker accent was motivating.

- 'They [students, and especially Europeans] know a course book is scripted and don't like that.'
- 'Most students will only ever speak to nonnative speakers.'
- 'We produce our own recordings. These are better than actors as they are real.'
- 'Authenticity is only a problem at higher level.'
- 'My students will probably never speak to an English native speaker, so we concentrate on meaning and understanding.'

The amount of material available in a published course book that can support teaching speaking was seen as rather limited, particularly as the level becomes higher:

- 'The speaking section is very small, so you have to develop that yourself.'
- 'Lack of supplementary materials.'
- 'Too rigid.'
- '[The importance of intonation is] underestimated in the course books.'
- 'We figure out what the students need and then adapt written stuff.'
- 'For the lower levels I tend to use the activities in the book as they are normally well structured and give students plenty of support.'

Teachers reported using a very wide range of alternative specialist books (around 30 titles across 12 respondents and, with adults, the British Council MyClass materials) to supplement their core teaching materials. Many of the teachers reported using the Internet, mobile phones, apps, YouTube, TEDtalks, and the flexibility and personalisation of different new media to engage with learners:

- '[Students] use social media a lot, which is a big influence.'
- 'Listening to each other on a recording and then transcribing it.'
- 'I record them and give them the sound files.'
- 'They record themselves on their phones.'
- 'There has been a move towards Internet materials and self-published materials such as YouTube, blogs etc.'
- 'Many students are keen to learn twenty-first century skills and therefore their teachers are also keen to keep up with their learners' interests.'

Finally, in relation to assessment of speaking and exam preparation there was a tendency to see the 'IELTS prep.' classes as separate from the general speaking classes and to empathise with the students' fear of the assessment processes:

- 'Learners need exposure to . . . work for exams separately.'
- 'Best to prepare them [for exams] without them knowing.'

- 'I found it most effective to assess students' speaking while they are working on a task or a communicative activity in pairs or groups. With Young Learners I would sometimes do this covertly, without the students realising they're being tested, in order to keep the affective filter low.'

When instructors were asked about the aspects they found most enjoyable and most challenging about teaching speaking, there was a unanimous sense of the fun that teaching speaking can be, although the challenges were many and varied. Teachers noted the humour and creativity that teaching speaking can bring to the classroom, the sense of growing confidence, a new 'voice' being acquired, and progress being quite tangible. The impact on the teachers was also mentioned, for example, the window given on individual lives and different cultural norms that speaking practice tasks allowed them (particularly in Arab-world contexts).

In terms of the difficulties of teaching speaking, they aspired to a level of relevant, personally engaging topics and felt that it was hard to differentiate activities to generate talk versus tasks that would improve speaking:

- 'Improving speaking skills as opposed to finding opportunities for students to speak, which is relatively easy.'
- '[M]aking a lesson plan that is challenging and fun at the same time.'

Some mentioned the accuracy versus grammatical correctness dichotomy being an issue particularly where students were risk averse or held ingrained ideas about correctness. The natural reticence of some students and the reluctance to work with peers (particularly those with accents they find culturally loaded) were issues for some. Others mentioned handling technical matters such as dealing with mistakes in task-based settings or teaching large or mixed-level groups. Two word clouds from the comments of the teachers are shown in Figures 3.3 and 3.4. Although it was not apparent from the survey or the webinar input directly, the dominance of the word 'pronunciation' suggests that this is a challenge in the minds of many of the respondents.

The small percentage of ELT staff worldwide that has the luxury of time and training in the specialist area of teaching speaking should not be forgotten. The much larger, hard-pressed, often nonnative speaker, teaching community still requires a range of modern published materials to support the development of speaking skills. Despite this very high demand, the needs of teachers for innovative materials into speaking may, in fact, be being addressed less rather than more in trends in modern ELT publishing. There has been some nervousness on the part of the commercial publishers to tackle the issues surrounding teaching spontaneous, richly contextualised speech data. The tendency in the publishing world has been simply to produce a greater variety of course books for different types of learners and levels and retain a strong focus on prompts for discussions, role-plays, and tasks to generate interaction (e.g. Gammidge, 2004). Rather than books that draw on research insights about spoken interaction, by far the most prominent development in recent years has been material developed to prepare for the speaking elements of the major international tests of English. A calculation based on web searches suggests that, in terms of materials for speaking/listening, around 50 new titles were produced for the two most widely known tests of English—the International English Language Testing System (IELTS) and the Test of English as a Foreign Language (TOEFL)—between 2000 and 2009, and a further 35 new titles published each year since then. This large number was prompted in part by significant changes to the test formats requiring new material to prepare students, but the paucity of commercial teaching material based on, for example, spoken corpora is stark in comparison. We may be witnessing a gap developing between two types of teaching community. The first, by far the largest, is the international community of often nonnative speaker teachers who depend on published materials and work in contexts where the use of a textbook is an imperative. The second is those who work in contexts that allow time and training to support the confident teaching of speaking skills by teachers of all backgrounds and languages. In general, the former group will be highly likely to teach speaking via standard course books and materials for test preparation such as those shown at the start of the next section.

3.4.1   *Two Contrasting Approaches: Teaching to the Test and Teaching Interactive and Pragmatic Skills*

The materials shown in Quote 3.18 are from a title published to help prepare students for the speaking module of the International English Language Testing System (IELTS) test. All materials for examination preparation tend to fall into very similar patterns. They introduce the main stages of the test, show typical tasks and model answers, propose hints and strategies for the test taker, and give plenty of practice materials. Quote 3.18 from Barron (2005) shows the typical stages in this process.

Quote 3.18   An examination focused approach

QUICK STUDY

Overview

There are three parts to the Speaking module, which lasts between 11 and 14 minutes. You will be alone in a room with one examiner who will ask you questions and ask you to talk on certain topics. The interview will be recorded. You will be able to take notes in Part 2 only.

The Speaking modules are the same for both the Academic and the General Training versions of the IELTS. Topics include discussions about you, your family, etc.

Speaking Module

Parts	Time	Tasks
Part 1	4–5 minutes	Introductions Identify self Answer questions
Part 2	3–4 minutes: 1 minute preparation, 1–2 minute speaking 1 minute follow-up questions	Talk on a topic given on a task card
Part 3	4–5 minutes	Discuss with examiner the issues related to the topic in Part 2

Question Types

There are a variety of questions and prompts the examiner will use to get you to talk during the IELTS Speaking module. You should be familiar with these types.

Part 1 *Wh*-questions
          Yes/No questions
Part 2 Describe and explain
          Wh-questions
          Yes/No questions
Part 3 *Wh*-questions
          Yes/No questions

Part 1

Practice A

Write the answer to the examiner's questions for Part 1.

1. What is your name?

_____

2. How do you spell it?

   _____

3. Do you have your proof of identification? May I see it?

   _____

4. Let's talk about where you live. Can you describe your neighbourhood?

   _____

5. What is an advantage of living there?

   _____

6. What is a disadvantage of living there?

   _____

7. Let's talk about jobs. What kind of job do you have?

   _____

8. What is the best thing about your job?

   _____

9. Let's talk about free time. What is one activity you enjoy doing in your free time?

   _____

10. How did you become interested in this activity?

   _____

Practice B

Pretend you are taking the Speaking module. The examiner asked you the questions in Practice A. Now give your answers aloud to the examiner's questions for Part 1.

Part 2

Practice C

Make notes to answer the questions on the Task Card for Part 2. Try to do this in one minute.

Task card

> Describe a place that you like to go.
>   You should say:
>   where the place is
>   how you get there
>   what it looks like
>   and explain why you like the place.

Notes:

   Place _____

   Location _____

   Transportation _____

   Appearance _____

   Why I like it _____

Practice D

Pretend you are taking the Speaking module. The examiner gave you the Task Card in Practice C. Now give you answers out loud to the examiner's questions for Part 2.

Practice E

Write the answers to the examiner's follow-up questions for Part 2.

1.   Do you go on your own to this place?
2.   Are there similar places you like to go?

Practice F

Pretend you are taking the Speaking module. The examiner asked you the questions in Practice E. Now give your answers out loud to the examiner's questions for Part 2 follow-up.

(Lougheed, 2006: 104–6)

The frame of reference in materials written for test takers is, understandably, the examination format and rubrics. Any mention of interactive behaviour is linked not to the norms of conversation, but to the best tactic for the candidate in the examination context. For instance, in Kaplan (2009) a useful conversational strategy—buying time by using conversational 'fillers'—is highlighted, but the conversational action is related to the outcome in terms of 'marks for fluency' rather than any wider understanding of pragmatic effects or goals (Quote 3.19).

Quote 3.19   Thinking or Hesitating?

Strategy 4: You can stall, but not for long.

   If you cannot think of an answer to an examiner's question right away, you can say some 'filler' phrases to acknowledge the question and to show the examiner that are [sic] thinking about your answer. However, avoid waiting too long before you speak. This will cause the examiner to give you lower marks for fluency.

(Kaplan, 2009: 172)

A contrasting approach can be seen in Viney and Viney (1996; see sample material in Quote 3.20).

Quote 3.20   Thinking Time

1. Hesitation Strategies

Often we want to give ourselves thinking time before answer a question, especially if we don't understand it! Here are four techniques:

Techniques	Examples	Advantages	Disadvantages
Pretend you haven't heard	*Pardon?* *Sorry?* *Eh?*	Simple—only one word to remember.	Everyone does it.
Repeat the question	*You mean . . . what is forty-five divided by nine?*	Lots of thinking time.	Can you remember the question?
Use delaying Noises	*Well . . .* *Um . . .* *Er . . .*	You can use them several times in the same sentence.	If you use them too often you sound stupid.
Use it depends	*It depends.* *It depends on (the situation).*	You will sound intelligent. (Stroke your chin at the same time.)	You can only use it when there is more than one possible answer.

Don't forget that you can use more than one technique.
   Sorry? You want to know what I think about this?
   Well . . . um . . . it depends, really.
Ask your partner questions. Your partner tries to get thinking time. You
   can ask:
   • mathematical questions *What's five hundred divided by twenty?*
   • factual questions *What's the capital of Mongolia?*

- moral questions *Should we kill animals for their fur?*
- personal questions *Do you believe in Father Christmas?*

2. Does this happen to you?

Ask a partner these questions.
- Do you interrupt people to correct their mistakes?
- Do you get angry when other people interrupt you?
- If there is a pause in conversation, do you feel embarrassed?
- Do you say something to fill the pause?
- In a conversation, are you the first person to give an opinion?
- If you get bored by a conversation, do you change the topic, or do you remain quiet?
- Do you like to be the centre of attention (the person everyone is listening to)?
- Do you feel shy in a large group?
- Do you notice when some people in a group are too shy to speak?
- Do you try to include them in the conversation?

(Viney and Viney, 1996: 79)

In Quote 3.20 the advantages and disadvantages of using different hesitation forms are weighed up and the conversational impact of them considered. This is followed by tasks to engage students in reflection on their own conversational style. Of the two approaches, that shown in Quote 3.20 will both motivate and engage learners in thinking about their own real-world needs in terms of conversation and will equip them for a wider range of context than a test but would also enable the test taker to perform naturally and fluently in the test context.

3.5   Bringing the Skills Together

It is salutary to remember how skilful the competent speaker of any language is and the multitude of tasks that have to be carried out simultaneously for talk to occur. Quote 3.21 gives a clear reminder of this. Acknowledging the unique complexity of the skill of speaking can help build confidence for teachers and learners in approaches to spoken language. It is not simply a matter of developing accurate mastery of structure and vocabulary combined with effective handling of phonetic detail. The spoken form, unlike the written, calls for the learner to draw on oral/aural, cognitive, processing, pragmatic, interpersonal, cultural, and motor skills simultaneously. This dynamic and complex set of achievements comes as naturally to the first language user as the smooth oper-ation of a car to an experienced driver (in contrast to the halting and some-times humiliating performance of the learner driver). Knowing how to speak is too often presented as a simple translation of linguistic knowledge into the spoken medium. Learners very often have a far higher passive knowledge of the language than the multiply challenging skill of speaking will allow them to deliver under real-time processing pressures. Explaining that the spoken medium brings processing and interpersonal pressures that even first language users will find challenging at times is a good place to begin for any level of learner. Finding the right response to anger in a friend or loved one, defending an idea in an aggressive business meeting or academic seminar, answering an unexpected question in a job interview—none of these are easy in the spoken channel, even in a first language under real-time processing constraints.

Quote 3.21   Florez on what a good speaker does

Speakers must be able to anticipate and then produce the expected pat-terns of specific discourse situations. They must also manage discrete elements such as turn-taking, rephrasing, providing feedback or redi-recting (Burns and Joyce, 1997). . . . Other skills and knowledge that instruction might address include the following:

- producing the sounds, stress patterns, rhythmic structure, and into-nations of the language;
- using grammar structures accurately;
- assessing characteristics of the target audience, including shared knowledge or shared points of reference, status and power relations of participants, interest levels, or differences in perspectives;
- selecting vocabulary that is understandable and appropriate for the audience, the topic being discussed, and the setting in which the speech act occurs;
- applying strategies to enhance comprehensibility, such as emphasiz-ing key words, rephrasing or checking for listener comprehension;
- using gestures or body language; and
- paying attention to the success of the interaction and adjusting components of speech such as vocabulary, rate of speech, and com-plexity of grammar structures to maximize listener comprehension and involvement (Brown, 1994).

(Florez, 1999: 2)

3.6   Summary

This chapter has looked at the issue of authentic speech and what model can be used for spoken grammar and for pronunciation. It also addressed the central questions of how far it is possible to teach 'real' speech, the influence of context on speaker choices, and what our expectations are when we teach fluency and pronunciation. Underlying each of these issues is the core question of how much we really know about the spoken form of any target language and how slow the processes are by which research into the spoken form reaches the classroom. The conservative and sometimes assessment-driven approach of the larger commercial publishing houses in relation to uptake of innovation in ELT materials for speaking was also discussed.

Further Reading

Dat, B. (2013). Materials for developing speaking skills. In B. Tomlinson (Ed), *Developing Materials for Language Teaching*. London: Continuum, pp. 375–393.

Folse, K. S. (2006). *The Art of Teaching Speaking*. Mahwah, NJ: Lawrence Erlbaum.

Low, E. L. (2014). *Pronunciation for English as an International Language: From Research to Practice*. London: Routledge.

Munro, M. J. and Derwing, T. M. (2011). The foundations of accent and intelligibility in pronunciation research. *Language Teaching*. 44(03), 316–327.

Nation, I.S.P. and Newton, J. (2008). *Teaching EFL/ESL Listening and Speaking*. London: Routledge.

Thornbury, S. and Slade, D. (2006). *Conversation: From Description to Pedagogy*. New York: Cambridge University Press.

Usó-Juan, E. and Martínez-Flor, A. (Eds) (2006). *Current Trends in the Development and Teaching of the Four Language Skills*. Berlin: Mouton de Gruyter.

4 Issues in Assessing Speaking

This chapter will . . .

- discuss the key issues underlying the assessment of speaking;
- describe and compare the speaking components of internationally recognised tests of spoken English;
- discuss the question of how far oral skills lend themselves to existing test paradigms and whether this is a problem.

4.1 Introduction

Quotes 4.1 and 4.2

The spoken performances of the test takers must be rated in some way. It is almost axiomatic that, because language use is a multicomponential phenomenon, requiring interlocutors to negotiate meanings, no two listeners hear the same message. This aspect of language use is a source of bias in test scores. It leads language test developers to severely limit which features of a performance they require raters to attend to in making their ratings. They hope that, if raters focus attention only on pronunciation, grammar, fluency and comprehensibility, for example, the many other features of the discourse will not influence them. There is mounting evidence that this is a vain hope.

(Douglas, 1997: 22)

[W]e give language learners tasks to do. The learners have to respond in some proscribed way to the tasks we set. We quantify their responses by assigning a number to summarise the performance. Then we use the numbers to decide whether or not they know the language well enough for communication in some real-world context.

(Fulcher, 2015: 1)

Language assessment is a complex field and one that even the most experienced and highly regarded experts remain challenged by. The two opening quotations to this chapter capture some of the central issues: how do you remove bias from speaking tests when, often, no two people hear the same thing? Can you solve bias and subjectivity by becoming increasingly compartmentalised and rigorous in what you decide to assess? How can we be sure that a simple score in a test really relates to what someone can do outside the test? A substantial research effort has gone on over the years to answer these kinds of questions, and this chapter deals with these along with an introduction to the key concepts of language assessment that most affect oral language testing.

The development of the assessment of speaking has gone hand in hand with the emergence of language testing as a recognised subfield of applied linguistics. Attitudes to oral assessment have been shaped by the changing currents of research paradigms in this field and in linguistics more generally. Early developments in language testing were strongly linked to governmental, colonial, and military requirements for effective language teaching and testing, particularly during the Second World War. This strongly practical focus meant that language assessment practices and theory tended to develop outside the discipline of linguistics, and it is only over the last 35 years or so (last 20 years of the twentieth century and the start of the twenty-first) that the somewhat isolated research in assessment has joined up with wider work in the discipline. This tendency has meant that the metalanguage of testing can be somewhat off-putting for those not trained in the field even if they are well-versed in applied linguistics more generally. The need for convincingly objective measures can also make the process seem very distant from the more humanistic discourse of the classroom that has tended to dominate our teacher training paradigms. Given the powerful influence of assessment on teaching, it is important for practitioners to become familiar with the basic terminology and concepts. This chapter brings together an introduction to some key concepts in language assessment more generally and weaves them into a specific set of issues for oral assessment.

Quotes 4.3, 4.4, and 4.5 Three aspects of the difficulties involved in assessing speaking

Why have oral tests generally received little attention? Many books have been written about language testing. They follow the changing fashions of language teaching, but they usually make the same basic assumptions about the nature of language testing. Generally, little space is devoted to oral testing compared to testing the other skills. This is partly because of the difficulty of treating oral tests in the same way as other more conventional tests.

(Underhill, 1987: 3)

The speaking assessment project is therefore primarily a practical one. The need for speaking tests has expanded from the educational and military domain to decision making for international mobility, entrance to higher education, and employment. But investigating how we make sound decisions based on inferences from speaking test scores remains the central concern of research.

(Fulcher, 2015: 198)

Measurement of a speaking performance . . . requires a different kind of scale, such as those used in rating performance in sports competitions. For example, the quality of a figure skater's performance in the Olympics is based on rank; there is no equal-interval unit of measurement comparable to ounces or pounds that allows precise measurement of a figure skating performance.

(Ginther, 2012: 3)

As is suggested by Quote 4.2 from the late 1980s, the focus on oral assessment *per se* was quite slow to emerge in the evolution of language assessment overall. This was for several reasons, some of which are still influencing the way that oral testing is viewed and carried out. During the 1970s and 1980s a primary concern for those engaged in professional test development echoed the tendency which had gained prominence in the middle decades of the twentieth century in linguistics generally. This trend involved a powerful interest in generalising away from particular instances of discourse to uncover more universal aspects of language. Whereas in linguistic theory this took the form of complex and sometimes arcane accounts of the structure of, for example, universal grammar, in the field of language testing this desire to generalise and to abstract away from particular examples of language emerged as a strong psychometric orientation in, for example, the work of John Oller. Oller (1983) provides a summary of his thinking as developed during the 1970s, which influenced a good deal of thinking at the time. This approach aimed to distil the complexities of language into 'facets' that could be captured by simple formats such as multiple-choice tests. These psychometric measures and techniques to capture a stable indication of performance across tests and domains remain accepted and influential in current test design circles. For the approach to work, there needs to be a clear and consistent link between the outputs and scores of the test and performance in the world outside the test. How to create this linkage is the fundamental question in all language assessment and is particularly difficult in the case of spoken language which, by its nature, is subject to many vagaries that affect its delivery. Many scholars have started to challenge the ethical and social effects of tests that are designed for large-scale delivery and at the same time have a powerful effect on life chances and on the priorities of the language classroom (see also Concept Box 4.5).

In ways that parallel the influence felt on textbooks and materials development for the skill of speaking, language testing is influenced to an extent by the interests of the major commercial publishers and the international organisations that research and deliver dominant, high-stakes (see Concept Box 4.5), and well-known tests of English such as IELTS (International English Language Testing System) and TOEFL (Test of English as a Foreign Language). These tests are hugely influential. They are run by substantial, commercially funded, international organisations that also provide significant contributions to the research arena in terms of deliverables and monographs on the work underpinning their tests. They fund independent research into their provision through competitive bids and tenders. Less positive, perhaps, is the powerful effect these major high-stakes tests have on what happens in classrooms as teachers 'teach to the test', and the spoken performance that is most highly valued becomes the output that scores highly in the test. Liz Hamp-Lyons' work on 'washback' (the effects a test has on the teaching given to candidates) and the culture that this promotes is relevant here (see Hamp-Lyons, 1997 and 2007 for the development of these ideas). In addition, the ethics of assessment generally, the power relations between test takers and designers, and the influence of testing in society have been questioned (see, e.g. McNamara, 2001; Shohamy, 2001; Bachman, 2005; McNamara, 2011; Shohamy, 2013). Kunnan neatly sums up the journey that scholars of language assessment have been taking in the early years of the twenty-first century as being one from 'how' and 'what' to 'why' and 'should we' (Kunnan, 2013: 13).

Within the scholarly community more generally the debate about oral assessment has gathered pace since the 1990s and in the early years of the twenty-first century has become particularly affected by the growing understanding of the differences between spoken and written language (see in particular Biber et al.,

2004, for a large-scale project on spoken versus written language in the context of test development research). There has also been a considerable and wide-ranging programme of research into how to assess speakers of a variety of backgrounds, cultures, and genders (O'Sullivan, 2000; Brown and McNamara, 2004; Lumley and O'Sullivan, 2005; Yu, 2010; Tong et al., 2010; Willingham and Cole, 2013). In the early years of the twenty-first century trends such as the English as a lingua franca, critical discourse analysis and the world Englishes movements all played a role in challenging what the norms and constructs of spoken assessment should be (McNamara, 2012, and see later in the chapter for further discussion in relation to models of language in assessment frameworks).

A further trend impacting on oral assessment in recent years has flowed from the improvement in speech recognition technology. This has in turn meant that automated assessment of spoken test performance has become increasingly prevalent. The speaking component of the TOEFL examination, for instance, is assessed in this way, as are newer-to-the-market tests such as Pearson's 'Versant'. This approach is based on the ability to validate online spoken assessment and other digital modes of testing against performance in more traditional forms of delivery and has led to suggestions that the online test reads across to the traditional more than adequately (Bernstein, Van Moere, and Cheng (2010).

It is in the context of the background factors outlined here about the history of the development and influence of wider trends that any discussion of testing speaking needs to take place. As in other fields of Applied Linguistics, there remains to this day a tension between the early very practical goals and the later more professionalised and research-oriented directions of language teaching, research, and testing. Assessment of spoken language asks difficult questions—both practical and ethical—of test developers and places particular demands on the research community. The considerations that are needed in relation to testing speaking are summarised in Concept 4.1. Even individual classroom practitioners attempting to create a small local speaking test for a particular group of learners will be influenced by similar issues to those outlined in the rest of this chapter once they start to reflect in detail on the questions of what they want their students to achieve, what they regard as stronger or weaker performance, how to distil this performance into a score, and how to evaluate this process consistently and fairly across several speakers.

Concept 4.1 Domains of speaking in relation to assessment

In his 2004 chapter on developing a principled approach to the complexities of teaching and testing speaking, Dan Douglas outlines eight aspects that the learner needs to be aware of in any communicative activities, including testing:

- setting
- participants
- purpose
- topical content
- tone
- language
- norms of interaction
- genre

He argues for far greater and more detailed understanding of the impact of these areas on spoken language than had previously been the case and for learners to be given a much richer set of contextual information before they try to produce spoken language. For instance, in terms of setting, he does not completely disallow the idea that in addition to normal written and pictorial prompts, other sensory input might be made available to set the scene, such as smells. He sees the impact of the contextual variables above as setting the research agenda for both teaching and testing speaking in future.

(Douglas, 2004: 40–1)

The nature of speech means that the potential for subjectivity, variation in test facets, and, due to these two factors, difficulty in maintaining consistency across tests are far higher in the spoken form than the written. As there are so many competing factors which can affect speech production under test conditions—from the health of the candidate to cultural expectations about how a conversation works—test designers have tended to focus on the more quantifiable aspects of language production (e.g. number of errors per stretch of speech) and to constrain the test procedure. The automated assessment of spoken tests online that was mentioned above is largely scored on these kinds of criteria, and research on the format suggests that interactive competence is less well captured (Ockey et al., 2015). A meaningful test of language proficiency rests on how objective, replicable and reliably consistent over time it is for comparative purposes. Speaking challenges all three concepts continuously, and it is only by handling it in terms of performance that is very different from the norms of daily spoken interaction that the examination processes can be carried out. The following sections look at these issues in more detail.

4.2   Why the Nature of Speaking Is a Challenge for Test Designers

4.2.1   *Understanding the Construct*

The first general question asked by any test developer is 'What is the construct that we are aiming to assess?' In lay terms this is simply asking 'What exactly is this a test of?' and our general layperson style answer here would be 'Speaking'. However, in the same way that many aspects make the spoken form harder to evaluate fairly, effectively and consistently than the written form, the nature of speaking also makes the definition of the construct challenging. Taken statistically, casual conversation is by far the most prominent genre of speaking. Setting aside formal or prepared public talk such as broadcast material or academic lectures the vast bulk of spoken discourse is commonplace, situated, informal, and as infinitely varied as the participants and their particular concerns at the time of talking. Through such discourse shared understanding of given and new information emerges; relationships, opinions and social identity are formed; and the performative and creative aspects of talk such as jokes, stories and word-play are carried out. However, as the second half of this chapter will show, 'everyday conversation' is clearly not the construct dealt with by the major tests of English, and the creative and affective aspects of talk do not appear in the criteria for internationally benchmarked tests of speaking.

Speaking is also carried out under severe processing constraints in which deleting and editing are impossible and planning difficult. A key skill for the speaker, therefore, is the ability to handle the pressures of speech production well and to maintain the flow of ideas and/or self-repair as needed. Unless a stretch of talk can be completely memorised (a skill some test takers try to master for their high-stakes language tests and generally fail), it must be created at the time of utterance by the speaker and will rarely—even when speech acts such as quoting the speech of oneself or others—be identical to what has been uttered before. As the analysis of descriptors and criteria later in this chapter shows, under test conditions the smooth and syntactically complete utterance will be valued more highly than the hesitant self-repair or choppy reformulation. Until oral assessment criteria value skilful handling of self-repair the pressure is on candidates to not produce these features in their test performance.

Quote 4.6   Preconceptions about conversation

[O]ne of the central characteristics of naturally occurring conversation . . . is that language users are largely unaware of how conversation is typically structured and managed. When asked to articulate conversational practices, native-speaker pronouncements are often at odds with what speakers actually do. . . . Much of how everyday conversation works is so deceptively familiar that people studying and testing language often overlook fundamental characteristics of conversation.

(Johnson and Tyler, 1998: 27)

In naturally occurring, spontaneous speech, interlocutors do not focus on the mechanics of their interaction but on the ideas/emotions/information being conveyed. The nature of language testing means that a strong focus is put on the actual samples of language used: their range, variety, complexity, or accuracy in relation to predecided criteria. This is a major cause of the tension between test criteria and natural oral production. To give an example, many native speakers are extremely hesitant in their speech delivery, particularly when being asked to do something such as form an opinion 'on the hoof'. However, listeners will not attend to the pausing, umming and erring in their interest to hear the answer to their question or the opinion of the speaker. When such discourse is held up for analysis after the event, it may appear incoherent and would probably be regarded as dysfluent if produced in a language testing context.

Quote 4.7 shows an example of a university student trying to express an opinion.

Quote 4.7

The plan was always . . .[=*pause*]. The plan was never to let go but to er assimilate em the Africans into er sort of wider France [inaudible] or whatever was to er assimilate the Africans into a larger France, never to sort of . . . like Britain. The plan was, I mean they saw an end to the road, they never said they would hold on to it.

(Carter and McCarthy, 1997: 137)

This (male) student had already given a presentation on the topic of 'Does France need Africa as much as Africa needs France?' in a politics seminar and therefore had time to think about the central concepts and opinions he held. However, set against oral proficiency criteria which value the ability to produce a smooth, literate, polished utterance, this native speaker of English would not fare particularly well.

Whether carried out via an external observer/rater, an interactive examiner, or self-assessment test, performance is held up against a set of beliefs about 'better' or 'worse' or 'more effective' or 'weaker' language use. Crucial in this area, therefore, is the state of knowledge (and beliefs or preconceptions) about speech and how this relates to a fundamental question in assessing speaking and defining the construct: what is authentic speech like in a variety of contexts, and what is regarded as good or appropriate speech in these contexts? As noted above, spontaneous interactive speech will be full of hesitations, false starts, and grammatical inaccuracies, have a limited vocabulary, tend towards repetition, and be structured around short thought units or quasi-clauses based on the constraints of breath and of spoken language processing. However, it would take a considerable change in preconceptions about language proficiency for, for example, single word answers or simple vocabulary in an oral proficiency interview setting to be regarded as good. The notion of vocabulary range, structural complexity, and quantity of utterances equating to valuable output is deeply embedded in the thinking of language test developers. Much attention is given to, for example, 'designing tasks that elicit spoken language of the type and quantity that will allow meaningful inferences to be drawn from scores to the learners' ability on the construct the test is designed to measure' (Fulcher, 2003; see also Quote 4.8). While it is not unreasonable to want candidates to speak as fully as possible to allow the measurement of their performance, there are contexts in which simple, single word, or fragmented utterances are not only more natural but better. The sophisticated interactive skill of 'listenership' or showing readiness to take up the opportunity to speak is often realised via monosyllabic utterances, for example (McCarthy, 2002; Holmes et al., 2013).

Quote 4.8   Riggenbach on the problem of preconceptions about speech

Conversation with friends calls for common, simple, familiar vocabulary. When students in my third year undergraduate/junior level 'Introduction to Language Studies' course at the University of Washington first listen in depth to an excerpt of dinner table conversation involving four native speaker adults, their first impressions often include descriptions of the native speakers as uneducated, based, in part, on their simple, unremarkable vocabulary usage.

This impression also applies to native speaker fluency. For novice conversation analyses, the amount of repair, hesitation, and lack of smoothness in normal native speaker conversation comes as something of a shock. Traditional definitions of fluency—reflected in rating scales designed to assess nonnative speaker speech such as the Test of Spoken English—include phrases such as 'smoothness of speech,' 'effortlessness', and 'speech exhibiting automaticity'. . . . Typical native speaker speech in conversation is often lacking in these qualities.

(Riggenbach, 1998: 63–4)

So far, we have looked at the construct (i.e. the model towards which assessment is oriented) in terms of the norms of spoken interaction and speech processing. However, a further strand of debate relates to the norms of speech in a different sense: whose language represents the standards for assessment?

Quote 4.9 from Taylor (2006) is from a rebuttal of a paper suggesting that the major test developers will be unable to cope with the growth of English as a dominant lingua franca (Jenkins, 2006). This debate introduces us to a further key question relating to what the model or target is, or should be, in relation to assessing speaking. The great bulk of the English language exists in the world in the form of spoken variants very different from those of native speakers; why is the norm of most assessment still taken to be the output of a much smaller community of native speakers? The answers given are generally twofold: first, as suggested by Taylor below, the test paradigms do shift, slowly, to recognise change in the use of language in the world, with an inevitable time lag allowing for carefully thought-through change to occur. The second, more theoretical, answer is that the spoken form has never been as homogenous as the written, and test designers have to create a model that, to their best efforts, reflects their understanding of the construct. However, there is a third position that could be pursued in future research in this area. This asks the extent to which the norms of native speakers are actually currently the basis of any of the major tests currently available and suggests they are not and never have been. Indeed, as I have been arguing in this chapter the construct is precisely not authentic spoken interaction between speakers, native or otherwise. As the lingua franca debates continue, scholars have been teasing out what English as an international language (EIL) and World English (WE) or World Standard English (WSE) mean. As a further dimension to this fertile work on English as a world language it remains clearly important to define those aspects of the construct that have always been underrepresented in test design (e.g. ability to handle disfluency or repair) and allow society in general to continue to influence what it regards as the norms of educated speech in a variety of contexts. Exciting work will still be needed to bridge the gaps between our emerging state of knowledge of the norms of speech—in both senses used here—and what it is realistically possible to assess fairly and consistently.

Quote 4.9

It's worth recalling that English language proficiency tests once looked
and sounded very different from the way they are today; they reflected
a standard usage known as 'Queen's English' and a manner of speaking
known as 'Received Pronunciation' (RP). As the case of ELTS/IELTS
shows, there is good reason to assume that over time other English varieties will take their place alongside the traditional NS Englishes in international as well as local tests. Over the next 10 or 20 years, emerging
Englishes—including EIL—may well grow in status and take on a role as
pedagogic and assessment models for English learners.

(Taylor, 2006: 59)

4.2.2   Formats and Interactions

A further influential aspect of oral assessment is that of the way in which candidate and examiner interact. Concept 4.2 summarises the main formats that
are generally used in assessing speaking.

Concept 4.2 Test formats and task types

Speaking examinations take many different forms. These vary from
noninteractive tasks responding to a prerecorded, written, or visual
prompt (as, e.g. in the Internet-based TOEFL speaking test) to one-
to-one interactive talk between examiner and candidate (as in the
IELTS speaking test) to two- or more party discussions between candidates rated by a nonparticipating examiner. The University of Cambridge ESOL general English certificate examinations (often referred to
as 'main suite' examinations) have several different task types in one
speaking test, in which two examiners and two candidates participate in
a variety of interactions.

The examiner and candidate participating in oral discourse under test conditions are in a fundamentally unnatural relationship in terms of everyday
speaking in several ways. A key skill in spoken language production involves
understanding listener needs and adapting speech in the light of this. For

instance, speakers using the same geographical dialect and from a similar social background will use distinctive forms and lexical items with people they feel close to in terms of social identity. The same speakers may, in different circumstances, monitor and adjust their way of speaking if, for example, they are speaking to someone of their own generation but from a different location or language background. They may adjust their talk again if they speak to someone much older than themselves who speaks their local dialect. A fine-grained and well-judged adjustment of talk is the mark of a proficient speaker and a skill that cannot be evaluated without reference to the recipient (see also Quotes 4.10 and 4.11). The reduction or elimination of how and how well one speaker adjusts to (or "accommodates") that of another is, on the one hand, a way of increasing the objectivity of the test and making it fairer, but on the other is also a further elimination of a defining set of characteristics of genuine talk in action. Some test formats call for interaction between two or more test takers. There is clearly no benefit to them to accommodate to one another to the point where the examiner does not understand them. Under examination conditions, inevitably, speakers are speaking for the examiner, not for their interlocutor.

Quotes 4.10 and 4.11

Because oral communication involves the negotiation of meaning between two or more persons, it is always related to the context in which it occurs. Speaking means negotiating intended meanings and adjusting one's speech to produce the desired effect on the listener.

(O'Malley and Pierce, 1996: 59)

Based on this instance, it is evident to us that a group oral discussion task of this kind has the potential to provide opportunities for students to demonstrate not only their linguistic competence, but also their inter-actional abilities to relate to each other in spoken interaction, for example, to initiate, expand, or close a topic, provided authentic conditions for communication are established, in particular topic engagement.

(Gan et al., 2009: 17)

Whether a candidate is asked to interact with an examiner or with another student, the interactive nature of speech and the level of personal involvement which even formal speaking will lead to mean that it is extremely hard to elim-inate the effects of one speaker on another. This is in part because good oral communication is founded on one speaker actually having an effect on another and on the reactions and responses that take place between interlocutors.

Quote 4.12 captures the problem of assessing interactive talk, and Quote 4.13 suggests that work in conversation analysis may be providing a way forward.

Quote 4.12   Butler et al. on the issue of test conditions and interactivity

It is important to recognize that a test imposes certain constraints on the character of the interactions that are created in the assessment and thus on the validity of generalizations from performances on the test to performance in ordinary interactions outside the test. Success in spoken interaction is determined by (a) the nature of the tasks that the interac-tion requires and the roles in that interaction; (b) the conditions under which the participants are required to perform; and (c) the resources the individual brings to the interaction.

(Butler et al., 2000: 2)

Quote 4.13   Fulcher on the issues of pairing test takers

First is the issue of who is paired with whom. Should the two test takers be familiar with each other, or does it matter if they are strangers?

- Does it matter if their first language is not the same?
- Should they be at roughly the same stage of learning the second language, or can they be at different stages?
- If the age, race, social class or profession of the two test takers is different, would it make a difference to how they would interact?
- What is the effect of personality differences between the test takers?
- Should test takers be paired if one is extrovert and the other intro-vert, for example?

Secondly in the paired format there is an interlocutor and an 'observer' whose only task is to rate the two test takers.

- What is the impact of this role on the test takers?
- The interlocutor also rates the two candidates, although he or she also participates in the interaction. Does this enhance the validity of the rating process?
- How do the raters assign grades to each of the test takers separately when, given whatever differences there may be in all the candidate variables listed above, one may be supporting another, one may not be providing the other with an opportunity to show how well he can 'negotiate' or take turns?

Thirdly, what is the role of the interlocutor in cases where the two test takers are incapable (as a pair) of undertaking the task?

- How much should the interlocutor intervene?
- What is the effect on discourse and scores if 'significant intervention' is required, or if one (probably the stronger) test taker gets more talking time than the other. . . .

Fourthly, in a 15-minute interview with four tasks that have to be explained by the interlocutor, is the speaking time for each of the test takers enough to elicit a ratable sample of speech?

Fifthly, does the test format result in a reduction or increase in test-taking anxiety, depending once again on the various combinations of 'pair types' that are possible?

(Fulcher, 2003: 187–8)

The more constrained the response types and interactive context, the more neutral and objective the test process would appear to be, and therefore the lower the effects of participant on participant and examiner on candidate. An extreme version of this is the physical separation of the candidate and the examiner and the use of a recorded sample of speech as the basis of the test. The advantage of this approach is that the aural and visual stimuli remain rigorously the same for all test takers and, given the impersonality of the test procedure, differences due to interpersonal factors will be minimised. Thus, the comparability of candidate responses is higher than in interactions that are more natural.

However, the question we return to here is whether the response to such inauthentic stimuli can be regarded as 'authentic speech'. This approach would not claim to be looking directly at interactive facets such as those outlined in Riggenbach's outline of discourse competence (see Quote 4.14).

Quote 4.14   Riggenbach's breakdown of discourse competence

Some of the skills that display a learner's discourse and strategic competence in conversation are listed here. These skills, micro both in the sense of relative length and functional scale, are necessary elements in coherent, fluid turn-taking (discourse competence) and in successful negotiation of meaning in the case of potential communication breakdown (strategic competence).

Conversation micro skills

- the ability to claim turns of talk
- the ability to maintain turns of talk, once claimed
- the ability to yield turns of talk
- the ability to backchannel
- the ability to self-repair
- the ability to ensure comprehension on the part of the listener (e.g. Comprehension checks such as Does that make sense? Are you with me? Get it?)
- the ability to initiate repair when there is a potential breakdown (e.g. Clarification requests)
- the ability to employ compensatory strategies (e.g. avoidance of structures or vocabulary beyond the learner's proficiency, word coinage, circumlocution, and even shifting topics or asking questions that stimulate the other interlocutor to share the responsibility for maintaining the conversation flow).

(Riggenbach, 1998: 57)

The counter-argument to criticisms of highly constrained oral test conditions is that a correlation exists between test performance and genuine speaking skills. That is to say, although there is an inevitable mismatch between the test criteria and conditions and naturally occurring speech, the test may still give an accurate indication of speaking ability. A number of TOEFL research papers have been produced which suggest this to be the case. For instance, Sarwark et al. (1995) found that the oral performance in class of teaching assistants correlated well with their performance in the SPEAK test (an easily administered test that can be given at an institution via a 'kit' of tapes and answer key and does not require trained examiners on site). A further line of research has been on automatic online testing in a variety of languages, with suggestions of a read-across between these and performance in oral interviews (Bernstein et al., 2010).

These questions of oral performance in and outside constrained test conditions remain a productive area for further research.

Quote 4.15   A summary of the problem of natural spoken discourse under test conditions

Speaking is . . . the most difficult language skill to assess reliably. A person's speaking ability is usually judged during a face to face interaction, in real time, between an interlocutor and a candidate. The assessor has to make instantaneous judgments about a range of aspects of what is being said as it is being said. This means that the assessment might depend not only upon what particular features of speech (e.g. pronunciation, accuracy, fluency) the interlocutor pays attention to at any time, but upon a host of other factors such as the language level, gender and status of the interlocutor, his or her familiarity to the candidate, and the personal characteristics of the interlocutor and the candidate.

(Series editors' preface to Luoma, 2004: ix–x)

4.2.3   *Genres and Skills*

Concept 4.3   Field-specific tests and/or assessing genres of speaking

Field-specific oral tests relate to the testing of speech in specific contexts and in a sense are tests of speech genres. The term 'field-specific' is an example of the particular terminology that assessment research has developed, and this is a well-established concept in the literature of assessment—more so, it could be said, than general speech genre work. Some professional contexts require very specific oral language use (e.g. air traffic control; doctor–patient encounters) and tests can be constructed which are designed to assess the test takers' ability to communicate in relation to the typical language of these target genres.

Field-specific testing is often regarded as superior to general proficiency testing as it is possible to examine the use, context, and variety of language (e.g. subject specialist or technical vocabulary) more clearly and in some depth when designing the test.

A wider issue is that of genres of speaking, a concept that has been less tied to the development of oral testing in general. This is possibly because the term 'speech genre' is somewhat underdefined and emerges in several distinct domains in language theory. It is associated with the work of Mikhail Bakhtin (1986) on utterance, dialogue, and texts, with the work of Michael Halliday on register and genre, and in corpus studies where the potential of large corpora has allowed some analysis of language variation and spoken genres.

A further issue in oral assessment relates to the question of what speech genres, if any, are being tested, and of 'field-specific' or specific purpose tests versus general tests. Both these issues are discussed in greater detail in Dan Douglas's book *Assessing Languages for Specific Purposes* (Douglas, 2000). In the case of speech genres, there is some evidence from the field of corpus linguistics to suggest that the language choices made by speakers are strongly influenced by the genre of talk in which they are engaged, for example, the densely informative (and therefore noun-phrase-packed) monologue of a seminar presentation versus the less densely structured conversational content which takes place during 'language-in-action' or service encounters. Webber (2005) constructed a corpus of medical conference presentations and noted the interactive features that were prevalent in what might have been predicted to be a formal monologue genre. Using such insights within a field-specific test of medical oral discourse in a range of genres is one way for speaking assessment to provide a more fine-grained and relevant set of criteria than are generally available in the generic tests of speaking (e.g. the Occupational English Test [OET] developed in Australia for health professionals).

However, much more work is needed if the oral test designer is to be able to construct test conditions in which realistic speech genres can be produced and if test criteria are to be matched more closely to real speech data. In addition, the extensive re-training of raters would also be essential. As noted above, in terms of a general test of informal spoken English, it takes a change of mindset to realise that hesitancy, short clauses (or even single word turns), ellipsis, repetitions, self-repair, and simple or inexplicit vocabulary may be the essence of excellent speech production in certain conversational genres. In contrast, long turns, explicit phrasing, and densely structured talk may be found in a spoken genre such as narrative. This is why the issues of speech genres, context, and purpose of talk need to be taken into account in relation to a full discussion of 'authentic' oral testing (see also Quote 4.16).

Quote 4.16   The role and influence of test methods

While it is generally recognized that [specification of the task or test domain] involves the specification of the ability domain, what is often ignored is that examining content relevance also requires the specification of the test method facets.

(Bachman, 1990: 244)

Another issue in the testing of oral skills is the degree to which it is possible to isolate speech from other skills in test design. This is known as the distinction between integrated versus discrete skills testing. The question arises in all language testing, for example, the degree to which reading ability influences performance in a written test; however, the matter is particularly acute in relation to the testing of aural/oral skills.

The two extracts shown as Quotes 4.17 and 4.18 are separated by nearly ten years. They give a sense of the continued difficulties, both practical and theoretical, felt by the academic community around teasing out the influence of one skill on another in any integrated skills test design. This led many to conclude that an individual test for each skill was desirable.

Quotes 4.17 and 4.18   The issue of integrated or discrete testing of speaking skills

At present, however, it seems to me that listening and speaking are theoretically and practically very difficult to separate. I recommend that serious consideration be given to integrating them, both methodologically and psychometrically. That is, I believe we should consider an oral/aural skills test, where the test taker uses his or her communicative language ability to produce and comprehend meanings in a variety of tasks and receives a single score reflecting the performance.

(Douglas, 1997: 25–6)

In terms of tasks, different types of tasks are associated with different types of input stimuli (e.g. a lecture, a reading passage, a stand-alone prompt) in the new speaking assessment. Thus, one intriguing research issue is whether examinees' performance on one task would be very similar to their performance on other tasks designed to measure a common construct of interest (i.e. speaking proficiency). Potentially, each of these task types might be tapping a somewhat distinct aspect of speaking and—if the speaking scores are based on a set of these heterogeneous task types—the reliability of the composite scores would be negatively impacted (or the impact of other skills may be confounded with speaking scores). In that respect, it is very important to examine the generalizability of speaking scores across tasks and task types in evaluating and validating a new speaking measure.

(Lee, 2006: 132)

However, a more challenging view in terms of the testing of oral-aural communication is that it is only our present, very 'literate', conceptualisation of language that brings us to the position where we consider it feasible to test discrete language skills in any meaningful sense (see also Hughes, 2004). The presence of the individually produced written text, such as the exam essay, which persists through time as a discrete object for analysis by assessors, encourages us to believe that all aspects of language can be tested in this assessment-friendly way. It would be refreshing and radical (and possibly fruitful) to regard the testing of fixed, decontextualised, 'product' as not the best model for all four language skills, and furthermore, that the assessment of the dynamic and interpersonal skills such as speaking and listening need to be assessed by criteria that incorporate and score interactive and prosodic competencies in detail. Such criteria would not be constrained and defined by the norms of the written mode and would reflect essential aspects of spoken mode. There is considerable room for a research agenda that addresses these ideas and for further scholarly work relating field-specific testing to genres, language output, and tasks.

4.2.4   Linking Performance Within the Test to Performance Outside the Test

Knowledgeable designers, deliverers, and users of tests of speaking and their scores would agree that there is no single test that can claim to be comprehensive and wholly predictive of speaking ability in a range of contexts beyond a test score reached on a particular day. The desire for objective, neutral,

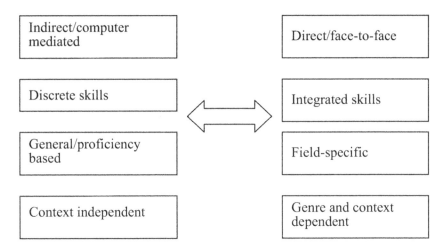

Figure 4.1 End Points of a Continuum of Oral Test Types.

decontextualised, and acultural testing is somewhat at odds with the nature of the spoken form when its distinctive properties are taken fully into consideration. At its most extreme, this view would imply that direct testing of speaking is not possible. There is, however, a huge amount of very valuable assessment of speaking that is undertaken together with considerable efforts by the creators of the major international tests to explain the usefulness and validity of their particular approach and to remain as convincing as possible in terms of ability accurately to test the construct 'speaking'.

Figure 4.1 attempts to summarise some of the various 'cultures' of test types by presenting them as a continuum with contrasting features at either end and on which different forms of assessment could be positioned. For instance, although they are not mutually exclusive, face-to-face tests will tend to favour and make possible the more 'holistic' approaches of integrated skills testing, and conversely an online test will tend to promote the more atomised approach to skills assessment.

Concept 4.4 Direct and indirect testing

The terms 'direct' and 'indirect' are used in two ways in relation to assessment. One use relates to oral test formats and simply indicates whether there is a present interlocutor ('direct' speaking tests) or not ('indirect'). The second use is also of interest in relation to the discussion of the complexities of spoken assessment but should not be confused with this first way of using the term. Within testing and assessment theory a direct test is one that claims a strong relationship between candidate performance under test conditions and the aspect being tested. In contrast, an indirect test will take the performance as indicative of but not the same as the type of language being tested. This is a very fundamental question in debates about test design and evaluation. It questions the correlation between language produced in the test and the extent to which you can extrapolate from it. Those who incline towards paradigms in which performance is tested indirectly (in the sense relating to theory rather than implementation) will be happy to argue that candidate performance in a one-to-one, asymmetric, formal, and nonspontaneous context will provide enough evidence of speaking ability to infer communicative level in very different contexts.

4.3   Oral Assessment in Three High-Stakes Tests

Concept 4.5 High-stakes testing

'High-stakes testing' is a term used to describe any test that has a major influence on the life of the test taker. While it could be argued that any test has an effect on the person taking it, significant barriers are placed before those who fail some tests and are raised for those who pass them. Examples of these kinds of tests outside language learning would be passing a certificate to practise law or medicine or, at an earlier stage, a test in a school context that permits a student to progress to higher examinations or limits their subsequent subject choices in some way.

By their nature, these tests draw a line between groups of people, and the opportunities and constraints of each group are defined by the outcome of the test. This is what makes them 'high stakes'. Some language tests are particularly significant in the lives of those who take them. Since 2004, the United Kingdom has had tests of English as a Second or Other Language (ESOL) for foreign nationals who want to settle in the country. The university systems in all Anglophone countries, and a growing number where English is the medium of instruction for higher education, require evidence of English language ability for entry to a desired programme of study. Both these are examples of high-stakes testing in the realm of language learning. When the stakes are high, the pressure on the assessment system is also significant. A small, local test provided in a class by a teacher to show relative progress of students may have little impact on their lives, but passing or failing one of these high-stakes tests will potentially change life chances considerably. This means that providers of such tests are somewhat conservative and cautious in their development. Their clients—whether individual or organisational—are very demanding. The conservative tendency in high-stakes testing has particular effects in relation to testing speaking—a form which is by its nature dynamic, interpersonal, context dependent, and fast changing.

The final sections of the chapter examine three contrasting tests of speaking to see what they reveal about the attitudes to the spoken form that underpin them and where they lie in relation to the debates presented in this chapter. The first two tests, IELTS and TOEFL, are the most popular tests worldwide for entry to university and are also used in relation to visas and immigration. The third assessment looked at is the 'Knowledge of Language and Life' test for those wanting to immigrate to the United Kingdom. The three types of assessment are all 'high stakes' for the test takers, as gaining a particular score in IELTS or TOEFL or a 'pass/fail' in KOLL will create significant opportunities or barriers for the individual in question. Whereas so far we have discussed the nature of oral test criteria in relation to language theory and the classroom, in this final section we look at the topic not only in this way but also at the political and social context of oral assessment that can make it a highly sensitive issue. It is interesting to note that it is in the arena of large-scale, high-stakes testing that the tensions between the norms of everyday talk and the needs of test developers are most evident.

4.3.1   *Internet-Based TOEFL Speaking Test*

Figure 4.2 shows the underlying relationships of the various aspects of speaking as conceived by the test development community in the highly influential Educational Testing Services (ETS; see www.ets.org). This is the organisation that researches, develops, and delivers the widely used and influential TOEFL test. At the time of writing the test was accepted by over 9,000 institutions and organisations worldwide as a recognised benchmark for English proficiency and is used in 'high-stakes' testing such as university entrance and immigration.

On the continuum of testing paradigms outlined in Figure 4.1, this test is firmly situated close to the left-hand end. The rhetoric surrounding it is allied to 'hard' science ('complexity', 'accuracy', 'precision'), objective measures that attempt to remove the individual and context from the picture (the test taker is not an element in the overview), and an atomisation of the skill of speaking into discrete levels and aspects that can be measured. Both the diagram itself and the descriptive language used to accompany it present a clear and stable framework on which to build the assessment of test takers' performances. Each level of the skill is regarded as built up of subcomponents and facets, and although the diagram itself does not represent the aspects hierarchically it is clear that they are regarded as 'nested', with 'Topic Development' being conceptualised

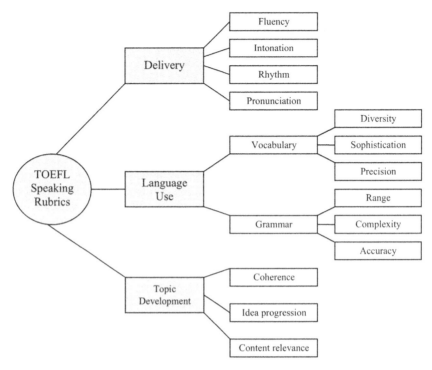

Figure 4.2 Categories Underlying the Speaking Construct.
Source: From Xi et al. (2008: 29).

as a higher order skill that builds on 'Language Use' which is in turn broken down into the specifics of 'Delivery'. This diagrammatic representation of the construct in terms of unique and clearly defined areas is itself closely connected to the ethos of the ETS test development approach in general.

The format and the rating process in the speaking element of the TOEFL test are deliberately impersonal. This is in order to sidestep a number of the issues concerning bias that can affect face-to-face assessments of speaking. Six tasks in TOEFL are designed to test different aspects of speaking. Two ('independent') call on the candidate to express an opinion on a familiar topic, and four others ('integrated') ask the candidate to speak in response to written or spoken material that provides input (ETS, 2015). The rubrics for the independent and integrated tasks are based on the same underlying facets, although the detail of the criteria differs slightly (ETS, 2014). Due to the nature of the test format, all responses are in recorded monologue. In essence, the difference between the independent and the integrated tasks relate to the source of the material, the topic being generated from students' own experience in the case of the independent tasks and from external prompts and visual stimuli in the integrated tasks. There is also a strong connection between ability to perform the task and the ability of the candidate to process and synthesise the written and heard material.

For the purposes of practice, since 2006, test takers can access online self-improvement materials which use automatic speech recognition (via the package Speechrater™); however, the TOEFL speaking test is still rated by human assessors. The performance of the candidate in the six different speaking tasks is captured as audio files and sent, separately, for scoring by the ETS team of trained raters via an online scoring network. At least three scorers rate the same candidate (i.e. the different tasks are not all sent to the same scorer), and some tasks are rated by two scorers to check reliability. The TOEFL speaking scoring consists of four levels, and each level is broken down into the facets represented in Table 4.1 (based on TOEFL Test ETS Independent Speaking Rubrics). These scores of between zero (no response or off topic) to four in each of the tasks are then translated into a single score of between zero and 30. The descriptive criteria for the highest and lowest scores are shown in Table 4.1. Overall, the key assumption underpinning the test is that the highly impersonal test delivery minimises rater bias and that the ability to perform in these contexts can be extrapolated to other, more interactive and informal, domains. In all six tasks the essential criteria for the four levels regard the target for good performance in speaking as smooth, error free, and coherent and low-scoring performance as lacking in content, hesitant, repetitive, and containing basic ideas. As has been noted earlier in this

Table 4.1 Based on TOEFL Test ETS Independent Speaking Rubrics

Score	General description	Delivery	Language use	Topic development
4 (descriptions of highest level performance)	The response fulfils the demands of the task, with at most minor lapses in completeness. It is highly intelligible and exhibits sustained, coherent discourse. A response at this level is characterized by all of the following:	Generally well-paced flow (fluid expression). Speech is clear. It may include minor lapses or minor difficulties with pronunciation or intonation patterns, which do not affect overall intelligibility.	The response demonstrates effective use of grammar and vocabulary. It exhibits a fairly high degree of automaticity, with good control of basic and complex structures (as appropriate). Some minor (or systematic) errors are noticeable but do not obscure meaning.	Response is sustained and sufficient to the task. It is generally well developed and coherent; relationships between ideas are clear (or clear progression of ideas).

(*Continued*)

Table 4.1 (Continued)

Score	General description	Delivery	Language use	Topic development
1 (descriptions of lowest levels of achievement above 'no attempt' or 'response unrelated to the topic', which gain 0)	The response is very limited in content and/or coherence or is only minimally connected to the task, or speech is largely unintelligible. A response at this level is characterized by at least two of the following:	Consistent pronunciation, stress, and intonation difficulties cause considerable listener effort; delivery is choppy, fragmented or telegraphic; frequent pauses and hesitations.	Range and control of grammar and vocabulary severely limit (or prevent) expression of ideas and connections among ideas. Some low-level responses may rely heavily on practised or formulaic expressions.	Limited relevant content is expressed. The response generally lacks substance beyond expression of very basic ideas. Speaker may be unable to sustain speech to complete the task and may rely heavily on repetition of the prompt.

chapter, care is needed when categorising these features quite so neatly, as in the native speaker they are consistent with many forms of casual talk or talk when attempting to form and express an opinion under pressure, and further discussion of this can be found later in this chapter.

In sharp contrast to the somewhat 'dehumanised' ethos of the approach to testing speaking that underpins the test, the TOEFL developers and ETS have an extremely user-friendly interface with their public. The chatty, communicative style and detailed tactical advice (ETS, 2016a and b and Quote 4.19) that can be tailored to your current score level give test takers a strong sense of systematic progress towards achieving the test result they need (and that individual, isolated, efforts will bring results). Since test performance is judged by scorers within the same frames of reference, this is good advice in terms of test outcomes. In addition, given the massive pressure on the English language teaching and testing community brought about by the continued growth of the use of the language in international business, commerce, and scholarship, having a means for individuals to practise by themselves and take tests that are well researched and rigorously benchmarked is a benefit for all concerned. Less easy to predict is the ability of the test taker to translate these scores that reflect largely nondialogic skills into a more dynamic and unpredictable context such as a seminar or fast-flowing conversation.

Quote 4.19   The TOEFL® iBT: improving your speaking skills

Advice for Speaking

Skill: Speaking about Familiar Topics
Performance Level: Fair
Score Range: 18–25

1   Look for opportunities to speak to native speakers of English. Interaction with others will help improve your speaking ability.

  • Find a speaking partner. Set aside time each week to practice speaking to each other in English.
  • If you can't find a native English speaker, find a friend who wants to practice speaking English and promise to speak only English for a certain period of time.

2   Practice speaking for a limited time on different topics without a lot of preparation. Time your responses to questions.

  • Make a list of some general speaking topics
    • people/persons you admire
    • places you enjoy visiting
    • things you enjoy doing

Think of a specific example for each topic (a parent, the market, reading books) and talk about each for one minute.

  • Select one of the topics above and write down three verbs and three adjectives relevant to the topic. Try to use the words as you speak.

3   Concentrate on speaking clearly with good pronunciation and intonation. Speak with confidence and open your mouth more widely than you normally do.
  • It is difficult to understand you if you speak word by word. Try to speak in "thought groups."
  • Take a reading passage and mark the thought groups first. Then read it aloud paying close attention to these groups of words and ideas.
  • Get a book on tape or get a transcript from a news report, interview or play.

- Listen to the performance and mark the pauses, stress and intonation on the transcript.
- Then read the transcript and try to imitate the pauses, stress and intonation patterns.

4   Use books that come with audio recordings to study pronunciation, stress and intonation in English.

4.3.2   The IELTS Speaking Test

In contrast to the TOEFL speaking test, the IELTS speaking test is conducted with a face-to-face examiner. It is a test with a stronger focus on holistic communicative skills than on the implicit hierarchy of separate language facets underlying the TOEFL test. Each test lasts 10 to 15 minutes and is recorded (IELTS, 2016a). A three-stage interview takes place, beginning with general and familiar topics for around four minutes. A card with a prompt is presented to candidates in the second stage of the test, and they are asked to prepare what they are going to say (around one minute) and then speak in monologue for two minutes about the given topic. A transition takes place to part three, in which a dialogue at a more abstract level is developed between the examiner and the candidate out of the material in part two.

Until 2001 the candidate's performance in the IELTS speaking test was judged against a single set of criteria, whereas from that date a new version launched that analysed performance in terms of four distinct areas: fluency and coherence; lexical resource; grammatical range and accuracy; and pronunciation. The full (public versions) of the descriptors are available at the IELTS website (IELTS, 2016a). An overview of the test criteria around the time of the launch of the new version is given in Quote 4.20. In more recent years the information for candidates has been presented in a different format and style, and the current information for candidates (IELTS, 2015) does not contain this level of detail.

Table 4.2 provides the top and bottom analytic descriptors of the rating scale: two, three and nine (zero being used if a candidate fails to attend the interview and the score of one being used for 'no communication possible' or 'no ratable language').

Quote 4.20   Marking and assessment

Fluency and Coherence

This criterion refers to the ability to talk with normal levels of continuity, rate and effort and to link ideas and language together to form coherent, connected speech. The key indicators of fluency are speech rate and speech continuity. The key indicators of coherence are logical sequencing of sentences, clear marking of stages in a discussion, narration or argument, and the use of cohesive devices (e.g. connectors, pronouns and conjunctions) within and between sentences.

Lexical Resource

This criterion refers to the range of vocabulary the candidate can use and the precision with which meanings and attitudes can be expressed. The key indicators are the variety of words used, the adequacy and appropriacy of the words used and the ability to circumlocute (get round a vocabulary gap by using other words) with or without noticeable hesitation.

Grammatical Range and Accuracy

This criterion refers to the range and the accurate and appropriate use of the candidate's grammatical resource. The key indicators of grammatical range are the length and complexity of the spoken sentences, the appropriate use of subordinate clauses, and the range of sentence structures, especially to move elements around for information focus. The key indicators of grammatical accuracy are the number of grammatical errors in a given amount of speech and the communicative effect of error.

Pronunciation

This criterion refers to the ability to produce comprehensible speech to fulfil the Speaking test requirements. The key indicators will be the amount of strain caused to the listener, the amount of the speech which is unintelligible and the noticeability of L1 (i.e. first language) influence.

(IELTS, 2016a)

What is noticeable in both these influential tests is that, despite the greater focus on interactive skills in the IELTS speaking test and the apparently stronger focus on proficiency in the more depersonalised TOEFL speaking assessments, there are large areas of agreement over what are perceived as positive and negative aspects of the construct 'speaking'. Tables 4.3 and 4.4

Table 4.2 Top and Bottom Criteria for the IELTS Speaking Test

Band	Fluency and coherence	Lexical resource	Grammatical range and accuracy	Pronunciation
9	• speaks fluently with only rare repetition or self-correction; • any hesitation is content-related rather than to find words or grammar • speaks coherently with fully appropriate cohesive features • develops topics fully and appropriately	• uses vocabulary with full flexibility and precision in all topics • uses idiomatic language naturally and accurately	• uses a full range of structures naturally and appropriately • produces consistently accurate structures apart from 'slips' characteristic of native speaker speech	• uses a full range of pronunciation features with precision and subtlety • sustains flexible use of features throughout • is effortless to understand
3	• speaks with long pauses • has limited ability to link simple sentences • gives only simple responses and is frequently unable to convey basic message	• uses simple vocabulary to convey personal information • has insufficient vocabulary for less familiar topics	• attempts basic sentence forms but with limited success, or relies on apparently memorized utterances • makes numerous errors except in memorized expressions	• shows some of the features of band 2 and some, but not all, of the positive features of band 4 [for example: 'attempts to control features but lapses are frequent']
2 (1 = 'no communication possible'/'no ratable language', 0 = 'does not attend'	• pauses lengthily before most words • little communication possible	• only produces isolated words or memorized utterances	• cannot produce basic sentence forms	• speech is often unintelligible

Source: IELTS (2016b).

Table 4.3 Summary of Perceived Negative Features in Oral Discourse Represented in iBT Speaking and IELTS Speaking (tick represents mention of feature in descriptors covering weaker performance)

Feature	IELTS	TOEFL
Repetition	✓	✓
Hesitation	✓	✓
Unintelligible	✓	✓
Pauses (long)	✓	
Pauses (frequent)		✓
Self-correction	✓	
'Finding words'	✓	
'Slips'	✓	
Lapses (in completeness)		✓
Lapses (pronunciation)		✓
Difficulties (pronunciation)		✓
Isolated words	✓	
Choppy		✓
Fragmented		✓
Telegraphic		✓
Memorised	✓	
Practised		✓
Formulaic		✓
Limited (content)		✓
Limited (grammar and vocabulary)		✓
Basic (sentence forms)	✓	
Basic (ideas)		✓
Insufficient (vocabulary)	✓	
Simple (linking)	✓	
Simple (sentences)	✓	
Simple (responses)	✓	
Simple (vocabulary)	✓	
Personal (information)	✓	

Table 4.4 Summary of Perceived Positive Features in Oral Discourse Represented in iBT Speaking and IELTS Speaking (tick represents mention of feature in descriptors covering stronger performance)

Feature	IELTS	TOEFL
Fluent	✓	✓
Effortless to understand	✓	
Intelligible	✓	✓
Fluid		✓
Well paced		✓
Clear (production)		✓
Automatic		✓
Coherent	✓	✓
Cohesive (devices/features)	✓	

(Continued)

Table 4.4 (Continued)

Feature	IELTS	TOEFL
Full (topic)	✓	
Full (range of structures)	✓	
Full (range of pronunciation features)	✓	
Complete		✓
Relevant (content)		✓
Precise (vocabulary)	✓	
Idiomatic	✓	
Accurate (vocabulary and idiom)	✓	
Accurate (structures)	✓	
Controlled (structures)		✓
Sustained/consistent	✓	✓

summarise these features. The combined criteria from these two major international tests of speaking allow us to consider the way in which a test and tasks are designed together and the attitude to 'good speaking' that the scoring system reveals. There is a clear set of assumptions revealed by the criteria in relation to what is being tested (the construct as defined by the developer), what is thought to be appropriate material to base a test result on (the output of the candidate in a task designed by the developer), and the categories of positive and negative features that will ultimately be used by each examiner in a standardised test (the descriptors designed to discriminate between levels). The tasks in major international tests of speaking are, therefore, generally designed to allow the candidate to perform at an imagined 'peak' that represents the highest level of achievement in the test and be given an opportunity to produce language with the features that are highly thought of in the test framework. It is notable that, as Tables 4.3 and 4.4 show, high-value performance will generally mean a full, coherent, lexically dense 'long turn'. Aspects of normal spoken conversational discourse such as simplicity, hesitation, self-correction, incompleteness, and using prepackaged, sometimes repetitious 'chunks' of language are regarded, conversely (again see Tables 4.3 and 4.4), as undesirable, while fluency, precision, accuracy, control, range, and completeness are valued highly. As noted earlier the ability to produce discourse that is free of the former and distinguished by the latter is not easy for anyone. It is not the norm for native speaker speech in spontaneous interactive setting.

A research topic of relevance here could be to investigate what, exactly, examiners perceive as self-correcting moments in the candidate's performance and compare these with moments in the candidate's discourse elsewhere or with native speaker performance in this area. It may show that an apparently negative feature is quite the reverse in spontaneous talk and is in fact a neutral or positive feature. A language learner who can handle this in a target language while maintaining the flow of ideas without allowing it to 'get in the way' is to be seen as a high achiever. Similar reconsideration of aspects of normal talk such as discourse that has low lexical range or is repetitive would be fruitful, as in many contexts listener-friendly speakers will be at their most effective when keeping the language clear, simple, and repeating the message.

4.3.3   *UK Border Agency Knowledge of Language and Life Assessments*

In 2005, the UK government began applying new criteria to foreign nationals seeking to settle in the country. This took the form of a Knowledge of Language and Life in the UK test (KOLL test), one function of which, as the name suggests, aimed to provide the immigration service (the UK Visa and Immigration [UKVI], which was at that time known as the UK Border Agency [UKBA]) evidence of some competence in English language. Applicants needed to show that they had reached Entry Level 3 in the UK National Qualifications Framework (equivalent to Common European Framework B1). When it was launched, the criteria for communication and for civic knowledge were combined via the Knowledge of Life or KOL test, which was a hybrid between an assessment of knowledge and of language. The criteria for the assessment were initially not designed directly for the KOL test but are taken from/link to the UK national literacy curriculum that included this level. In 2013, the KOL test and the assessment of language level became clearly separated. It was no longer the case that passing the KOL test would give you the language pass for the English level at B1 in the Common European Framework. Two levels of English competence were set up: for 'further leave to remain' as a spouse or parent requires A1 level, and indefinite leave to remain and naturalisation require B1. At the same time the link between the national ESOL framework and curriculum was lessened and the tests that would be recognised restricted as part of a general tightening of UKVI border policies around this time. The concept of a Secure English Language Test (SELT) became linked to the process more overtly, and the only two examining bodies for all Visa purposes became the Trinity College London suite of examinations and IELTS examinations. As the chapter has dealt with the IELTS criteria for speaking, the latter part of this section deals with the Trinity criteria.

The Trinity suite of spoken examinations (Graded Examination of Spoken English [GESE] and Integrated Skills in English [ISE]) use the same four level descriptions whatever the test and whatever the level. These are shown in Quote 4.21. UK naturalisation regulations accept GESE level 5.

Quote 4.21   Trinity Suite of examinations generic criteria for speaking examinations

Band   Task fulfilment

A   The candidate's contributions are very effective, clearly comprehensible, highly appropriate and obviously fulfil the task. There is comprehensive coverage of the communicative skills, functions and language items of the grade/level. These items are used with consistency and with a high level of accuracy and appropriacy. Any inaccuracies which occur rarely impede the overall communication of meaning. The interaction proceeds smoothly, with the candidate contributing promptly and fluently.

B   The candidate's contributions are generally effective, comprehensible, appropriate and adequately fulfil the task. There is good coverage of the communicative skills, functions and language items of the grade/level. There is evidence of a good level of accuracy and appropriacy in the use of the language items although this may not be maintained throughout the phase. Inaccuracies do occur and at times they may affect the communication of meaning. The interaction generally progresses well but the flow may be affected by some hesitancy.

C   The candidate's contributions are moderately effective, comprehensible and appropriate and partially fulfil the task. There is coverage of the communicative skills, functions and language items of the grade/level although this may be characterised by the provision of only isolated samples. There is some control over the accuracy and appropriacy of the use of the language items of the grade/level. Inaccuracies can affect the communication of meaning and require remedial action. The flow of the interaction may be halted by hesitancy, requests for repetition or pauses while searching for language. The candidate may need some support.

D   The candidate's contributions are very limited, lack comprehensibility and appropriacy and, although there is some attempt at the task, this is not fulfilled even with support.

There is very little evidence of coverage of the communicative skills, functions and language items of the grade/level. Inaccuracies and inappropriacies are highly evident and cause communication breakdown. Lack of understanding and severe hesitation impede communication and prevent the interaction from proceeding as required.

(Trinity College London Graded Examinations in Spoken English and Integrated Skills in English (Interview Component) Performance Descriptors, http://www.trinitycollege.com/site/?id=3109).

The language specifically required for the B1 for immigration purposes is shown in Quote 4.22.

Quote 4.22   Language functions

- Talking about the future—informing and predicting
- Expressing preferences
- Talking about events in the indefinite and recent past
- Giving reasons
- Stating the duration of events
- Quantifying

Grammar

- Present perfect tense including use with for, since, ever, never, just
- Connecting clauses using because
- Will referring to the future for informing and predicting
- Adjectives and adverbials of quantity, e.g. A lot (of), not very much, many
- Expressions of preference, e.g. I prefer, I'd rather

Lexis

- Vocabulary specific to the topic area
- Vocabulary specific to the subject areas

- Expressions relating to past and future time, e.g. Two days ago, in the future
- Phrases and expressions relating to the language functions listed above

Phonology

- The correct pronunciation of vocabulary specific to the topic and subject areas
- The combination of weak forms and contractions, e.g. I've been to . . .
- Avoidance of speech patterns of recitation

(Trinity College London Graded Examinations in Spoken English, Language Requirements, Grade 5, August 2014)

These criteria are assessed in the GESE level 5 via a face-to-face interview on a topic prepared by the candidate in advance. There is a strong emphasis in these criteria on structure and delivery over interactive speaking skills.

The assessment of language for immigration purposes and the broader issues surrounding integration of people from other language backgrounds into a society is an interesting example of what happens when a test of speaking is being used in a very high-stakes context but one that is hard to specify and deliver without controversy (McNamara and Ryan, 2011; Kunnan, 2012). In 2016 the UK government started actively encouraging ethnic minority Britons to improve their English, and this led to considerable debate. Countries have been setting clear and demanding language requirements for those wanting to remain long term in the country or apply to be citizens. Australia, for instance, states that evidence is needed for all four language skills and that the language of the nation is English. Canada requires listening and speaking from all applicants and has requirements that can be met in either English or French. Germany caused huge controversy when it started to apply language and cultural knowledge tests to prospective immigrants in 2005. However, the discursive practices in spoken language testing for such high-stakes assessments highlights and clearly links back to current concerns about the ethical and social responsibilities of the academic and professional language testing community.

As Quote 4.23 suggests, there may be challenges to the underlying paradigms of these large-scale tests. Testing informed by the ethos of a 'culture of learning' that, as Hamp-Lyons suggests, would require attention to 'the individual, the changing, the changeable' (2007: 487) resonates with much that, I have been arguing, defines the spoken form.

Quote 4.23   Cultures of testing versus cultures of learning

The contexts and needs of classrooms and teachers are not the same as those of large scale testing. The large scale needs to discriminate, to separate, to categorize and label. It seeks the general, the common, the group identifier, the scaleable, the replicable, the predictable, the consistent and the characteristic. The teacher, the classroom, seeks the special, the individual, the changing, the changeable, the surprising, the subtle, the textured, and the unique. Neither is better but they are different. We have only started to realize the extent of the difference in recent years.

(Hamp-Lyons, 2007: 487)

4.4   Summary

A number of questions surrounding oral assessment have been raised in this chapter including three central ones:

- What can we learn about attitudes to speaking from analysing how the assessment community defines the construct and how it goes about the practicalities of testing it?
- Are the criteria for assessing speaking more aligned to the norms of writing than of speaking?
- If we had a better understanding of 'good', 'effective', or 'appropriate' speaking in different contexts, could we move towards oral test criteria which are more closely aligned to the micro-skills and structures which constitute speaking ability?

As with the issues raised in Chapter 3 surrounding materials development, the inclusion of real people and real speech contexts, and the dynamic, personal orientation of key aspects of speaking, raise crucial issues for assessment. There is a considerable tension between the dynamic, transient, and interpersonal nature of speech and the underlying principles of professional language testing. These questions are interesting starting points for research projects into speaking proficiency. Such research, together with further work on the correlations between test performance and communicative ability outside test conditions, would form a basis for answering the bigger question, of how far it is realistically possible to assess speaking from a perspective other than 'language proficiency'.

Further reading

Bachman, L. and Palmer, A. S. (2010). *Language Assessment in Practice: Designing and Developing Useful Language Tests*. Oxford: Oxford University Press.

Fulcher, G. (2015). *Re-Examining Language Testing: A Philosophical and Social Inquiry*. London: Routledge.

Luoma, S. (2004). *Assessing Speaking*. Cambridge: Cambridge University Press.

McNamara, T. and Knoch, U. (2012). The Rasch wars: The emergence of Rasch measurement in language testing. *Language Testing*. 29(4), 555–576. 0265532211430367.

Shohamy, E. (2001). *The Power of Tests: A Critical Perspective on the Uses of Language Tests*. London: Longman.

Taylor, L. (2011). *Examining Speaking: Research and Practice in Assessing Second Language Speaking* (Vol. 30). Cambridge: Cambridge University Press.

5 Approaches to Researching Speech

This chapter will . . .

- introduce qualitative, quantitative, and theory-driven approaches to researching speaking;
- consider the effects of researcher stance and research approaches described in these projects;
- present summaries of case studies into various aspects of research particularly relevant to broadening our understanding of speech.

5.1 Introduction

Approaches to researching speaking are very eclectic and cover many fields in linguistics and applied linguistics, including phonetics, phonology, sociolinguistics, pragmatics, intercultural communication, and second language pronunciation. This reflects the fact that the spoken form touches many aspects of life and of society, and spoken language data are seen as relevant to a variety of research domains and research questions. These can range from the qualitative end of the spectrum of methods, for example, analysing roleplays using conversation analytical techniques with a view to understanding business negotiation in intercultural contexts, to the highly quantitative, for instance, a statistical analysis in a laboratory setting of how listeners perceive accent. The reasons for choosing one approach over another are perhaps best understood by beginning from the relationship between research topics, data, and the conclusions that can be drawn from these. As noted elsewhere in this book, there is a particularly interesting relationship between spoken language and theories of language. Our view of language is strongly shaped by the means we have to collect, describe, and then analyse it, and this is particularly the case in researching speaking. This chapter examines both quantitative and qualitative approaches to research questions in the domain of speech and discusses the role of speech data in relation to the methods used in each.

The studies described here are presented in terms of three broad (often in reality overlapping) categories. Two approaches—the quantitative and the qualitative—are clearly oriented towards data. The third covers work that would not be described by either of these terms and can be thought of as primarily theory or ideas-led. These terms relate to the overall methodological framework or approach being used for the research and are closely linked to the underlying philosophy of the researcher. They are not by any means mutually exclusive categories, but it is helpful to understand that research into speaking, as with any of the language skills, is not carried out from within a single or neutral perspective. The epistemological standpoint of researchers significantly affects what they consider important and the way in which they approach their investigations.

Concept 5.1 The influence of epistemological standpoint

Epistemology is a branch of philosophy that studies knowledge. Terms such as 'epistemological standpoint/perspective/stance' are derived from this discipline for more day-to-day use in academic life. In this broader context they are used to set the compass points of 'where the researcher is coming from'. Obvious examples of differences in epistemology would be between a religious and a nonreligious person in relation to accounts of the origins of the earth or between someone living before the discovery of the shape of the earth and the majority of people today. One's standpoint affects beliefs about a topic and what is regarded as valid evidence or proof of what is true. In terms of research this also relates to how you proceed with your investigation. If you believe in the gathering, comparison, and analysis of 'hard facts', you will be drawn towards quantitative approaches. If, on the other hand, you are more convinced by the importance of relationships between people, ideas, and contexts, you may be less convinced by the quantitative way of working and want to approach a research topic through detailed, qualitative work. Both approaches are equally valid when used to investigate speaking.

A small number of academics in applied linguistics engage in work that is neither quantitative nor qualitative but, rather, attempt to work with ideas in order to consider the theoretical underpinning to a topic. These studies are quite rare but can be highly influential.

The overall approach and standpoint of researchers will shape what they regard as a relevant question and coherent outcome. The scholarly community reads an article or evaluates findings with a certain understanding that the terms of reference are clear both to them and to the researcher. What would be unacceptable in a statistical survey (e.g. allowing findings from a small sample to inform a more generalist perspective) is perfectly acceptable in a research project that does not orient towards that framework. It is important for the novice researcher approaching an investigation into spoken discourse and carrying out initial literature reviews and searches to be aware of the influential relationship between the assumptions of the researcher and the framework(s) available for research. There is not one best way to investigate a topic; there are a multitude of ways. The approach used needs to have internal consistency and show awareness of any discrepancies between what is regarded as the standard research procedures and assumptions and what is being carried out.

In addition to these groupings (quantitative, qualitative, theory/ideas driven), which apply to all research methods, the approach used affects how speech data are regarded in the process of research. For instance, researchers might gather speech data to test an idea, model, or hypothesis, or they might be primarily concerned to put forward a new theoretical model and are merely using speech data to exemplify this; in contrast, an investigation might deliberately start with the unmotivated collection of natural discourse in order to avoid preconceptions and be driven entirely by the data in its description of new phenomena. In broad terms, these differences between the role of speech in the research process map onto the more quantitatively oriented approach (testing a hypothesis), the qualitative methods that have been gaining some ground since the 1980s (beginning from data to possibly challenge pre-existing models (or the idea of a 'model' itself) and discover new patterns and practices), and the rather small number of researchers who engage in trying to construct a theory.

5.2 Quantitative and Qualitative Approaches Towards Researching Speaking

Quantitative approaches are very prevalent in researching speaking. They have been used to carry out research at all levels, from the way a very specific acoustic feature affects clear speech (Maniwa et al., 2009) to how a medical discourse community shows trust (Kvarnstrom and Cedersund, 2006). The apparent preponderance of quantitative methods does not mean that there is a necessary affinity between the spoken form and quantitative approaches, and, in fact, the situation may simply reflect the balance between the approaches generally found in the discipline of applied linguistics. Research by Benson et al. (2009), among others, suggests that overall around 20 per cent or less of research in applied linguistics is carried out by qualitative means. Therefore, the likelihood is that spoken language research, like other areas of language, will be carried out in the dominant quantitative paradigm. Quantitative approaches provide a powerful and a well-tested framework for an investigation by moving from pre-existing questions/hypotheses to the appropriate methods to investigate these—for instance, looking at the frequency of a feature in natural data or designing a laboratory-based experiment to elicit speech data and then analyse this. Very often, whatever the method of data gathering, the findings are analysed by means of statistics, and these give the researcher the basis for generalising from particular results to something beyond the data in question. *Not* finding what you predicted in this approach is almost as interesting as finding evidence for what you imagined would be the case, and this is part of the strength of the approach.

Quantitative approaches tend to analyse data in terms of pre-existing categories, and the researcher then seeks to investigate the nature of these items in the data. For something as dynamic and socially grounded as spoken discourse, this use of predetermined categories can be unhelpful. The strength of the qualitative paradigm is that it works from the 'inside' of instances of talk towards patterns and regularities and is able to uncover aspects that the investigator may not have imagined existed.

A widely used method among the qualitative approaches to researching speaking is conversation analysis (CA). This method puts high value on the careful qualitative analysis of examples of real (i.e. nonelicited) talk to understand how speakers create meaning and organise their discourse as social action. The CA analyst is interested also in what linguistic and other resources (syntax, prosody, gaze, laughter, silence, and so on) speakers use to 'do talk' and how these are different in specific varieties of language and discourse contexts. The 'pure' CA approach, therefore, is unique in that it seeks to understand the nature of speech primarily from observation of nonelicited data and through this process gain insights about broader patterns and meaningful regularities appearing in the interaction. In recent years some researchers in the CA tradition have begun to adopt quantitative methods, especially for comparisons of conversational practices across different languages. This has helped with firming up the claim that some aspects of conversational structure are shared across most or all languages. For example, conversational turn-taking can be seen to display very similar characteristics, even across languages that are extremely different with regard to their linguistic typology (Stivers et al., 2009). Similarly, question-response sequences show the same basic functional make-up, even if the spread of certain functions varies across languages (Stivers, Enfield, and Levinson, 2010).

A quantitative approach allows researchers to count and compare occurrences of the same phenomenon and their frequency across varying types and sizes of corpora. However, when dealing with empirical data, the question is how interpretations of linguistic functions are arrived at. For instance, a corpus-linguistic approach (see Chapter 1, Section 1.2.5) will draw conclusions from the purely numerical information resulting from, for example, the electronic search for a specific word or phrase in a large speech corpus. Individual instances are not considered; instead, the numbers of different occurrences and co-occurrences are seen to speak for themselves. A more qualitative approach, such as conversation analysis, may at times use statistical methods to strengthen an argument concerning the spread of a certain conversational practice. However, underlying this interpretation are nevertheless the painstaking qualitative analyses of each individual occurrence.

Two contrasting studies dealing with the same linguistic phenomenon can show the differences between quantitative and qualitative approaches to researching speaking. Watanabe et al. (2008) and Mushin and Gardner (2009) both deal with the topic of pausing or silence in conversational inter-action. The former follows a classic quantitative approach using prediction based on previous work (evidence from corpora that filled pauses precede complex utterances): a hypothesis (that listeners interpret a filled pause as a precursor of a complex utterance of some kind), an experiment designed to test the hypothesis (participants asked to listen to a description of a shape with and without a filled pause preceding it and press a button when they have matched description to shape), and analysis of the time taken to make the match in the different conditions by means of statistics (two-way ANOVA). Their findings supported the idea that a filled pause appears to 'prime' a lis-tener to expect a complex description. Interestingly, when proficient and less proficient language users were compared, the effect was not significant, sug-gesting a link between proficiency level in the language and understanding the predictive link between the pause and the ensuing material.

Mushin and Gardner (2009) were also interested in understanding more about conversational pauses but in sharp contrast to Watanabe et al. (2008) used a conversation analytical approach to probe the topic. In something of a return to CA's ethnographic roots, they investigated Australian aboriginal talk and began from assumptions from cross-cultural studies that silence is used differently in Aboriginal and in white Australian talk. Rather than trans-form this into a formal research question and hypotheses as the quantitatively oriented academics might, they use it as a jumping-off point for a series of rhetorical questions. These provide the link between previous findings and the current study and explain to the reader what interests them and motivates the study (see Quote 5.1).

Quote 5.1   Using rhetorical questions to show research focus

Such characterisations [that Aboriginal talk tends towards more silence] are presented as evidence of the considerable differences in interactional styles between Australian Aboriginal people and mainstream white Australians. Yet we still have little understanding of how Aboriginal conversation is organised outside of cross-cultural settings. What does it mean to be 'comfortable' with longer silences? What constitutes 'quite lengthy silences'? Are comfortable lengthy silences a feature of an Aus-tralian Aboriginal conversation style (i.e. a cultural feature), or are they a reflection of more general interactional features (i.e. a consequence of the local interactional context)?

(Mushin and Gardner, 2009: 2034)

Their analysis was based on extensive samples of speakers of the Garrwa language (four audio recordings and one video recording, the latter lasting for approximately two hours). What is important to note is that while the authors use a quantitative feature (length of pauses in interaction), the dominant paradigm is a qualitative, CA, one. They are principally interested in how the speakers orient towards one another and in what emerges as salient for these speakers. In their attempt to understand more about the role of silence in this speech community, what concerns them is not, primarily, the length of the silence (although this can be measured and is one useful source of data) but seeing how the speakers handle turns and respond, or do not respond, to one another in a variety of speech contexts. Quote 5.2 gives an example of this type of analysis.

Quote 5.2   An example of a CA interpretation of interactive behaviour

For an Anglo-Australian, the acknowledging response . . . seems to occur so late as to lack relevance, yet here it is treated as unproblematic. The falling terminal intonation contour suggests perhaps that this Mh hm is proffered as a sequence closing device, rather than as a continuer. . . . This is supported by Daphne's overt termination of the sequence in the very next turn with barriwa, a form which is conventionally used to finish a sequence. This extract is thus a nice example of the ordinariness of long silences in this interaction.

(Mushin and Gardner, 2009: 2047)

The key phrase in Quote 5.2 indicating the qualitative ethos of the paper is 'is treated as'. Unlike the quantitative tendency to map pre-existing constructs to the data and use them to test a hypothesis, the CA tradition assumes that linguistic resources are handled and shaped by participants in the process of communication. Further, they would argue that any analysis must give primacy to the apparent importance of different features as they emerge at the time of interaction.

The distinction between the orientation of a researcher towards quantitative work or otherwise is not, in real-life research, as clear cut as this introductory outline has been suggesting. The examples chosen here have been selected to give a clear taste of work that falls mainly into one camp or the other in relation to investigating some aspect of speech or of using spoken data to investigate a broader question in linguistics. In addition, the field of applied linguistics appears to be becoming more interdisciplinary as the twenty-first century progresses, and some of the boundaries between what have been opposing disciplines are becoming more blurred. For instance, among the second language acquisition (SLA) community there is a growing desire for ecologically valid methods and an increasing acknowledgment of the potential benefits of borrowing from disciplines that study actual instances of the spoken form and the situated practices of interaction. Mori (2007) provides a thoughtful overview of the relationships between SLA and conversation analysis (CA), for example. The field of interactional linguistics that started to emerge at the start of the century (Couper-Kuhlen and Selting, 2001) also draws on the detailed analysis of the spoken form, and the boundaries between this and CA are particularly permeable.

5.3   Theory-Driven, Positional, or Ideas-Based Approaches to Researching Speaking

All research is about theory and ideas; however, in some work the questioning of the theory or the discussion of a possible alternative theory is the *primary* focus of the study. These studies are interesting because they can question how an aspect of speaking is conceptualised and researched and, if they lead to challenging debate about their strengths and weaknesses among other scholars, they are extremely influential. Liberman's article (Liberman, 1998), 'When theories of speech meet the real world' is as example of what is known as a 'position paper'. This means that the research text in question—such studies are generally journal articles—encapsulates an academic's stance on a broad topic, and they generally deal with an issue that is open to debate. These can be difficult to write, as there is a need to understand the ideas being criticised, summarise the relevant arguments, and present a coherent alternative to them.

The idea under attack in Liberman (1998) is that the stream of speech is made up of individual segments of sound that are in turn decoded by the brain into comprehensible discourse. The whole article revolves around a single underlying question: why is it so much easier to learn to speak than it is to learn to write? The more subtle point that Liberman is making is the following: if there really is a rough parity between arbitrary symbols that make up writing systems and arbitrary sounds which make up speech, why is speech not as cognitively challenging as writing? Quote 5.3 summarises the question.

Quote 5.3   Liberman's main research question

What did evolution do for speech that gave it such a biological advantage over writing/reading? A theory of speech—or more broadly, language—can avoid that question, as most do, but it cannot avoid implying an answer; and if that answer does not sit comfortably with the priority of speech, then the scientists should consider that they have got hold of the wrong theory.

(Liberman, 1998: 112)

Theoretical research questions very often begin life as 'what if . . .?' thoughts, and in a 'position paper' these can and are often intended to present fundamental challenges to existing paradigms. It should be noted, however, that even the most robust theoretical thinkers are selective in what they present as 'given' and what is challenged. Liberman, for example, does not question his own fundamental assumption that speaking really *is* easier than writing. Nor does he address the issue of the extent and quality of the differences in the two learning processes. It could be argued, for instance, that it takes several years practising for ten or more hours a day for children to become fluent, grammatically standard (within the norms of their own social or family group) speakers.

Nonetheless, by framing a question which sums up his position so completely (the 'why is speaking easier than writing?' question), Liberman is able to develop a coherent line of thought which contrasts the inadequacies of conventional theory and generative phonology in the first half of the paper against the satisfactory nature of his less generally accepted stance presented in the second half (see Research summary).

Research summary: The structure of Liberman's discussion of his research question regarding the biological advantage of speech over writing and subsequent questions

Conventional theories of speech sounds suggest that they are not intrinsically any different from any other sounds in the world but are the vehicles of meaningful segments of sound roughly equating to visual segments in a writing system.

↓

If there is no biological basis for speech sounds, 'how is it that people who cannot spell a single word—lacking even the awareness that words

---

can be spelled—nevertheless find, each time they speak, that producing perfectly spelled phonetic structures is dead easy?'

↓

Conventional theories also suggest that speech perception is a two-stage process in which the primary sounds are translated into phonetic elements by the brain. '. . . [T]he two processes are exactly parallel, requiring the same kind of cognitive step to endow their ordinary auditory and visual percepts with phonetic significance. Why, then, should the one be so much easier and more natural than the other?'

↓

If ease of perception of discrete elements is the key to language, then the oral/aural channel is in fact *less* suitable than the visual/motoric.

↓

Liberman proposes that language as it evolved merely appropriated sounds to put them to the use of the language system, whereas traditional theory has difficulty answering his initial question: what exactly was it that evolved?

In the rest of the paper Liberman proposes a 'phonetic module' which deals directly with the sounds of speech and which requires no intervening processing or translation of these into any other form. These 'articulatory gestures of the vocal tract' are, he argues, the product of an evolutionary process rather than being standard sounds appropriated for the use of language. In discussions of Liberman's work it has often been referred to by an acronym 'SiS' (speech is special). A powerfully influential theory frequently has a very elegant basic idea such as this which assists with its understanding and acceptance by people in a range of contexts, whether or not they agree with it.

Liberman's discussion here also shows the way a questioning technique can be used as the basis of both a critical evaluation of a theory and a framework for presenting that evaluation. By taking a step back from the data a theoretical approach can ask questions at a very universal or general level (some might argue too general and abstract) and provide a clear framework for others to use or to challenge. His work was widely cited, was contentious as soon as it was published, and yet has proved to cast a very long shadow. In the first decade of the twenty-first century, debate about the 'Motor theory' of speech remains ongoing and sometimes heated (e.g. Fowler. 2008). Liberman's work has also influenced and is still cited as a key source in the scholarly 'landscape' in the emerging studies of speech processing using magnetic resonance imaging (Lotto et al., 2008). Outside speech processing, his ideas are regarded as relevant (and often still controversial) in fields as diverse as the study of dyslexia (Uppstad and Tønnessen, 2007; see also Quote 5.4) and the evolution of language (Fitch et al., 2005).

Quote 5.4   The lasting resonance of a theory-driven paper

As a consequence, we have a situation where the phoneme is both rejected and accepted, which naturally only enhances the confusions. The inductive character of theory-building is especially clearly seen in the writings of Alvin and Isabel Liberman (Liberman, 1997, 1999; Liberman and Whalen, 2000), where dogmatic arguments are deployed against features of theoretical positions which are not at all compatible with the authors' own position. While this kind of controversy is of course not unusual in science, the proportion of arguments belonging to the dogmatic category is alarming. These arguments are clearly not sufficient to prove A. M. Liberman's claim about the relationship between spoken and written language. In our view, dogmatic positions should be avoided in order to maintain high standards of empirical science. This can be done by studying behaviour in written and spoken language, without a priori assumptions of causal relationships.

(Uppstad and Tønnessen, 2007: 163)

5.4   Examples of Contrasting Approaches in Researching Speaking

This section provides summaries of different approaches to researching speaking ranging from more examples of 'position' papers, to qualitative work, to technically oriented papers reporting experimental findings. The papers are organised so that the more quantitative papers are grouped together later in the section and the more theory-oriented or qualitative work is presented earlier. The intention is for the reader to gain a sense of the richly diverse approaches that have been taken to the investigation of speech.

5.4.1   *A Position Paper Combining Language and Ethology: Universal Meanings of Intonation According to the 'Biological Codes'*

Similarly to Liberman (1998), two influential phonologists, John J. Ohala and Carlos Gussenhoven, have put forward a position that is first and foremost grounded in a theory rather than in empirical research findings.

Research summary: Introducing an 'against the grain' position and relating it to current theory

In contrast to Liberman, Ohala and Gussenhoven do not start with a question but by asserting an association between language, specifically intonation, and humans' evolved physiology. They then use other writers' empirical research findings to underline their own claims and interpret them in a way that best supports the new theory. Both writers are very open about the fact that their assertions have not been 'proven' scientifically but that doing so can be left to future research.

In three papers spanning over a decade, Ohala (1983, 1984, 1994) proposed that:

> '[C]ertain global uses of intonation across languages exhibit sound symbolism, i.e. they show a motivational link between the shape of an intonation pattern and its meaning or function. This is not a new claim . . . But there are several good reasons for being sceptical of such claims, including those I make here. First, it runs counter to the dominant Saussurian dictum that "the sign is arbitrary," i.e. that the link between sound and meaning is conventional, not natural. . . . Second, there has typically been no convincing theory offered as to why sound symbolism should exist in languages. . . . Third, most of the evidence offered for sound symbolism lacks the rigor found in linguistic argumentation at its best. . . .

'The most I can hope to do in this paper is to reduce the level of scepticism surrounding sound symbolism by proposing a unifying, ethologically based and phonetically plausible theory. . . . To the extent possible I will cite experimental results in support of my claims although, admittedly, much more empirical work needs to be done.'

(Ohala, 1994: 325–6)

Ohala's fundamental claim is that there is a natural, ethologically based link between high pitch and 'feminine' attributes such as friendliness and submission, which has its linguistic expression in 'uncertainty', resulting in rising pitch for questions; and between low pitch and 'masculine' attributes such as dominance, which communicates 'certainty' in language and thus results in falling pitch for declarative statements. Ohala refers to the fact that the male human larynx is twice the size of the female organ, particularly in the front-to-back dimension, allowing for the vocal folds to be longer. The longer the vocal folds the lower the frequency. Other physiological facts also add to a lowering of the overall frequency, such as any lengthening of the vocal tract.

Among the physiological facts that Ohala draws on are the position of the male larynx, which is lower in the vocal tract than for women and thus results in lower overall pitch, and the fact that lip spreading (i.e. smiling and being friendly) shortens the vocal tract and thus raises the frequency with which speech is delivered. This sound-meaning correlation is referred to as the 'Frequency Code' as it affects fundamental frequency (F0), i.e. pitch.

Carlos Gussenhoven adopts Ohala's theory and adds two further codes: the 'Effort Code' and the 'Production Code.' Together, he refers to all three as the 'biological codes' (Gussenhoven, 2002, 2004). The Effort Code states that the more breath force and energy it takes to produce an utterance the higher its overall pitch value will be. This is closely related to emphasis in language; in terms of human attributes, Gussenhoven links high effort/high pitch to helpfulness and argues that the effort of producing high pitch is being interpreted by humans as being obliging. The argument becomes decidedly difficult when it has to address rising or falling pitch, as the question is whether the sound-meaning mapping occurs on the starting pitch value, for example, a high pitch accent, or the movement towards the end value, such as falling. In the first case the utterance would have to display signs of the 'natural' meaning for high pitch, in the second case 'low pitch' meanings would apply, both in terms of the Effort Code and the Frequency Code. Finally, the Production Code refers to how breath force depletes towards the end of an utterance and thus overall pitch does, too. Therefore Gussenhoven asserts that pitch declination towards the end of a turn or sentence is a 'natural' pattern, signifying finality.

Neither Ohala nor Gussenhoven fail to note that many linguistic patterns do not follow the rules and predictions of the biological codes. This is a fundamental problem, given that the writers' claim is that the form-meaning connection is a 'natural' (Gussenhoven) and 'motivational' (Ohala) one. Gussenhoven in particular faces this issue head-on. He argues that while the biological codes are natural and as such tied to the basic human experience and physiology, language change can affect forms to such an extent that they lose their natural meaning. This argument provides Gussenhoven with the opportunity to identify any case that might otherwise be used to falsify his theory as 'grammaticalisation' without the need to consider nonconforming phenomena individually or in any detail.

Quote 5.5   Cementing the theory: An explanation for deviant cases

A discussion of intonational meaning typically raises the issue of whether such meaning is universal or language-specific (. . .). The position defended here is that both the universal and the language-specific per-spectives are true, simultaneously, for any language. . . . The universal meanings are based on metaphors of biological conditions that influence the speech production process, in this case F0. Three such metaphors, or 'biological codes,' as I will call them, have been identified. Together they amount to a theory of paralinguistic meaning in intonation. . . .

Unlike paralinguistic meaning, linguistic meaning is potentially arbi-trary, although the form-function relations between tones and meaning frequently mimic the paralinguistic form-function relations employed in phonetic implementation (. . .). Grammatical meanings are like paralin-guistic meanings, as when final H% indicates non-finality or final H% signals interrogativity. However, this is by no means always the case. Language change may create 'unnatural', arbitrary forms.

(Gussenhoven, 2002: 47)

Given that the discipline of linguistics is grounded in the widely accepted view that the relation between language form and language meaning is arbi-trary, the assertion that 'linguistic meaning is potentially arbitrary' (Gussen-hoven, 2002: 47) represents a significant qualification. However, it is needed to prepare the ground for the theoretical position of biological codes and their ethologically motivated nature, given the vast number of counter-examples in all languages of the world.

The biological codes and the potential explanations they offer for the meaning of intonation have an intuitive appeal initially. Some writers have fully accepted the theory of biological codes and attempted to extend the concept. For example, another famous phonologist, Julia Hirschberg, sug-gests that the theory should be aligned with Grice's Maxims of Coopera-tive Conversation (Grice, 1975) and proposes new maxims in line with the biological codes: a Maxim of Pitch (Frequency Code), a Maxim of Empha-sis (Effort Code) and Maxims of Range and Phrasing (Production Code) (Hirschberg, 2002).

However, such universalist claims have been in the minority. Ladd's (1996: 115) words of caution echo the majority view in the discipline of linguistics: 'there are good reasons for scepticism about the universalist view. . . . [M]ost of its generalisations are so broad or so vague ("high or rising pitch") that it is virtually impossible to falsify them.' Similarly, the theory-driven approach adopted by Liberman, Ohala, and Gussenhoven is rare in linguistics and even rarer in applied linguistics, as the following sections show.

5.4.2   *How Methods and Research Questions Are Woven Into a Position Paper: A Study of First Language Acquisition and Prosody*

A different way of constructing a position paper from Liberman's can be seen in Speer and Ito (2009), 'Prosody in First Language Acquisition—Acquiring Intonation as a Tool to Organise Information in Conversation'. Rather than an adversarial style, the authors present a comprehensive survey of approaches to researching first language acquisition with a particular focus on prosody.

The authors combine the review of previous work with a discussion of the implications of the various approaches. In particular, this article aims to convince the reader that an aspect of spoken language development has been underresearched, to map out the potential for research to fill this gap, and to explain the major problems with previous methods which this new research programme would need to consider if it were undertaken (see also Quote 5.6). The topic the authors are interested in is the relationship between prosody and the development of very young children's comprehension of the presentation of information and subsequent handling of similar prosodic resources to signal focus on different information as they learn to speak. They suggest that two aspects of prosody could be a source of information 'packaging' and focus drawn on by listeners: grouping of words into 'chunks' or phrases and intonational prominence. They discuss through a wide-ranging literature review the state of knowledge and the methods used in previous studies in the area and, by doing this, make the case for the centrality of these questions for the comprehension and production of spoken syntax and for language development in general. As much of the work is with infants of less than 12 months, the methodological challenges are fascinating and provide insights into the relationship between research methods design and wider theoretical issues, especially the care needed in reaching conclusions about the implications of findings made via a particular experimental method.

Quote 5.6   Presenting a position and showing relevance

Recent research on children's acquisition of prosody, or the rhythm and melody in language, demonstrates that young children use prosody in their comprehension and production of utterances to a greater extent than was previously documented. Spoken language, structured by prosodic form, is the primary input on which the mental representations and processes that comprise language use are built. Understanding how children acquire prosody and develop the mapping between prosody and other aspects of language is crucial to any effort to model the role of prosody in the processing system. We focus on two aspects of prosody that have been shown to play a primary role in its use as an organizational device in human languages, prosodic phrasal grouping, and intonational prominence.

(Speer and Ito, 2009: 90)

Comprehension of speech in very young infants has been measured by a variety of standard methods. These include correlations between attention to language phenomena and head turning in the very young infant, actions carried out in response to visual or oral prompts, and analysis of actual utterances in children as they become able to produce them. However, experiments carried out by these means have to be designed extremely carefully in relation to the research question. This is due to the potential influence of the restricted cognitive development of the child, the difficulty of the task in relation to a child's state of development, and the need to interpret linguistic phenomena, often through paralinguistic evidence such as gaze and gesture.

Concept 5.2 Methodological challenges in investigating very young infants' understanding of speech

Evidence for a child's language development begins from a very early age, four months or possibly earlier, as the infant becomes able to show attention and share this with others. The challenge for the applied linguist is how to uncover what is happening in this process, and a number of creative research design methods have been used to investigate this. These range from an artificial nipple with an electronic sensor to assumed correlations between gaze or gesture and underlying linguistic functions or structures. In the case of the former method, the speed and strength of sucking are linked to renewed interest in the child in the sounds he or she is hearing and therefore can be used to test what linguistic features are noticed by the child—for instance, attention paid to phrases in mother tongue versus nonmother tongue or phrases pronounced with and without standard intonation boundaries for the mother tongue. Özçalışkan and Goldin-Meadow (2005) provide a particularly convincing account of the relationship between the progress of child language development and the links to gesture. Electroencephalography and event-related potential (ERP) methods have also been used, allowing researchers to investigate brain activity in young children in relation to spoken and visual input (e.g. Tan and Molfese, 2009). These methods use electrodes placed on the scalp of the child and analyse the correlations between input (e.g. video scenes that match or do not match a simple spoken description) and the levels of activity in the brain in response to these events.

Speer and Ito (2009) report a series of studies on the relationship between the development of syntactic and prosodic processing in infants from the late 1980s to the time of writing and note the inconclusive nature of some of these when fine-grained investigations of the relationship are undertaken. They support the idea that the relationship between the processing demands of the tasks and the nature of the child's cognitive development will play a key part, and results will be skewed or contradictory if this is not taken into account. For example, they note the difference between studies that have simply indicated a child's preference for phrases that fall into syntactic groups over those that do not and the evidence that would be needed to show the child's ability to understand syntactic relationships. A child, they imply, may hear that appropriate groups of words are being said and what the boundaries are between these, and yet this may not translate into a precise understanding of the relationships between these groupings and the underlying syntax, nor would it be clear from previous work at what age the comprehension of syntactic information via prosody was evident nor, similarly, how and when the child develops mastery of prosodic-syntactic relations in their own speech. Such issues are at the heart of their position paper, and they build on the idea through a summary and critique of work that has attempted to deal with similar questions. They note that the testing of hypotheses regarding syntactic awareness in relation to prosodic cues has generally been carried out by asking children between the ages of around three to seven years to respond to syntactically ambiguous sentences by means of an action. For instance, Snedeker and Trueswell's (2001, 2004) toy-moving experiments in which children heard the sentence 'Tap the frog with the flower' presented in two ways: [Tap] [the frog with the flower] and [Tap the frog] [with the flower] and differentiated by prosody. They go on to give a balanced summary of other similar experiments but point out that task complexity and the experimental setting may undermine the ability to reach firm conclusions about the level of the child's understanding. Different results (better correlation between syntactic cues and actions) were found, they noted, when the child was given the prompt first without the visual excitement of the toys and instruments to manipulate, which may have led them to be distracted from the language element under scrutiny (Meroni and Crain, 2003). Speer and Ito suggest that the areas they are promoting for further research (child's understanding of phrasing and information focus in relation to prosody) are critical to developing our understanding of the acquisition of language more generally. They conclude that the programme of research they have been exploring in the rest of the article is well worthwhile, nevertheless: 'As experimental techniques continue to be refined over time, we may continue to find evidence for children's surprisingly sophisticated use of intonation at younger and younger ages' (Speer and Ito, 2009: 106).

Overall, this paper provides a carefully structured case for further research and unites theoretically interesting questions with the practical issues of how to probe them. The methodological challenges of investigating the spoken form are magnified in the context of child language experiments, and understanding the implications of these is a good starting point for researchers aiming to deal with this transitory and context-embedded mode.

5.4.3   A Position Paper on Qualitative Principles: Clause, Grammar, and Interaction

In their paper 'The Clause as a Locus of Grammar and Interaction' (2005), Sandra Thompson and Elizabeth Couper-Kuhlen present a case for the clause as a fundamental linguistic feature towards which speakers orient in interaction. Quote 5.7 provides a summary of their position and approach.

Quote 5.7   Making the case for a new conceptualisation of spoken clauses

This article draws on work at the interface of grammar and interaction to argue that the clause is a locus of interaction, in the sense that it is one of the most frequent grammatical formats which speakers orient to in projecting what actions are being done by others' utterances and in acting on these projections. Yet the way in which the clause affords grammatical projectability varies significantly from language to language. In fact, it depends on the nature of the clausal grammatical formats which are available as resources in a language: in some languages these allow early projection of the turn unit (as in English), in others they do not (as in Japanese). We focus here on these two languages and show that their variable grammatical projectability has repercussions on the way in which three interactional phenomena—next-turn onset, co-construction, and turn-unit extension—are realized in the respective speech communities. In each case the practices used are precisely the ones which the clausal grammatical formats in the given language promote. The evidence thus suggests that clauses are interactionally warranted, if variably built, formats for social action.

(Thompson and Couper-Kuhlen, 2005: 807)

They use the term 'format' to discuss the 'patterns or templates' that speakers use to create their utterances and interact with one another and build a discussion and argument around the significance of this as an important topic for the field of interactional linguistics. The significance of this lies in the fact that it provides an alternative explanation for grammatical forms as emerging from human communicative practice rather than vice versa. The article provides a tightly argued case building on key types of speaker behaviour—how speakers start a turn, co-construct a turn with others, or add an incremental phrase or utterance to an apparently completed turn (providing a 'turn-unit extension'). The paper is strengthened by its use of cross-linguistic comparisons—Japanese and English—to help make the case that the nature of the clause in a given language constrains and affects the way speakers handle these three types of conversational action. They argue that whereas in English the verb phrase allows relatively early projection of the rest of an utterance (a subject leading to a verb and then the expected additional words and phrases linked back to this, e.g. direct objects or obligatory phrasal elements), in Japanese the construction remains far more open and clausal elements are less frequently made explicit. Despite this, they argue, speakers in both languages show clear sensitivity to clause boundaries, whether or not elements are fully expressed, in terms of how they handle incoming turns, co-construction, and increments.

Whereas Speer and Ito (2009) are interested in the relationship between experimental methods and what can be concluded about spoken language development, Thompson and Couper-Kuhlen (2005) are working in a very different paradigm. Their methods, those of conversation analysis, are a given, and they build their argument—extremely convincingly—based on the internal logic of this approach. Quote 5.8 shows a typical example of how conversational evidence is interpreted and then related to the central topic of the article.

Quote 5.8   A typical CA analysis

Ford et al. (2002) point out that English increments [words or phrases tagged on after a possible completion point by a speaker] typically involve adverbial constituents. We note that all of these elements— although they can in principle be placed within the clause—are more typically positioned at its edges. This reflects the fact that they are external to the clausal format. And they are frequently overlapped by an incoming next speaker. Here is an example from our data collection:

(4) Carsales 5 (Ono and Thompson, 1995: 87)

1   G: . . (H) the only thing you can do is be the best you can.
2   . . [right]?
3   D: [but definitely].

In this example, G comes to a point of possible completion at the end of his clause in line 1. It is just at this point that D concurs with *but definitely*, but inadvertently, D's turn unit overlaps with the tag *right* (as shown by the brackets), which G has just appended at the same time to his possibly complete clause in line 1. Yet D's turn is exquisitely 'well-placed' in the sense that it comes just at the end of a clausal format with prosody suggesting completion of a turn. This is reflected in the fact that none of the characteristic speech perturbations found to accompany violative incomes are present here (French and Local, 1983; Schegloff, 1987).

(Thompson and Couper-Kuhlen, 2005: 820)

The point to note is that the CA approach does not simply assume that a given linguistic resource/feature equates to a particular interactive function; rather, it develops a tentative interpretation of the events in context based on the local context ('. . . exquisitely "well-placed" in the sense that'), and on previous work in the field ('. . . none of the characteristic speech perturbations found to accompany violative incomes are present here (French and Local, 1983; Schegloff, 1987)'). A further point to note is that, in keeping with the qualitative paradigm, a multiplicity of pieces of evidence are gathered to make the case for a particular interpretation rather than a single dominant or authoritative piece of evidence being promoted. In this example it is both the prosodic features of the completing turn (indicating closure), the syntactic features of the turn, the timing of the increment, and the lack of features normally associated with a problematic interruption in the incoming turn that are put together by the authors to infer that the speakers are orienting towards the clause format and positioning turns and increments in relation to something that has salience for both of them. A further significant point related to the lack of a one-to-one relationship between linguistic features and their interpretation out of context is the case made by the authors that the nature of the grammatical formats differ from language to language and significantly affect how speakers handle turn, increment, and collaboration. Although the authors do not mention it, the implications for second language teaching and learning are clear, and further work on this area would be of great interest.

5.4.4   *A Qualitative 'Privileged Insider' Approach*

An unusual but effective approach to gaining understanding of speech genres is taken by Janne Morton in her paper 'Genre and Disciplinary Competence: A Case Study of Contextualisation In an Academic Speech Genre' (2009). Spoken genres are an underresearched topic, and the article is interesting, therefore, not only in its own right but also as providing a distinctive method of evaluating them. Two main strands of work on spoken genres have been evident in applied linguistics: one more ethnographically focused and the other more linguistically focused, often with a link to corpus studies and the analysis of the features of language that correlate to particular genres (e.g. Biber, 2006). Morton (2009) is in the former tradition and takes as a given that the student architectural presentation is a distinct genre and that it is one of the means by which the novice becomes accepted into the professional community. Showing an understanding of the genre and handling information in an appropriate rhetorical framework is as important, if not more important, than the content of the presentation. By performing the spoken genre the students align themselves to their discipline with greater or less success and become socialised into it (see also Quote 5.9).

Quote 5.9   Introducing the idea of socialisation into a profession

The process of disciplinary socialisation has been linked to a gradual mastery of a discipline's genres. This article takes a view of genre, as indexing a wide range of often implicit understandings about knowledge creation and use within a discipline, and as fully rhetorical. Within such a framework, novice and near-expert examples of one academic assessment genre—the student architecture presentation – are compared. The face-to-face nature of the academic presentation directs attention to the interpersonal dimension involved in the speaker persuading the audience of the value of their design. The analysis thus focused on identifying the rhetorical strategies that successful students used to accomplish this interpersonal dimension in a manner valued by disciplinary experts. From our data, it seemed that the contextualisation practices that students drew upon to facilitate intended interpretations of their design distinguished successful from less successful presentations. These practices were found to include a narrative style, metaphorical images, and dynamic grammar. Such practices served to animate students' design artefacts and to help take the audience beyond the design artefacts into the world of the students' designs that the artefacts represented.

(Morton, 2009: 1)

In terms of methods, Morton compared presentations in two groups, first- and fourth-year students, and categorised them as successful or not according to an insider perspective—that of their lecturer—without any additional comments, criteria, or analysis from the researcher. This approach is in line with an emerging strand of work on assessment in which 'indigenous' criteria (rather than those imposed by an outsider's perspective) are highly valued (see Yu, 2007, for a useful summary of literature and a research project investigating this idea). From this then flowed the detailed analysis of three presentations selected as typifying three levels of socialisation towards being a fully fledged architect: (least successful) 'The "Janitor's Tour"'; (more successful) 'Novice emerging architect'; and (most successful) 'Playful near-expert'. The analysis of rhetorical features, linguistic, and nonlinguistic devices incorporated (images, models, gesture, and so on) and cross-comparisons between the presentations lead the researcher to conclude what aspects of each may be correlated to 'success'. While all students managed to handle and incorporate linguistic and nonlinguistic elements into something which could be recognised as the architecture presentation it was, Morton suggests, the capacity to draw on certain 'contextualisation practices' that distinguished the successful from the less successful presentations. These included handling embedded narratives and storytelling, shifting narrative voice and stance, humour, and the overall ability to contextualise the designs being presented within a rhetorical narrative. Whereas the novice presenter used images in simple 'technical' manner, the near expert would use them in a more associative and metaphorical way, for example, bringing historical and artistic references into the presentation. Noteworthy also in the successful presentations was what Morton describes as 'dynamic grammar', including active verbs of motion, to describe the often static blocks of the architectural structures (e.g. a building being described as 'stretching' or 'folding'). Finally, in terms of what is valued by those judging architecture presentations there appeared to be a requirement for the student to project a sense of an architectural 'self'. This self needed to be involved closely with the ideas being presented rather than to simply describe the work as something objective and distanced from the presenter (an approach which may, in contrast, be highly valued in a different discipline, such as engineering; Darling, 2005).

This in-depth look at three presentations based on insider perspectives provides a good example of the strengths of the qualitative approach. The links between spoken discourse, context of delivery, the handling of linguistic and nonlinguistic features, and socialisation practices in a professional community are probed in a multifaceted analysis that a less 'open' approach would find difficult to achieve.

5.4.5   An Experimental and Control Group Approach With Pre- and Posttesting to Investigate Fluency Improvement

In contrast to the preceding examples this paper presents work firmly in the quantitative paradigm. Blake (2009) ('Potential of Text-Based Internet Chats for Improving Oral Fluency in a Second Language') was interested to learn whether exposure to online chat room discourse would increase the oral ability of students in off-line settings. The topic is clearly of great interest to anyone working on second language oral development, as the details of cross-modal effects on language proficiency have rarely been considered. In addition, the paper links ideas about theories of language processing (Levelt's (1989) model of articulation) to pedagogic environments. It also provides a clear example of a very frequently used approach to reaching a conclusion about a research question in a pedagogic setting. This is to establish a hypothesis or hypotheses relating to your research question, decide on a teaching intervention to test this, and then carry out a programme of instruction with testing of the students on the feature(s) before and after the intervention (see also Quote 5.10).

Quote 5.10   Introducing an experimental method

Although a number of studies have reported on the positive effects of Internet chats in the second language classroom, to the best of my knowledge no studies to date have examined the effect of text-based chats on oral fluency development. This exploratory study addressed the above question by examining the oral fluency development of 34 English as a second language learners who participated in the same 6-week course but in separate instructional environments: a text-based Internet chat environment, a traditional face-to-face environment, and a control environment that involved no student interaction. The study found that the gain scores of participants in the text-based Internet chat environment were significantly higher on the phonation time ratio and mean length of run measures than the gain scores of participants in the face-to-face and control environments (prior to Bonferroni adjustment). Gain scores on the three other measures were not significant. The author discusses these findings in relationship to Levelt's (1989) model of language production and argues that text-based Internet chat environments can be a useful way of building oral fluency by facilitating the automatization of lexical and grammatical knowledge at the formulator level.

(Blake, 2009: 227)

Generally this approach is strengthened and made more methodologically robust by using a control group (given standard instruction) and an experimental group (given different instruction involving the factor under investigation). In this way the results of the pre- and posttest can be interpreted in relation to the effects of the differences in instruction between the control and the experimental group. These interpretations are generally based on statistical analyses which allow the researcher to comment on the level of significance of the results in ways that are meaningful to other researchers. Blake (2009) is a model of this approach. He uses three groups to probe the effects of the medium of instruction on fluency development. This is because he wishes to tease out the differences between a simple online environment with no 'real-time' interaction between students, a face-to-face traditional classroom environment, and an online chat room context (more technically a context of synchronous computer mediated communication 'SCMC' as opposed to asynchronous interactions online such as bulletin boards or discussion forums). The control group in his experiment was therefore a group who studied online, carried out the listening and vocabulary exercises which formed the syllabus for all groups, but simply received e-mailed feedback from the tutor rather than experiencing immediate feedback and interaction with other students. The two experimental groups differed in that one participated entirely online with a tutor participating simultaneously with them and the other entirely in a face-to-face environment with classmates and teacher together. The obvious need to select participants at a similar level and to take into account gender, first language, syllabus content, and who was providing the instruction were all carefully planned for in the experiment. The fascinating result that Blake reported was that the group using chat room as the medium of instruction showed the greatest gains in terms of oral fluency in the posttest. He suggests that whereas the face-to-face environment may seem the most likely one to support the development of oral skills, the dynamics of a class actually lead to very few students having the chance to speak, and the norms of turn-taking mean that a learner will assume that when someone else is speaking they will not be called on to speak. In contrast to this, a discussion carried out via instant messaging allows all participants to be actively putting forward their ideas simultaneously. In line with the paradigm he is using, Blake also has a thoughtful section on the limitations of his findings, some questioning of his definition of fluency, and the need for more researchers to investigate the kinds of questions he asked in this project. All in all, the article provides both a model for the novice researcher and a starting point for further work.

5.4.6   Using a Single-Factor Within-Participant Group Experimental Design to Investigate Oral Performance

Quote 5.11   Introducing different experimental conditions

This article reports on an experimental study that investigated the effect of different conditions of listener backchannels on the fluency of L2 [i.e. second language] speakers. Participants were 14 non-advanced Japanese learners of English who each performed three oral tasks in three different backchannel conditions: (1) verbal/nonverbal (V/NV), (2) nonverbal-only (NV), and (3) no backchannels (NB). Verbal backchannels included 'mm-hm' and 'uh-huh' while the nonverbal backchannels involved head nodding. Fluency was assessed via five temporal measures. As hypothesized, the results showed that the 14 Japanese participants were, on average, most fluent in the V/NV condition, less fluent in the NV condition and least fluent in the NB condition. The differences obtained in fluency between the V/NV and NB conditions were found to be significant. These results lend support to the 'backchannel output hypothesis' which suggests that backchannels may facilitate the fluency of non-advanced learners of English during oral tasks depending on the nature of backchannel use in their L1 and sociocultural environments.

(Wolf, 2008: 279)

The second example of a quantitative approach to investigating speaking looks at speaker interaction and asks what effects different kinds of listener response in terms of 'backchannels' (short often nonverbal responses by a listener to acknowledge understanding or encourage continuation) have on oral production. In the article 'The Effects of Backchannels on Fluency in L2 Oral Task Production' (2008) James Wolf uses a classic research question plus experimental approach to test a hypothesis and reach quantifiable results. The framework he uses is based on the statistical approach he will adopt for the analysis. He describes it as a 'single-factor' (i.e. the independent feature being investigated, in this case backchannel) 'within-participant' approach (i.e. the variable is tested on a single group of subjects with similar language background and levels of proficiency; see also Quote 5.11). This means that researchers take a single main feature they want to investigate and see it in action under slightly varied conditions in relation to the same subjects. The differences in output from the subjects can then be interpreted in light of the varied conditions. A multifactor/factorial approach would look at two (or more) independent features (e.g. backchannel and syllable rate) and a between-group approach would have two clearly defined categories of subjects (e.g. Japanese L1 versus Mandarin L1 speakers). The approach is therefore embedded in the quantitative paradigm, as its success depends on the ability to delimit and categorise features and groups clearly, to demarcate the conditions you wish to apply to subjects, and to have some reliable and objective form of measurement of the output from the participants.

Wolf's fundamental question is how English backchannel cues might influence Japanese EFL learners' fluency during oral tasks (Wolf, 2008: 281). More specifically he is intrigued by the differences between Japanese and English in terms of typical use of backchannel and hypothesises that for the intermediate EFL student this will have a significant effect on oral fluency. He argues that, whereas there is some evidence that advanced EFL students adopt the back-channel behaviour of the target language, the lower proficiency students will be influenced by what the norms are in their first language. He also assumes that the Japanese learners will show a preference for a combination of ver-bal and nonverbal backchannel signals (head nod plus short utterance, which previous literature suggests is typical for the Japanese context) and will be more fluent under these conditions than when a nonverbal gesture is made or no backchannel is forthcoming. He designs an experiment in which 14 intermediate Japanese speakers tell a narrative from pictures in these three conditions—with the researcher either giving a combination of verbal and nonverbal signals, head nods without verbalisation, or no backchannels. The design is exemplary in that factors such as the effect of the different story type and the repetition of the story task are all factored into the methods.

Wolf (2008) found that his hypotheses were generally supported, with the highest levels of oral fluency being found in the condition when the narrative was told in a combination of both verbal and nonverbal backchannel cues. The differences between the other two conditions were less marked, but the lowest scores for fluency were found in the condition of zero feedback through backchannel signalling.

A weakness of the paper is the leap to a conclusion that what is being uncovered is a fine-grained relationship between L1 backchannel expecta-tions and L2 behaviour. The evidence presented could equally support the hypothesis that the intermediate learner is encouraged and made less anxious by the quality/quantity of feedback from an interlocutor, not the nature of it in relation to L1 expectations. Nevertheless, the paper provides a carefully thought-through experimental approach with findings that can clearly be ascribed to the three conditions under which the learner is producing the oral narratives. As such it provides an interesting starting point for further work on cross-linguistic comparisons of interaction and has clear implications for other domains, for instance, oral assessment.

5.4.7 Using a Video Corpus Approach to Investigate How Gesture, Language, and Speech Processing Work in Combination

Quote 5.12 Explaining a multimodal approach to a research question

Speakers monitor their own speech and, when they discover problems, make repairs. In the proposal examined here, speakers also monitor addressees for understanding and, when necessary, alter their utterances in progress. Addressees cooperate by displaying and signaling their understanding in progress. Pairs of participants were videotaped as a director instructed a builder in assembling 10 Lego models. In one group, directors could see the builders' workspace; in a second, they could not; in a third, they gave instructions by audiotape. Two partners were much slower when directors could not see the builders' workspace, and they made many more errors when the instructions were audiotaped. When their workspace was visible, builders communicated with directors by exhibiting, poising, pointing at, placing, and orienting blocks, and by eye gaze, head nods, and head shakes, all timed with precision. Directors often responded by altering their utterances midcourse, also timed with precision.

(Clark and Krych, 2004: 62)

The final example of how research into speaking has been carried out deals with the emerging field of multimodal analyses. This field attempts to understand the spoken mode via one or more forms of traditional linguistic analysis (here, e.g. number of words, types of turn, and length of utterances). It is carried out by means of videoing interactions that allow speech, gesture, gaze and contextual references to be looked at in combination (see also Quote 5.12). Clark and Krych (2004) present a quantitatively oriented research project in which they develop a radical view of spoken language. They argue that theoretical frameworks that do not take into account the effects on speakers of the availability of visual signals provide a fundamentally incomplete picture of the mode. Their conclusion can be seen in Quote 5.13.

Quote 5.13   The case for a multimodal view of language

[Speakers] rely not only on each other's vocal signals, but on each other's gestural signals such as exhibiting, poising, pointing at, and placing physical objects, nodding and shaking heads, and directing eye gaze, and on other mutually visible events. They use the signals to create projective pairs by which they ground what they are currently saying. Dialogues are the artful orchestration of these actions. Models of language use that are limited to only part of this process are necessarily incomplete and, for many purposes, incorrect.

(Clark and Krych, 2004: 79)

They work towards this conclusion through a meticulous study of a small corpus of videotapes of dyads (pairs of speakers) attempting to carry out a simple task together. The aim is to put together ten 'Lego' models correctly and as quickly as possible. In the task, one of the pair is the director and the other the builder. The directors can see the prototypes of the models; the builders cannot and rely on the directors to guide them in building the models from loose bricks. To investigate the relationship between spoken interactions, gesture, and shared visual 'workspace', the authors created two different conditions under which the tasks were carried out. They termed these 'interactive' and 'noninteractive'. In the former both the director and builder could interact verbally, and in half the pairs could see the builder's workspace as well as interact verbally (a subcondition was set up in which faces could be seen or not seen, but the researchers noted that this made no significant difference and they do not report on it further). These were analysed as 'interactive-workspace-hidden' and 'interactive-workspace-visible'. In the noninteractive condition, the director recorded the instructions and was told that the builder would make the model a week later. The builders were then given the task of creating the models from the recorded instructions and were allowed to play the instructions as often as they liked and to rewind and repeat sections of the instructions.

Clark and Krych measured a range of aspects of the task performance including the average time taken to complete a model under the different conditions; the number of words per task and per turn used by director versus builder in the three conditions; time spent checking actions had been carried out correctly; percentage of errors made; number of deictic expressions (*here, there, this, these, that, those, like this, like these, like those*); and action and gesture types (e.g. show a block to the director, position a block tentatively). To show the relationships between speech and actions they created 'action graphs' (see Figure 5.1).

Their results suggested that there were significant differences on all measures between the interactive and the noninteractive conditions and between the interactive conditions where the workspace was visible to both participants and where it was not. For instance, hiding the workspace from the director doubled the average length of time taken to create the model and significantly increased the number of words used by both the director and the builder to carry out the task. The noninteractive conditions (builder responding to instructions on a recording) increased the task time further and hugely

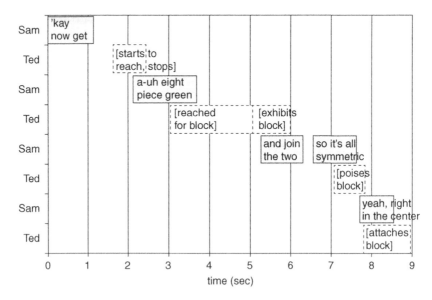

Figure 5.1 Action Graph Showing Gesture Timings in Relation to Spoken Directions.
Source: From Clark and Krych (2004: 72).

increased the errors in the final models (by eight times in final model structures and by 14 times in terms of misuse of individual blocks, e.g. wrong colour). At the level of detailed analysis of gesture, efficiency, and verbal behaviour, the authors note the increases in deictic references when the workspace is visible. They ascribe the increased efficiency in the interactive-workspace-visible conditions to the delicate interplay between gesture, action, and verbal input, for instance, the builder being able to 'poise' a block in a location to seek assurance that it is both the correct block and correct placement. It is this interplay that the authors see as key in terms of the theoretical stance they are promoting, and they provide compelling evidence for the need to see spoken discourse in terms of fundamentally bilateral processes: 'Our findings have general implications for models of speaking. Perhaps the most basic is that speakers and listeners do not use the same processes in dialogue—the primary site for language—as they do when they are alone' (Clark and Krych, 2004: 76).

5.5   New Directions

This section ends the chapter with a brief overview of current trends in applied linguistics that will have particular significance for researching speaking. It is an exciting time for those interested in the spoken mode, as major trends continue to emerge that have reshaped and will continue to reshape the research landscape. The first of these is the breaking down of some of the barriers between different 'camps' in the discipline, the acceptance of a less adversarial, more eclectic, approach to language theory and respect for interdisciplinarity. Choi and Richards (2016) note the 'end of paradigm wars' in their introduction to the special issue of *Applied Linguistics* on research methods. This trend can be seen in the field of spoken language research as linkages are made between areas that have traditionally not had much dialogue, for instance, conversation analysis and second language acquisition (Kasper and Wagner, 2011; Hughes and Szczepek Reed, 2010) or assessment of second language speaking and critical linguistics (Shohamy, 2014; Elder and McNamara, 2015) or learner corpora and cognitive linguistics (de Knop and Meunier, 2015). It can also be seen in cross-disciplinary work where the interface between applied linguistic insights into talk is transferred into work in fields as diverse as business studies or health sciences. The approach shown in Burns and Moore (2008) towards gaining a better understanding of accountancy discourse described in Chapter 7 provides an example of this.

A second major trend is that of the effect of the rising access to English via the processes of globalisation and new technologies, the world Englishes (WE), and English as a lingua franca (ELF) movements. In these contexts, the notion of whose spoken English is the norm and the political, pedagogic, and policy-related issues that flow from seeing English as not, primarily, owned by those who speak it as a first language are creating a source of interesting debate. As noted in earlier chapters the impact of these debates on issues of assessment and language pedagogy will take considerable time to filter through to syllabuses, published materials, classrooms, and examination boards. In terms of education systems around the globe, the introduction of English as a core subject at increasingly younger ages is on the rise and is not without its critics (Kirkpatrick, 2011). The use of English in academic settings and the increased size and international diversity of research projects are also driving changes to language teaching needs (Hughes, forthcoming). These are phenomena which everyone who teaches or researches speaking is being affected by at some level. Work in the subdiscipline of 'variational pragmatics' is starting to both provide theoretical underpinning and the stability to allow some of the insights to reach the classroom (Barron, 2005; Murphy, 2012). The research article described in Chapter 7 reporting work by Cheng and Tsui (2009) provides a further example of work in this area. Work at the interface between corpus linguistics and ELF also appears to be becoming particularly strongly established, and major sources of data showing the norms of interaction between nonnative speakers are now available for scholars and teachers to examine and begin to ask what the 'core' of this language is like and whether they wish to teach it (Prodromou, 2008). Two projects in Chapter 7 exemplify this: Lam (2010), which contrasts corpus data and materials for the classroom against the backdrop of Hong Kong English, and Hincks (2010), which looks at the issue of the effects of using English as a lingua franca on the content and speech rate in student presentations.

A third trend is the recent increase in cross-linguistic and cross-cultural comparisons of interactional practices, especially in the field of conversation analysis. The first few decades of research on natural talk were characterised by a rarely questioned use of (US American) English as the data source and an almost naïve assumption that findings from English could be generalised across other languages and cultures. While non-English language data became a more frequent subject of CA inquiry in the 1990s, it was only in the early years of the new century that comparisons across languages and cultures began to be conducted more systematically. For example, Enfield and Stivers (2007) compare person reference in a range of languages, while both Fox, Maschler, and Uhmann (2010) and Dingemanse and Enfield (2015) look at repair cross-linguistically. From the perspective of speaking, two developments within this trend are particularly relevant. Sidnell and Enfield's (2012) investigation of agreeing with a previous assessment in three languages shows that the variations in the linguistic means by which speakers of the different languages accomplish this activity result in 'collateral effects': in each language the linguistic form being used for agreement has different accompanying functions, making agreeing a slightly different social action depending on the language being spoken. A related programme of research has been started by Szczepek Reed and Persson (2016), who study confirmations in two languages (French and German). They find that although the pronunciation rules for the two languages prescribe the opposite rule with regard to how words should be linked together phonetically, when it comes to extending a confirmation with more talk, speakers of both languages use the same articulation patterns, irrespective of what pronunciation dictionaries tell us. Both of these developments show how empirical research can yield surprising results with regard to the assumed commonalities and differences in spoken language practices across the world.

Finally, the consolidation of technological advances over a 25-year period and the incorporation of entirely new technologies have had, and will continue to have, a major effect on our understanding of spoken mode and how to research it. At its most basic, technology has allowed the development of large corpora of speech, and at its more sophisticated, this has permitted multimodal work combining speech, transcriptions, and digital audio and video material for the researcher to probe. This brings a wealth of data for the researcher and will probably be particularly effective in helping us gain insights about spoken grammar. In 2006, Christophe Rühlemann noted: ' . . . it seems reasonable to assume that these are just the early days of "conversational grammar" and that what little we already know about it may well appear as just the humble beginnings in the decades to come' (Rühlemann, 2006: 406), and in 2015 Carter and McCarthy were reviewing the decade and more of work and the challenges to norms of grammar that it entails, particularly in relation to metalanguage (Carter and McCarthy, 2015). Interactional linguistics is gradually beginning to tap into these large corpora, and with the increasing capacity to combine audio files with transcriptions it will be fascinating to see this development continue. There is great strength to an approach that could take an account of an emergent and collaborative structure and seek parallels in other contexts and languages very speedily.

Two further technological advances may have significant impact on our understanding of spoken language. The first of these is the adoption of brain scanning techniques to the analysis of language processing. This has tended to be mainly at the level of semantic processing but will soon develop into other linguistic domains. The 'hard' evidence that fMRI scanning provides has the potential to answer some of the major theoretical questions in terms of speech production in due course. Straube et al. (2010) describes in some detail how this work is carried out, and a summary of the article and ideas for further work are given in Chapter 7. These techniques are beginning to have even more fundamental applications. Chai et al. (2016) applied neural scanning to begin to understand the differences in the brain functions and structure of adults with and without an aptitude for learning a second language. The second major development is that of the World Wide Web in the twenty-first century. A search on the term 'conversation' in a popular website on which users can display video brings the user a 'corpus' of many million more words than have ever been designed by a linguist. These insights and access to online resources are being brought into mainstream research in linguistics and into the language classroom (Tribble, 2013; Flowerdew, 2015) In addition, the ethical position of many who are developing the next generation of the web means that the open sharing of data will be the norm, and protocols to allow different sets of data to talk to one another and to be analysed by different groups will be developed (Chiarcos et al., 2012). This open access to vast quantities of multimodal data and tools to describe and analyse it may well drive our understanding of the norms of speech in future.

Further Reading

Boxer, D. and Cohen, A. D. (2004). *Studying Speaking to Inform Second Language Learning*. Clevedon: Multilingual Matters.

Brown, J. D. and Rodgers, T. (2003). *Doing Second Language Research*. Oxford: Oxford University Press.

Dörnyei, Z. (2007). *Research Methods in Applied Linguistics: Quantitative, Qualitative, and Mixed Methodologies*. Oxford: Oxford University Press.

Hughes, R. (2010). Researching speaking. In B. Paltridge and A. Phakiti (Eds), *Continuum Companion to Research Methods in Applied Linguistics*. London: Continuum, pp. 147–158.

Kormos, J. (2014). *Speech Production and Second Language Acquisition*. London: Routledge.

Larson-Hall, J. (2010). *A Guide to Doing Statistics in Second Language Research*. London: Routledge.

Litosseliti, L. (Ed) (2010). *Research Methods in Linguistics*. London: A&C Black.

Mackey, A. and Gass, S. M. (2011). *Research Methods in Second Language Acquisition: A Practical Guide*. Oxford: Wiley-Blackwell.

Wong, J. and Waring, H. Z. (2010). *Conversation Analysis and Second Language Pedagogy: A Guide for ESL/EFL Teachers*. London: Routledge.

Section III
Researching Speaking

6 Spoken Language and the Classroom

This chapter will . . .

- discuss some theories of language development that have strongly influenced classroom practice;
- review some key features of speech and relate these to the treatment of the spoken form in the language classroom;
- outline some of the issues at the interface between language teaching methodology and research into spoken mode.

6.1 Introduction

As Quotes 6.1 and 6.2 imply, speaking has for a long time played a special role in language education and applied linguistic theory beyond what might be simply regarded as 'teaching speaking'. This fact has affected how speaking is regarded in the classroom and in teacher training. An aim of the current chapter is to highlight and explain these links.

Quotes 6.1 and 6.2   The Importance given to speech in language pedagogy

It is evident that our strongest and most direct associations ought to be with the spoken language, for in speaking we must have all our associations between ideas and words in perfect working order: we have no time to pick and choose our words and constructions, as when we are writing. . . .

If, then, we first get a thorough knowledge of the spoken form of the foreign language, and then proceed to learn its literary form, we shall be in exactly the same position as regards relative strength of associations as the natives themselves: we shall think in the spoken language, because our associations are directly with it.

(Sweet, 1900: 52–3)

For the teacher, understanding classroom communication, being able to 'shape' learner contributions and making strategic decisions in the moment-by-moment unfolding of a lesson are regarded as being crucial to developing SLA in the formal, L2 classroom context.

(Walsh, 2006: 133)

6.2   The Status of Speaking in Classrooms

Historically, there are several reasons for the special status of spoken interaction in applied linguistics and language pedagogy. These perspectives strongly influence what is regarded as good classroom practice whether the explicit name of the component in the syllabus is speaking or not. Spoken interaction is seen as an important, if not key, aspect of the language learning process and has been for over 100 years. The spoken form is variously conceived of as:

- the primary mode in which 'natural uptake' can occur (as in 'The Natural Method' or 'The Oral Approach' prevalent in the early years of the last century until the early 1960s),
- a powerful tool for developing automatic and fluent output, together with consolidation of grammatical patterns (as in 'The Direct Method' or 'The Audio-lingual Approach'),
- the ideal medium for the exploration of language and one that allows a focus on communication to take precedence over form (a fundamental aspect of 'The Communicative Approach' and later developments such as 'Task-Based Language Teaching').

In terms of approaches, methods, or techniques (to use Anthony's (1963) often used and still useful categorisation to distinguish different levels of teaching methodology), the spoken form has for a long time retained a very significant status in the language classroom.

However, the status and handling of the mode has not remained static and, in particular, the decade of the 1970s marked a significant transition. The language learner in a 1950s and 1960s classroom, whether in the UK or the United States or contexts influenced by these major Anglophone communities, would have had a very high chance of being exposed to the spoken form. Indeed the influence of early British applied linguists such as Henry Sweet remained powerful throughout the first half of the century and, as Quote 6.1 suggests, led to a strong emphasis on oral mode. What emerged as 'The Natural Method' relied on introducing language items systematically and almost entirely through speech and then on the very accurate (in phonetic terms) oral practice of explicitly taught language rules and features. In the United States, the influence of ethnographic approaches which depended on close and careful scrutiny of the oral form were also influential, and these were superseded by what eventually became known as 'The Audio-lingual Method'. This again relied heavily on oral input, exposure to native speaker models, and repetitive oral work ('drilling') which could be carried out with very little reference to meaning or context. The role of speech in the language classroom during these post–Second World War to late 1960s years was rather similar to a Petri dish in an experiment. It was the 'medium' or container of carefully selected (in the better programmes) linguistic items that would flourish in this sheltered environment and then become automatic and natural for the learner who had absorbed and internalised them through extensive practice. The focus was not primarily on communication but on structure and accurate production.

There was, however, a gradual acknowledgment from the late 1960s onwards that language rules and explicit focus on input and practice could only take the learner so far. Quote 6.3 gives an example of an early statement of the issues.

Quote 6.3   Widdowson on the role of communication in language teaching

The difficulty is that the ability to compose sentences is not the only ability we need to communicate. Communication only takes place when we make use of sentences to perform a variety of different acts of an essentially social nature. Thus we do not communicate by composing sentences, but by using sentences to make statements of different kinds, to describe, to record, to classify and so on, or to ask questions, make requests, give orders. Knowing what is involved in putting sentences together correctly is only one part of what we mean by knowing a language, and it has very little value on its own: it has to be supplemented by a knowledge of what sentences count as in their normal use as a means of communicating. And I do not think that the recommended approach makes adequate provision for the teaching of this kind of knowledge.

(Widdowson, 1972: 16)

The acknowledgment of the limitations of 'putting sentences together correctly' came about at the same time as a changing ethos in educational circles in liberal Western thinking. These repositioned 'The Teacher' and 'The Student' and made the idea of an authoritative model presented by a native speaker less attractive. Several simultaneous factors therefore combined to mean that the learner in a 1980s classroom would be asked to carry out a very different set of tasks from his or her counterpart of the postwar era. This language learner would, in classrooms influenced by Western academic applied linguistic thinking, be far less likely to be asked to carry out structured oral practice of a language feature and much more likely to be involved in a student-led task involving negotiation and discussion with peers carried out in the medium of speech and with little explicit focus on rules and 'getting it right'. In this early 'communicative' classroom the spoken mode was, and still is, vitally important, but it was no longer merely the receptacle or tool of instruction; rather, it was coming to be seen as the actual medium through which the learner's state of linguistic knowledge is shaped and altered.

To understand this change in the status of speech in the language teaching classroom it is necessary to go back to another highly influential set of trends and discussions in linguistics and applied linguistics that took place from the mid-1960s and which continues to be relevant today. In particular, there was a strand of debate from that period onwards about how to incorporate the theories outlined by Noam Chomsky into the language teaching arena: how could language practitioners approach second language teaching in ways that reflected his insights about first language development?

One answer was based on the premise that there is no real difference between the two acquisition processes. These ideas were not new but were most extensively explored as a method or approach for the ELT classroom by Stephen Krashen (Krashen, 1981 through Krashen, 2008) in what came to be called 'The Natural Approach' (not to be confused with the early twentieth century 'Natural Method' which emerged as part of the reaction to 'Grammar Translation' methods). Like the communicative language teaching movement, this theory suggested that a second language is best acquired not by a learner being presented with grammatical information and rules by a teacher but by active engagement in meaningful communication (the 'learning–acquisition' distinction) and by students needing to comprehend discourse which is slightly beyond that which they can express themselves (Krashen's 'input hypothesis'; see also Quote 6.4 and Concept Box 6.1).

Quote 6.4   Krashen on the role of spoken interaction in language acquisition

Language *acquisition* [original emphasis] is very similar to the process children use in acquiring first and second languages. It requires meaningful interaction in the target language—natural communication—in which speakers are concerned not with the form of their utterances but with the messages they are conveying and understanding.

(Krashen, 1981:1)

The input hypothesis runs counter to our usual pedagogical approach in second and foreign language teaching. . . . [O]ur assumption has been that we first learn structures, then practice using them in communication, and this is how fluency develops. The input hypothesis says the opposite. It says we acquire by 'going for meaning' first, and as a result, we acquire structure!

(Krashen, 1982: 21)

The idea underpinning Krashen's theory was that in the process of exposure to the target language just beyond a student's current capacity and in the engagement of meaningful and enjoyable communication in it, something akin to a child's acquisition of language would occur. This was an exciting idea offering to bridge the gap between classrooms and the current dominant language theories that dealt with language as an idealised system difficult to relate to the realities of the language teaching classroom. The reason it was well-received, therefore, was that it gave a theoretically convincing answer to language practitioners who had faced the issue of how to relate the specifics of language 'performance' in their classrooms to underlying development of L2 'competence'. Krashen's model appeared to provide the solution: the process will happen as naturally as L1 acquisition, if you provide the right conditions. Because spoken interaction was the primary channel for child language development, this perspective placed great emphasis on the spoken mode in second language learning theory and was one of the major drivers of change to what was regarded as good practice in the language teaching classroom by the late 1980s.

Rather quickly, however, Krashen's theory became the subject of heated debate concerning how to apply and how to verify it (e.g. White, 1987), together with the growing sense in the field that L2 acquisition differs from L1 in a variety of ways (e.g. Ellis, 1986). The significant impact that the ideas had mean that Krashen's ideas are retained in the standard English language teacher training syllabus and the focus on interaction rather than explicit instruction that they promoted provides part of the explanation for the strong focus on speaking in language acquisition that remains to this day. As noted, the change of emphasis from explicit tuition and drilling to looking at language in use was also shared by the communicative language teaching movement that began to be highly influential from the early 1970s.

Concept 6.1 Learning versus acquisition and input hypothesis in the 'Natural Approach'

During the early 1980s Stephen Krashen developed his influential theory of second language development in what came to be referred to as the 'Natural Approach'. This has been challenged on several fronts, but some of the central ideas helped to shape second language acquisition theory (SLA) and remain influential to this day. Two of his ideas—the distinction between learning and acquisition and the input hypothesis—are relevant to how spoken interaction is handled in the language classroom today.

In this framework, consciously learning a language was at best a secondary process and the real focus of interest was acquisition. The L2 student, Krashen posited, like the child learning a first language, engaged with language at a deeper level than superficial grammatical knowledge and by exposure to it tapped into the underlying 'hard wiring' of the brain (i.e. the system which would be called 'competence' in Chomskyian theory). The strongest version of this theory suggested that one simply could not 'learn' a language and that too much emphasis on learning versus finding the right conditions for acquisition were harmful to L2 development.

In discussing the question of what the conditions for acquisition might be, the second key concept became relevant: the input hypothesis. This was presented in a formula 'i+1' (Krashen, 1982: 20–1) in which 'i' represents the current state of knowledge of a language and '1' equates to the next stage of its acquisition. The ideal conditions for acquisition were, Krashen suggested, those in which stimulating and motivating input at the level just beyond 'i' were presented to the student leading them to naturally engage with it and thus reshape their state of knowledge towards '1'. This very neat statement, although soon challenged as unverifiable (McLaughlin, 1987), provided a paradigm or framework for SLA which remains highly influential.

6.3 The Role of Spoken Interaction in Communicative Language Teaching Classrooms

The communicative language teaching (CLT) approach that has dominated English language teaching from the 1980s, if not earlier, and the natural approach that retains a strong influence on teacher training were developed around the idea of meaningful interaction and the focus on communication rather than linguistic facts. Both therefore valued and were interested in encouraging students' engagement in copious amounts of spoken language in the classroom.

The handling of classroom talk has therefore become something of a marker of ability to promote good language learning environments. It is also used as a measure of the level of learner versus teacher centredness of a class, with a correlation being between low levels of teacher talking time (TTT) and higher levels of student engagement and autonomy. The focus on the importance of speaking and its links to a dominant philosophy in the teaching of English has markedly affected the nature of classroom management at a global level and also influenced how particular instances of spoken interaction are valued. At the global level, teacher training in the communicative method explicitly discouraged too much teacher input and, taking this to its logical conclusion, one of several 'alternative' approaches was 'The Silent Way' (Gattegno, 1976). This, as its name suggests, promoted the reduction of teacher talk to an absolute minimum. The popularity of small group and pair work that emerged as teachers began to make constructs such as the communicatively oriented 'notional-functional' syllabus real during the 1980s was also linked to the high value placed on students' spoken interaction in the classroom.

Considerable attention is still paid to how to handle classroom dynamics effectively to promote greatest output from the student and position the teacher as a facilitator of exploratory and autonomous learning through negotiation rather than the dominant voice of authority on what is correct (Juswick et al., 2013; Boyd and Markarian, 2015). This philosophy has continued to shape what is regarded as good practice in the classroom over the last 30 to 40 years. The emergence of, for example, task-based learning and focus-on-form has been a refinement rather than a sea change in the primary status given to the role of spoken interaction and its management in the ELT classroom. The emphasis has shifted more recently from a concern about the relative 'air time' of the teacher versus the student towards gaining a better understanding of how spoken interaction between teacher and student or student and student can influence language learning (see, e.g. Quote 6.2, with which the chapter opened). The emergence of phenomena in other areas of teaching such as massive open online courses (MOOCs) in higher education and the 'flipped classroom' in pedagogic thinking generally have, similarly, placed even more emphasis on what students learn from one another through peer-to-peer discussion, online chat, and social networking support than from direct instruction from a face-to-face teacher (Wong et al., 2015; Nwosisi et al., 2016).

CLT has itself become more refined and diverse over the years, but the basic assumption that language is best approached as action and interaction rather than a set of rules has remained the bedrock of English language teacher training. An example of how classroom management of interaction is seen as influencing language acquisition is in the role of feedback and error correction by a teacher. In the focus-on-form movement, for instance, the handling of immediate feedback by drawing attention to an item just said by a student is part of the approach. It is felt to enhance the process of becoming more aware of a correct form and promote accurate spoken output by the student (see Quote 6.5 for an example of this process in action).

Quote 6.5   Example of didactic focus-on-form

In Example 3, the student leaves out the definite article 'the'. The teacher has no difficulty in understanding him but focuses attention on the error by correcting the utterance. The focus-on-form episode that results from this type of error treatment constitutes a kind of pedagogic 'time-out' from meaning-focussed communication and for this reason can be considered 'didactic'. It involves a 'negotiation of form' rather than a 'negotiation of meaning'. It is possible that students do not notice the target of such negotiation as no meaning is at stake. There is no evidence in Example 3 that the student has paid attention to the teacher's feedback. Ellis et al. (1999) found that didactic focus-on-form was far more common than conversational in communicative ESL lessons involving adult learners.

Example 3: Didactic focus-on-form

S: I was in pub
(2.0)
S: I was in pub
T: in the pub?
S: yeah and I was drinking beer

(Ellis et al., 2002: 434–5)

Another influential development in CLT that places great emphasis on the spoken mode was the still influential task-based language teaching (TBLT) movement (see Concept Box 6.2). This approach has not been without controversy—in particular the role of explicit versus implicit focus on linguistic items—but the ideas underlying it chimed particularly clearly with the ethos of CLT and have meant that the TBLT remains a current topic for scholarly debate and classroom applications (e.g. Guchte et al., 2015).

Concept 6.2   Task-based language teaching—TBLT

This is an approach to language learning based on insights first outlined in the late 1980s by Prabhu (1987) and which has remained a central topic in syllabus design and debate about language learning generally. Reporting on his work in India, Prabhu suggested that learners who were mainly focused on a real-world task made as good if not better progress than language learners given explicitly language-focused instruction. This led to a variety of attempts to implement 'task-based learning' more widely and to relate them to the language classroom more generally. This was done by designing tasks that promoted the use of authentic language and required active engagement by the student in their completion, generally with a high level of spoken interaction being required. A typical pattern for a lesson would be to provide an introduction to the task in the form of a 'warm-up' discussion to focus the attention of the students on the topic in question and help to generate some of the language required, a phase introducing the task and checking that students have fully understood the task and their roles (depending on the stance of the teacher to explicit linguistic input, this phase may include focus on particular language items needed to complete the task, or not), a phase in which the students carry out the task with the teacher taking the role of facilitator and interlocutor, and a phase of rounding up and reflection on the task and the language used. One of the aspects that teachers found refreshing was that the typical pattern of structured input and very constrained practice of particular items was abandoned. In the task-based classroom students are placed in a role of greater independence and, in a carefully constructed task, the idea is that they will generate language before getting further feedback and clarification of it both from other students and from the teacher.

A useful overview of how these ideas developed can be found in Bygate et al. (2001), *Researching Pedagogic Tasks: Second Language Learning, Teaching, and Testing*, and Samuda and Bygate (2008), *Tasks in Second Language Learning*. A more practically oriented title with ideas on how to implement TBLT in detail is Willis and Willis (2007). On the theoretical side, Peter Skehan went on to develop TBLT thinking in relation to task design and the balance between cognitive demands, focus on language, and maintaining some level of authenticity in the task. Skehan (2007) gives a balanced summary of thinking on TBLT, including an account of why it had its critics. This related to the difficulty of correlating language uptake with task and the role of explicit focus on linguistic features that different adherents promoted. Bygate et al. (2015) and Robinson (2011) note the gradual trajectory of TBLT from, in effect, a popular method to an important element in second language acquisition research, allowing spoken language to be both the tool for language improvement and assessment and a window on language development processes.

A very extensive investigation of how to transfer TBLT theory into the classroom was carried out in Belgium and reported in van den Branden (2006). Quote 6.6 shows the importance of the spoken mode in this approach and gives a sense of the relationship that develops between teacher and student as the approach is implemented.

Quote 6.6   The role of teacher–student spoken interaction in the task-based classroom

In task-based language teaching (TBLT), the teacher can be regarded in many ways as the learners' most privileged interlocutor. Although the teacher's role in TBLT differs from the role teachers assume in more 'linguistic', structure-oriented approaches, it is equally crucial. . . . In a nutshell we will argue and illustrate that there are two core actions that we believe the teacher should take in order for tasks to elicit rich learner activity and to enhance the chances that this activity turns into actual learning. These are:

a)   motivating the learner to invest intensive mental energy in task completion;
b)   interactionally supporting task performance in such a way as to trigger processes such as the negotiation of meaning and content, the comprehension of rich input, the production of output and focus on form, which are believed to be central to (second) language learning.

(Van Avermaet et al., 2007: 175)

The trends in language teaching theory outlined here have meant that it is almost commonplace to say that it is better for students to talk in the classroom than teachers and that there is a strong link between talk in the classroom and language acquisition processes. This in turn affects how spoken mode is handled in the classroom. However, its dominant role in some theories may, paradoxically, not be a good thing for teaching spoken language, *per se*. Promoting student talk and providing tasks that allow 'meaningful interaction' may not promote fluent, accurate, and stylistically diverse talk. Furthermore, the apparent focus on spoken mode in the classroom may mask significant issues for understanding the nature of speech and how best to teach and assess this skill in its own right. Quote 6.7 also captures something of this tension.

Quote 6.7   Interaction, important but underresearched?

Despite this enthusiasm for 'interactivity' as a defining notion in language teaching, a model of 'Language as Interaction' has not been described in the same level of detail as those models that have been developed for structural and functional views of language theory.

(Richards and Rodgers, 2001: 22)

The rest of this chapter provides a brief overview of some of the implications of the nature of speech for the classroom. It looks at some of the needs that practitioners may have in relation to handling spoken discourse in the speaking class as opposed to a class in which speaking is treated as the medium for language acquisition more generally.

6.4   Drawing on Classroom Practice for Research and Vice Versa

Activities based around speaking need to be managed and fostered through careful planning and direction by the teacher and through a choice of suitable tasks to stimulate speech. Where there are groups of students from different language backgrounds co-operating to carry out a task, there is rich potential for reflective practitioners to draw on existing research or to carry out their own classroom-based project in this area. There are also, however, factors that need to be taken into account, some of which have been underresearched in relation to the language classroom.

When we consider the complex nature of speech interaction, it is perhaps unsurprising that even the most advanced students still feel most at a loss when they are trying to take part in spontaneous, informal conversation in a new language. While the communicative classroom gives abundant opportunity for the student to interact, it is fruitful to raise awareness of the fundamentals of spoken discourse in order to give students a better understanding of how very different speaking is from the stringing together of grammatically correct (or incorrect) sentences. Language awareness activities based around the norms of spontaneous interaction in the target language can provide both an increased understanding of the problems, pitfalls, and skills needed for successful communication with native speakers and provide learners with a metalanguage to ask further questions about the difficulties they are encountering.

Three basic aspects of spontaneous speech that language learners need to be aware of and which language teachers may find helpful to reflect on are:

- speaking is fundamentally an interactive process and is defined by interactivity;
- speaking happens under real-time processing constraints;
- speaking is more fundamentally linked to the individual who produces it than the written form is.

These are the elements that stem directly from the way speech is produced and distinguish it from standard written forms. I will discuss each of them further in the following three subsections and outline the implications for the language learner.

6.4.1   *The Higher Interactive Potential of the Spoken Form Than the Written*

There is a far greater potential for interactivity in the spoken mode than the written. Even online 'chat' that takes place in writing cannot match the interplay of speakers in face-to-face or mediated (telephone or online) oral interactions. This leads to features such as not only interruptions, corrections, and overlaps but also the potential for speaker co-operation as two or more people seek to speak and understand one another in real time. A written text and classroom tasks that are based on written mode are therefore generally more predictable and easy to manage than tasks involving large amounts of 'free' speaking. As the earlier sections have suggested, generation of peer-to-peer talk is a commonly seen goal in the current language classroom. There may be several underlying issues to consider.

In the context of group task completion learners need to become aware of the potentially different mechanics of interaction in their own language and the target language (see Concept Box 6.3 for some examples). Practitioners may also find that learning more from the literature on conversational norms in the cultures of their students can explain the dynamics of what they see happening between students in their classroom. A classroom-based research project on the impact of different cultural expectations in spoken communication when completing a particular task would be valuable. Larsen-Freeman and Anderson (2013) is a highly readable introduction to classroom teaching methods that pays particular attention to the demands of handling spoken tasks and how these may challenge the teacher but also increase reflection on motivations and beliefs about why tasks are being undertaken.

Concept 6.3   The nontransferability of conversational patterns across cultures

A fundamental issue for the language teacher is the extent to which the norms of a target language's interactions mirror those of the learners' mother tongue. Nelson, Mahmood, and Nichols (1996), for example, investigated the different ways in which Syrians and Americans respond to compliments. Although there were a number of similarities (e.g. mitigating the compliment, that is, saying something to play down the thing that is being complimented), there were also some significant differences. Americans were more likely than Syrians simply to say 'thank you'. Syrians were more likely to produce a long or a formulaic response (e.g. offering the object of the compliment to the giver of the compliment). Where there is a combination of similarities and differences in the ways that cultures handle conversational functions, there can be particular difficulties for the teacher of spoken forms.

These issues of intercultural expectations and their impact on communication extend beyond the language classroom and are particularly relevant for teaching staff involved with professional language training. For example, Meeuwesen et al. (2007) examined doctor–patient discourse between Dutch doctors and patients from different ethnic and linguistic backgrounds. They discovered that the Dutch patients were much more capable of signalling a lack of understanding to the doctor than those from other backgrounds. Therefore intercultural communication awareness raising and training for L1 and L2 users may be vital in a range of settings other than 'simple' language acquisition. Interestingly, more work was originally carried out in professional settings on these issues than on their impact in language for specific purposes classrooms. Applied research to consider the implications of cultural difference in spoken settings for language teaching has started to feed into professional training (Yates et al., 2016).

6.4.2   The Production of Speech Happens Under Real-Time Processing Constraints

While the written form can generally be edited, rewritten, and 'polished', speech—even speech that is prepared in advance—is delivered to the listener with no possibility for the recall of a word or erasure of a grammatical error. The exception is, of course, spoken discourse that is prerecorded and can be retaped if necessary. However, the greater part of speech, that is, conversational data, is created in real time. This means that speakers tend to use simpler vocabulary, use a higher frequency of coordinated clauses, and use many fixed, filler expressions, such as 'you know', 'you see', to buy processing time. Learners need to realise that simple, even repetitive vocabulary is not unacceptable in speech, or rather that they should not spend so long making lexical choices that they lose the chance to speak. Equally, they need to gain a repertoire of natural time-buying devices to help them plan and process their discourse more easily.

Concept 6.4   Speech processing and language demands

Recognising what is said in any language is a remarkable feat. Recognising what is said in an unfamiliar language is a more difficult task but one that shares the basic processing system with L1 comprehension. Rather than presenting the learner with a binary of L1 (in which they are expert) versus L2 (in which they are currently in deficit), it is preferable to consider the demands of speech processing generally. Current thinking on how this process happens neurologically may help learners understand the challenge they are facing and the strategies that they need to adopt to help them participate in spoken interaction. Interlocutors are constantly analysing spoken input and matching this against their linguistic expectations. Consensus in neurolinguistics suggests that ' . . . candidate words are identified immediately, considered in parallel, and compete in some way' (McMurray et al., 2010: 3), and these insights have been applied to a deeper understanding of speech processing development beyond early years with 16-year-olds showing greater facility than nine-year-olds, for instance (Rigler et al., 2015). The acoustic clues in this process are, naturally, crucial as the stream of speech unfolds and is interpreted. In considering the capacity for successful spoken interaction in the L2 classroom it is worth bearing in mind that the student in a multilingual group performing a task is processing not only the competing lexical items that are normal for L1 speech processing but also mapping a diverse set of realisations of phonemes from a variety of L1 background speakers and dealing with these against a perhaps partial understanding of the target language syntax. These processing demands are in addition to the potential cultural and pragmatic differences already mentioned. It may, therefore, be fruitful for the practitioner to address the L1 differences and levels of mutual intelligibility at an early stage in planning communicative tasks.

6.4.3   A Strong, Perceptible Link Exists Between the Deliverer of the Discourse and the Discourse Itself

Spoken discourse reaches the world directly from the human vocal tract. As such it is a less mediated form than the written, which is transferred onto (or, with technological advances such as computers and personal communication devices, into) another medium before it is read. Something of this is reflected in the greater evidence of personal involvement shown by the spoken form, for example, high frequency of personal pronouns, especially first and second, and verbs showing stance to the topic such as 'think', 'feel', 'believe', and so on.

Concept 6.5 Stereotype effects on speech perception

Perception of speech is strongly affected by preconceptions about the person who is producing the speech. Unlike written mode, where, to a far greater extent, the content of the discourse can be disconnected from the author, the message carried by the stream of speech is processed in real time as output from a particular person and is interpreted by an interlocutor not only as speech sounds but also as the production of this person. This means that whatever preconceptions the listener carries with them about the race, age, gender, and personality of the speaker can have a powerful effect on how the spoken discourse is understood. To investigate these issues researchers have created a method known as the 'matched-guise' approach. In this, listeners are played an extract of talk and are told a fact about the speaker, often their nationality. The results suggest that the perception of sounds and attitudes to the presumed fact about the speaker correlate and influence what is heard to the point that perception and input are clearly at odds. For example, Hu and Lindemann (2009) conducted an experiment on attitudes to Cantonese-accented English. All the examples played to the subjects were spoken by American speakers of English, but half the time the subjects were told that they were Cantonese speakers of English. When this was the case, listeners were more likely to perceive one of the features associated with the accent—missed final consonants. These 'hidden' biases that influence what a listener hears provide a fascinating insight into how strong the connections are between perception and attitude to the individual speaking. Gaining a greater understanding of stereotype effects can help promote good classroom dynamics, can indicate to the learner that spoken mode is fundamentally dependent on interpretation, and is of clear importance in the assessment of speaking.

An awareness of the effects of the interactive, spontaneous and personally oriented nature of speech can, therefore, be of great benefit to learners, both in terms of confidence in production and to help to improve global listening skills. If, however, speech is taught without greater regard for some of the basic features that shape the process of listening and speaking, then learners will constantly be striving, and failing, to speak in the complete, grammatically standard, and impersonal discourse that is untypical of naturally occurring speech.

6.5 Summary

The chapter has outlined some of the reasons for the emphasis on the spoken mode in language acquisition theories and the influence this has had on classroom practice. Some instances of the use of spoken interaction to promote language acquisition were given. I suggested that there are possible tensions between the importance given to spoken interaction for general language uptake and the particular needs of teaching speaking as a skill in its own right. The chapter ended with a review of the issues involved in teaching speaking *per se* due to its interactive and context-dependent nature.

Further Reading

Berns, M. (1990, reprinted 2013). *Contexts of Competence: Social and Cultural Considerations in Communicative Language Teaching*. New York: Springer Science & Business Media.

Garrett, P. (2010). *Attitudes to Language*. Cambridge: Cambridge University Press.

Kumaravadivelu, B. (2012). *Language Teacher Education for a Global Society: A Modular Model for Knowing, Analyzing, Recognizing, Doing, and Seeing*. London: Routledge.

Richards, J. C. and Rodgers, T. S. (2014). *Approaches and Methods in Language Teaching* (3rd edn). Cambridge: Cambridge University Press.

7 Research Project Ideas and Frameworks

This chapter will . . .

- introduce a cross-section of research projects which have been carried out on spoken discourse;
- describe further related projects which could be carried out in similar areas;
- discuss the research approaches and frameworks for these projects.

7.1   Introduction

The projects selected here for summary show different approaches to moving from investigations into spoken mode towards generalisations that can be used either in wider descriptions of spoken discourse or applied in the language classroom. Articles have been selected to show a diverse range of approaches to researching speaking and include qualitative, quantitative, corpus informed, conversation analytic, ethnographic, phonetic, pragmatic, and recent neurological techniques. In the commentary, key skills and features for the novice researcher are also highlighted, such as the benefits of a null hypothesis, explaining limitations of results, and the potential criticism of an approach.

In each case, some further topics for research are included which could grow naturally from the findings described, and ideas for reader projects are outlined.

7.2   A Project on Spoken Language Found in Textbooks Versus a Corpus

Quote 7.1   From (Lam, 2010) 'Discourse Particles in Corpus Data and Textbooks: The Case of *Well*'

Discourse particles are ubiquitous in spoken discourse. Yet despite their pervasiveness very few studies attempt to look at their use in the pedagogical setting. . . . [T]he present study compares the use of discourse particles by expert users of English in Hong Kong with their descriptions and presentations in textbooks designed for learners of English in the same community. Specifically, it investigates the similarities and differences in the use of the discourse particle *well* between the two datasets in terms of its frequency of occurrence, its positional preference and its discourse function.

(Lam, 2010: 1)

7.2.1   *Commentary and Ideas for Further Work*

This study of the use of 'well' (as a discourse marker/particle) as presented in textbooks and as found in authentic speech is interesting because it covers many areas that are relevant to current debates in applied linguistics and aims to provide an analysis that integrates insights about spoken language, research, and pedagogy.

Lam (2010) compared a corpus of speech with a range of textbooks supporting the development of oral skills for high intermediate English learners in secondary schools in Hong Kong. She was interested in particular in how a well-researched linguistic item that is typical of speech (the discourse particle 'well') was presented in the textbooks both in terms of frequency and function/context and in what the implications of any differences might be for the classroom. She found significant differences in terms of the frequency and nature of the particle both in the two sources and between genres. Lam focused on both less interactive and more interactive contexts in the two sources. For example, sample 'made up' presentations from the textbooks were compared with prepared business presentations from the corpus, and sample discussions created for the former were contrasted with interviews and meetings in the latter. Overall, she discovered that textbook discussions strongly over-emphasised the use of 'well' in comparison to overall use in the corpus (over 80 instances per 10,000 words in the textbook discussion genre versus around 20–30 in the corresponding number of words in the corpus). In contrast, the sample material for presentations greatly underrepresented the particle—by up to five times—leading, Lam suggests, to a false impression of the use of the word being formed in the minds of the learner. She then goes on to give a detailed analysis of the functions of 'well' in the different sources, concluding 'textbook writers seem to pay excessive attention to *well* in responses while ignoring other important discourse functions such as framing which are also highly common in naturally occurring spoken examples' (Lam, 2010: 16–17).

At the most general level, the work is a useful starting point for the new researcher with an interest in the classroom because it asks several questions about the contrasts between speech that can be heard outside the classroom and the material presented to learners in the medium of published textbooks. Phoenix Lam comments: 'One might . . . quite reasonably, query whether such textbooks are so detached from reality that they have ultimately lost their pedagogical value' (Lam, 2010: 18). Novice researchers interested in continuing this debate might be moved to ask the extent to which they agree with this statement and what further work they might carry out to reach their own conclusions. One underlying question is the precise meaning of 'pedagogical value', as the discrepancies between the bulk of published material and the complexities of spontaneous talk have been discussed elsewhere in this book. A natural next step would be to write some sample materials that are closer to the norms Lam has pointed to and try these with an experimental and a control group. A simpler variant of this would be to use the same published materials with two groups and provide additional awareness-raising input with the experimental group.

From a different perspective, the article also deals with the issue of what the best model or target for the learner should be—'native speaker' or high-achieving 'nonnative speaker'. The corpus of speech and the textbooks Lam analyses are not internationally focused but rather both are defined by a local setting: that of the high-achieving Cantonese speaker of English living and working in Hong Kong (the majority of the corpus data participants) and the learner with a similar language background aspiring to this level of achievement. The article deals with this more at the stage of setting out the methodology than in the discussion, and the issue of local versus general models would be an interesting area for further work. If the reader works in a different language acquisition setting where there is a source of English as a lingua franca data and published materials tailored for the local market, a replication study could be carried out. Alternatively, a different discourse feature could be analysed using the same approach and the same corpus and textbooks. A more theoretical paper could also be written on the pros and cons of a local model as a basis for materials and some consideration given to the constraints imposed by the publishing world on what is made available in a variety of contexts. The questions to ask here are:

- Are there, and should there be, differences, in principle, between materials produced in a context where English is a strong second language alongside the mother tongue (such as Hong Kong) and materials produced for the learner where it is not (such as rural China)?
- Are there always benefits in seeking to reproduce the exact frequencies found in corpus data in classroom materials?

7.2.2 *Potential Reader Project: Extension to Classroom Talk*

Lam (2010) suggested that an important use of 'well' in her authentic data was the function of framing (see Quote 7.2).

Quote 7.2   Finding patterns in speech data: the 'framing' use of *well*

The framing use of "well" to insert a point of division or transition for easy comprehension is one of the most frequently occurring functions in the corpus data. In these examples, "well" acts as a boundary marker in discourse to signal transitions in topic and discourse stage. At times, it plays a role similar to punctuation marks in the written language in dividing words into clauses and sentences. In example 6, the speaker uses well together with a metalinguistic comment "let's talk a little bit about conflict" to indicate a topic change:

(6)
. . . but yet at the same time not violate our group harmony (.) yea it can be done (.) It can be done okay well let's talk a little bit about conflict why is conflict management so important . . .

(HKCSE, B123)

Apart from segmenting texts, "well" could be used as a link to introduce explanations and additional information to the preceding discourse.

(Lam, 2010: 11)

She notes that this use is helpful to the listener in extended speech as it marks transition points or slight divergence from the expected flow of ideas (such as giving some additional information or a self-correction). In the data she has analysed, it would seem that students are being presented with a model that over-represents a different function—simple response at the start of a turn, particularly when disagreeing with someone. A possible research question is 'how do students actually use 'well' in their own discourse?' A related question is what relationship, if any, there is between this and the input they have received from materials in their speaking classes.

Stage 1: Preliminary Decisions

A first stage would be to decide the discourse type to be the main focus in relation to the categories found in Lam (2010)—these were presentations or discussions. A further decision would relate to whether the goal is a small-scale classroom-based project or an investigation that is aimed at a peer-reviewed journal or similar. These factors would affect the amount of data required and the criteria against which the findings would be judged.

Stage 2: Data Gathering

There are two possible approaches to gathering data for this project. The first is to design a task in which students will be asked to carry out one or other of these genres of talk. This has the advantage of being under the control of the researcher, and decisions about the topic, length of task, and instructions given to the students can all be carefully tailored to the project. Alternatively, in the context of practitioner-led research a speaking class that is already available could be used as a source of data, as such classes often contain both individual presentations and discussions. In the latter case, the researcher would simply record sessions of the appropriate type as they occur to create the data set for analysis.

Stage 3: Preliminary Analysis

Record as many student presentations or discussions as appropriate. As noted earlier, this will be different depending on the overall aim of the research. If this is intended as a small 'action research' project, a data set involving around four to five students would be enough. If the project is to be published, a more substantial number of examples would be required for statistically useful findings. In this case, the researcher will also need to think through issues such as the gender and first language of subjects and try to ensure that the classroom context and task are well matched. In either approach, the larger the data set, the more that can be said in relation to the findings.

In terms of how to find and analyse the frequencies, contexts and functions of 'well' the approach will also be influenced by the nature of the overall approach. For a small-scale project, simply listening to the recordings/watching the videos and noting the instances of 'well' being used would be adequate. For a large-scale project, the data should be transcribed more fully, and a searchable corpus could be created from the electronic transcripts and the audio recordings. This would automate the process of finding instances of 'well' and would allow concordances of the context to be pulled out easily for further analysis.

In addition, data regarding the input in the speaking materials would also need to be gathered so that a comparison could be made between what the students have been exposed to in relation to the discourse particle and their subsequent use in a task providing free practice.

Stage 4: Results and Discussion of Findings

Even in a small sample, something very significant may be seen. For example, the investigator may find that the students only use the term 'well' for the function that they have been taught (perhaps 'introducing disagreement' that Lam suggested was never actually seen in her authentic data). This would lend some credibility to the argument that students' pragmatic behaviour may be affected negatively by the inappropriate model being found in a textbook. Alternatively, the students may not use the particle when they might be expected to, or they might use it for functions that they have not explicitly been taught. In either of these cases, there would be support for a counterargument to Lam in terms of the significance of the effects of input from teaching materials on student behaviour. That is to say, although the model does not match authentic material, students are not directly transferring the uses and contexts to their own speech anyway, and therefore the impact is less than might be assumed.

7.3   A Project on the Effects of Speech Rate in the Context of English as Lingua Franca Presentations

Quote 7.3   From (Hincks, 2010) 'Speaking Rate and Information Content in English Lingua Franca Oral Presentations'

This paper quantifies differences in speaking rates in a first and second language, and examines the effects of slower rates on the speakers' abilities to convey information. The participants were 14 fluent (CEF B2/ C1) English L2 speakers who held the same oral presentation twice, once in English and once in their native Swedish. The temporal variables of mean length of runs and speaking rate in syllables per second were calculated for each language. Speaking rate was found to be 23% slower when using English. The slower rate of speech was found to significantly reduce the information content of the presentations when speaking time was held constant. Implications for teaching as European universities adopt English as a medium of instruction are discussed.

(Hincks, 2010: 4)

7.3.1   *Commentary and Ideas for Further Work*

The growth of English as a medium of instruction internationally means that work such as reported in Hincks (2010) will have increasing usefulness and relevance. This paper is interesting in that it analysed the same speakers (Swedish mother tongue with a good level of fluency in English as L2) doing a speaking task—a presentation—in their L1 and their L2. Very often conclusions are drawn about L2 speaking without reference to the characteristics of the speaker in their first language. One of Hincks' findings was that speech rate transferred from L1 to L2, and when a speaker was slower than average in Swedish, this would also be the case in English. She comments on the importance of bearing in mind L1 speaker norms in reaching conclusions about L2 performance. Hincks developed a system to analyse difference in terms of both speech rate and, more significantly, 'points of difference' or PODs. The latter were, for example, the number of information items that could be included under time constraints in the presentation in each language. She concludes:

> The least fluent English speaker, S1, was so hampered by his L2 that his L1 presentation included three times the PODs when time was normalised. However, the gap between the two languages was also apparent for more fluent speakers, such as S13 and S10. These two participants were exceptionally knowledgeable about their topics (one was a salesperson and one went on to do a PhD related to the subject of his presentations), raising the worrisome concern that the more one knows about a topic, the bigger the differences that appear when one is required to talk about it in an L2.
>
> (Hincks, 2010: 16)

In addition, she points to more subtle contrasts between the presentations in the two languages; for instance, although a speaker can communicate a definition literally, the stylistically engaging use of resources such as metaphor were missing in the L2 context. This was not counted as a POD but noted in the discussion as a noteworthy difference and one that adds to the overall conclusion she makes, that students working in the English medium may not be able to reach their fullest potential.

This work could be taken further in several different ways. Hincks herself suggests some of these. They include the links between comprehension ability of a mixed audience of L1 and L2 and speaking speed in lectures, the development of an electronic monitor for speakers to international audiences to show when their syllable per second rate becomes too high for comfortable comprehension, and the question of the amount of content that a L2 lecturer can include in a given amount of time compared to an L1 user. Her findings suggest that around 25 per cent more time might be expected to be taken by the L2 speaker in similar contexts, for example. At a more theoretical level, the work also raises interesting areas for further work and debate. For example, her article includes a reference to the fact that speakers in conversation adapt their speech rate to their interlocutor if they are speaking to someone who has a different first language and needs this. Speakers in monologue rarely do this. However, as Hincks herself noted, not all L1 speakers behave in the same way conversationally. It would be intriguing to gain a better understanding of the conditions under which a speaker adjusts speech rate and whether there are other conversational contexts or speaker types who do/do not do this.

7.3.2   *Potential Reader Project: Extension by Replication and Additional Qualitative Phase*

The work reported by Hincks (2010) is in the quantitative tradition. It would be interesting to do two things to follow up on these findings. First would be to replicate the study with a different language or with several languages, and second would be to add a reflective phase to the study where the speakers are interviewed about the experience of presenting in each language.

Stage 1: Preliminary Questions

If the research is being undertaken in a classroom with a monolingual setting and the researcher has good competence in both the local language and English, it will be relatively simple to replicate the study. If the investigator is not familiar with the language of the students then he or she will need to employ an assistant to help with the analysis. Factors such as the level of the students and the amount of input and practice before the presentations were gathered should also be matched as closely as possible to the Hincks study.

A particular decision will be how central the subsequent interview data will become in this project. It could be handled as a very simple feedback session or a more elaborate semi-structured interview. In the latter instance, the interview could be designed around some of the key findings in Hincks (2010) such as being able to convey less in the time available or having to use literal versus metaphoric language to get a point across.

Stage 2: Quantitative Data Collection

The data collection section in Hincks (2010) should be adapted to the circumstances of the current research and the context of the investigator. In the original study, students were asked to choose a topic for themselves on a semi-technical theme and speak for ten minutes in English. This was part of their programme. They were then invited to repeat the presentation at a later date for research purposes, for a small fee, in their first language. Where the current study deviates from the approach in the original article significantly, a comment should be added to any methods section. This allows the reader of the eventual research report to understand the points of exact similarity and difference between the new study and the original. The presentations would then be recorded and transcribed using the method described in Hincks (2010: 9).

Stage 3: Qualitative Data Collection

Having decided on the general approach of the reflective interview in the preliminary phase, the material from the students would be gathered after the second presentation in the mother tongue had been completed. Small focus groups of students could be arranged to discuss the experience of presenting in the two languages and record them. Alternatively, you may wish to conduct a full one-to-one interview with all subjects, basing this around the core topics you are interested in.

Stage 4: Analysis, Results, Discussion

The kinds of questions that the researcher will expect to be able to answer by the end of the replication of the study are as follows. Do the students in the new study find that they are also unable to deliver the same amount of content in the two languages? Are the differences as marked as those discovered between the advanced English learners and the Swedish native speakers? Do they show differences in speaking rate when syllables per second in the two languages are compared? Are there any significant differences in the findings in comparison to Hincks? Is there evidence of a more literal style in the lingua franca versus the mother tongue? How do the students feel about speaking in the two languages? How do you explain the difference, if so? What do their reflections suggest to you in terms of helping them in future?

7.4   An Exploration of Intercultural Expectations in Conversation

> **Quote 7.4   From (Cheng and Tsui, 2009) ' "Ahh ((Laugh)) Well There is No Comparison Between the Two I Think": How Do Hong Kong Chinese and Native Speakers of English Disagree with Each Other?'**
>
> [C]ontrary to the stereotypic accounts of Chinese culture, HKC [Hong Kong Chinese] are not at all shy to disagree with their NSE [Native Speakers of English] interlocutors. Neither are HKC less likely, if not more likely, to disagree in order to present their different, or alternative, views. However, when they disagree, they are more inclined to address the face-want of both themselves and the addressees by using redressive language and mitigating devices. Qualitative analysis of sequences of disagreements in a conversational excerpt has shown the varying efforts HKC and NSE speakers make to align themselves with the interlocutor to manage interpersonal relationships and negotiate common ground.
>
> (Cheng and Tsui, 2009: 2365)

7.4.1   Commentary and Ideas for Further Work

This article presents work on intercultural pragmatics. The authors are particularly interested in probing the conversational behaviour of native and Chinese users of English when they find that they disagree with each other and need to re-establish some kind of consensus. Through their analysis they reach wider conclusions about conversational behaviour and relate them to previous preconceptions and conclusions about Western versus Asian behaviour and values. The project is thus presented via a 'classical' research paper structure including a review of previous work, hypotheses, data against which hypotheses are compared, and a revision and conclusion in light of the starting point of the article. The project is interesting in that it combines quantitative analysis—for example, proportions of disagreements with and without redressive (efforts at 'softening' the level of disagreement) language—with conversation analytic tools. In the first sections of the article, three main hypotheses are set up about what conversational behaviour the researchers think they may see on the basis of earlier work on language users from Anglophone cultures (called here native speakers of English, NSE) versus their interlocutors, who are Hong Kong Chinese (HKC). Quote 7.5 provides the broad hypotheses that the researchers were interested in.

Quote 7.5   Hypotheses developed by Cheng and Tsui (2009)

1. HKC will disagree with NSE less frequently than NSE will disagree with HKC.
2. HKC will use bald-on-record strategies in their disagreements less frequently than NSE will use bald-on-record strategies in their disagreements.
3. HKC will use redressive language in their disagreements more frequently than NSE will use redressive language in their disagreements.

(Cheng and Tsui, 2009: 2368)

After collecting and statistically analysing 13 hours of conversation between NSE and HKC speakers, the researchers concluded that the first hypothesis was not supported in their data but that the other two were supported. HKC speakers were less blunt in their expression of disagreement (using fewer than half the frequency of 'bald-on-record' strategies shown by NSE) and used more softening language. Whereas nearly 90 per cent of the instances of disagreement were surrounded by redressive language in the turns of HKC speakers, just over 70 per cent of similar conversational moments were 'softened' in this way by NSE. The finding that HKC speakers did *not* avoid conversational conflict is a particularly clear instance of why a 'null hypothesis' (one that does not find evidence to support it) can lead to a very valuable research result. While earlier work might have suggested that the orientation towards harmony, face saving, and consensus would dominate the conversational input of the HKC, the findings showed that these speakers differed with their interlocutors just as much but had different strategies and styles to handle these moments. The second analysis presented is a conversation analytical one dealing with an interaction between two police officers who differ over the route and the benefits of a charity walk. The researchers show how the HKC user of English handles the disagreement by shifting the conversational topic back to common ground, is ready to concede, and uses ambiguity as well as praise for the NSE's ideas. At this point the NSE becomes critical of his own position, and the researchers conclude, 'We have an interesting example which illustrates how contributions made by participants in discourse not only shape the contributions made by other participants but are also shaped by them' (Cheng and Tsui, 2009: 2377).

The clarity of the structure of this paper means that it would readily transfer to other language groups and could be replicated by readers in other contexts. A straightforward comparison could be made between NSE and non-NSE handling of disagreement in conversational settings where the non-NSE is from a different linguistic and cultural background from the HKC users analysed here. The point could be made that it is not necessarily 'being a HKC' user of English that is the most prominent effect but 'being a nonnative speaker speaking to a native speaker'. Replicating the study with a range of speakers from different language backgrounds and cultures would be one way to test this idea. A practitioner may wish to take the conclusions of this paper and see how students in his/her class deal with disagreement and also use the findings to raise awareness for students of the potential for cultural norms to affect how they 'come across' in a conversation. The findings may be particularly relevant to English for specific purposes contexts, where handling disagreement in business or professional contexts may be very delicate.

7.4.2   Potential Reader Project: Replication and Extension to an Online Environment

Cheng and Tsui (2009) suggest that the frequency of expression of disagreement does not differ between a native speaker of English and a Hong Kong Chinese speaker using the same language. They conclude, however, that the HKC speaker will handle the divergence of opinion differently and will use more strategies to soften and mitigate the effect. It would be interesting to probe this further and to understand more about what is inherent to the cultural background of the speaker and what may be affected by particular context and mode. One way to begin this process would be to look at disagreement in an online environment. It has been suggested that explicit markers of politeness tend to be missing or greatly reduced in, for example, chat room discourse (Carlo and Yoo, 2007). Will HKC speakers show a higher incidence of politeness markers when disagreeing in this environment than NSE? More generally, will speakers from Chinese and similar cultural backgrounds handle disagreement in online environments differently from speakers of other ethnic origin?

Stage 1: Preliminary Decisions

It may not be possible to directly replicate the pairings of Cheng and Tsui (2009), and it would be necessary to make it clear to the reader how you are defining the speakers' language backgrounds that you eventually analyse. Are you going to use authentic chat room data available online, or are you going to set up targeted discussions? The study described next uses the latter approach. Rich and authentic data may be available online; however, the difficulty would then be checking the language background and other aspects of the users such as age, gender, and so on.

Stage 2: Data Gathering

If the project is being carried out by a teacher with students from a range of linguistic backgrounds and access to online resources that allow 'chat', it would be possible to set up a structured discussion and retain the 'threads' as the basis of the analysis. For instance, the students could be allocated to three to four different 'rooms' and a theme or a problem-solving task that will naturally generate differences of opinion set up in each. The archive of these electronic discussions together with the identity of the students involved would become the basis for findings about differences between students from different cultural backgrounds in relation to confrontation in an online setting.

Stage 3: Analysis and Findings

One of the advantages of this approach is that data are readily available in written form to be analysed without the need for transcription. It would be good practice to work with another researcher to check exactly how 'disagreement' is being defined and to code instances according to an agreed system. It would then be possible to carry out both quantitative and qualitative analysis to see whether there were behavioural patterns to the handling of disagreement across the different cultural groups. The quantitative analysis would measure the incidences of expression of disagreement in users of different language backgrounds, and the qualitative work would look at whether Asian speakers mitigated disagreement more than users from different backgrounds. A comparison could be made to the finding of Cheng and Tsui (2009) and some discussion presented of the implications of what is found. Whether or not the same tendencies are perceived, there will be interesting conclusions to be drawn. Either these would be concerning the strength of the cultural tendency to mitigate disagreement even in online contexts or, if these patterns were not visible, questions would arise about the interaction of cultural and pragmatic factors in face-to-face interaction versus the online environment.

7.5   A Project That Analyses a Professional Speaking Genre So It Can Be Handled in the Classroom

Quote 7.6   From (Burns and Moore, 2008) 'Questioning in Simulated Accountant-Client Consultations: Exploring Implications for ESP Teaching'

This paper reports research investigating spoken accounting discourse derived from simulated accountant–client consultations. It draws on the work of Drew and Heritage (1992), in which questioning is identified as a key discursive feature in institutional talk, and also the more recent work reported in Heritage and Maynard (2006), in which the complexity of the formulation of questions and responses is revealed in doctor–patient consultations. The paper discusses the use of simulations in cases where access to actual workplace settings by ESP teachers is unattainable, as well as the usefulness of the interactional data these simulations generate.

(Burns and Moore, 2008: 322)

7.5.1   *Commentary and Ideas for Further Work*

This paper deals with the interface between spoken interaction in professional contexts (in this case accountancy advice giving) and the English for specific purposes (ESP) classroom. It is an interesting article in several respects. First, this is a little-researched genre in a field that has high levels of training needs for international students. Second, the main focus of ESP has tended to be written rather than spoken discourse. Finally, it discusses a number of methodological issues raised by the approach used to gain data and gives a wide range of suggestions for further work. The authors analysed the question and answer patterns between trainee accountants on a master's programme and volunteers who role-played members of the public asking for advice about how to complete a tax form. Based on this they tentatively produced a taxonomy of question types used by advice-seekers and advice-givers in these contexts. In terms of how to transfer this idea to the classroom they suggest: 'Learners can be given opportunities to enhance their understanding of the functions of each questioning technique and the kinds of responses they are intended to elicit. They can be introduced to the questioning techniques primarily utilised by the accountant in contrast with those that clients might introduce' (Burns and Moore, 2008: 333). They also note the lack of interpersonally oriented questions asked by the trainee accountants and note that raising awareness of the acceptability of using these kinds of questions and also humour may be beneficial for the students and 'improve the overall tenor of consultations'.

The use of simulated interaction is the fundamental point in relation to the question methods used. The authors are very clear that, in terms of a research paper without direct reference to the classroom, this source of data would be questionable (see also Quote 7.7).

Quote 7.7   Justifying a method

[W]hile simulation may be criticised for lacking the features of natural-istic data from the authentic worksite (and given the absence of such data this criticism is itself speculative), it also offers, we have argued, a way for ESP teachers to raise their own and their students' awareness of the nature of accountant–client interaction. Given the problems of access, recording, and analysis of workplace data for most ESP teachers, such simulations, as a means of preliminary analysis and insights into discoursal patterns, present a promising alternative.

(Burns and Moore, 2008: 333)

In the research-into-practice domain, the data elicited in the simulations serve multiple functions, therefore, rather than the single function that would be the norm more generally. In other research contexts, data would be pri-marily elicited/captured for linguistic insight without reference to the needs of, or constraints on, the practitioner. In the current context, they are both a model on which to base preliminary assumptions about the target genre in authentic communication and to raise the awareness of the student and the ESP teacher of what may happen in general terms in these types of interac-tions. At the same time, they represent the product of students aspiring to be fully fledged accountants who are themselves potentially recipients of the insights in a future ESP classroom. In this sense the simulations become part of a needs analysis for the future development of an ESP curriculum (what the students may lack) and provide indications of some basic input for that cur-riculum (the patterns of questioning that were seen and the different input of client and advisor).

The need to tackle the issue of the lack of access to authentic data and explain why there are good reasons not to be concerned about this provides a good example for the novice researcher to understand. In terms of the dialogue with the reader, experienced researchers can explain the level of limitation clearly (hence pre-empting criticism) and show the features that add to the validity of what they are concluding. To do this well the writer of the article needs clearly to set out the frame of reference that he or she wishes to be judged against. Crucial to this paper is the fact that it has been written from the outset with direct teaching applications in mind. This allows the multiple functions for the data to work well, permits a level of sketchiness to the generalisability to all such interactions, and generally motivates and provides a solid rationale for the defence of the use of simulated data.

The authors provide several avenues for further work. First, at a very general level they note the lack of any detailed research into accountancy discourse. They suggest that this is therefore a fruitful genre for more investigation. They also suggest widening the participants from master's level trainees to other levels to help gain a sense of what ESP students may need and may lack at these different points in their study career. In addition, they point to the work that could be carried out in terms of analysing interactions between dyads from different linguistic and cultural backgrounds. At a more theoretical level, it could be interesting to pursue the idea of the benefits and limitations of the use of simulated interactions in applied research settings. In particular it might be beneficial to explore further the idea of the students as model generators and reflective users of the insights gained from the experience of role playing their future self interacting with others in their future career role.

7.5.2 Potential Reader Project: Extension of Approach to Placement Learning

The aim of Burns and Moore (2008) is to gain some insights about accountancy-client interaction and to discuss the usefulness of simulated role-play as a tool for gaining these insights and in then embedding results into an ESP curriculum. This approach could also be beneficial in the context of university level assessed placements that are commonly found in the later stages of undergraduate programmes and master's training for vocational and professional purposes. In these contexts, advanced learners need to handle complex spoken interaction and manage semi-professional relationships outside the educational setting. In this context, they are regarded both as students and as emerging 'experts' with a developing professional identity. It would therefore be interesting to investigate the usefulness of simulated role-play in preparing students for placement learning. A control and experimental group approach could be used. In this approach, two groups of students are trained in the same area, but in the case of one group, the input or approach differs in respect to the research question. In this case, one group (experimental) would be exposed to simulated role-play; the other (control) would take the standard preparation.

Usually some measure of performance is taken at the start and end of the training programme, and differences between the two groups are evaluated in relation to the different input. In this way the approach seeks to connect the differences in achievement to the difference that has been designed to link to the topic under consideration in the research. It will be clear from this that a key point is to try to match as far as possible the experimental and the control groups in all other respects, such as age, gender, curriculum, teaching methodology, language level at start of experiment, and so on. In reality, in the context of a 'live' teaching environment, it is actually quite unrealistic to match all features of the experience of students in both groups apart from the 'intervention' (in this case, use of simulation). However, researchers will make every effort to match the conditions and the subjects and will then provide a narrative to explain any significant points of departure. For instance, if a different teacher teaches the groups, they will include some discussion of the possible impact of this variable both at the outset in relation to the design of the project and then again in the discussion when they are looking at the results and giving possible explanations or reasons for particular findings.

Stage 1: Preliminary Decisions

This project would work well if carried out by an ESP/EAP practitioner team in tandem with a researcher who would provide the theoretical background and design the experimental framework. Given access to two groups of students preparing for professional or vocational careers decisions, care would be needed about several aspects. First, there would be the general approach to embedding simulated role-play into the curriculum for the experimental group, the nature of students to be involved in terms of benchmarking oral skills at the start of the project, and consideration of their linguistic and cultural background(s).

Stage 2: Experimental Phase

It would be good practice to carry out a small pilot study with a different group of students from the two that will be in the main study. This will allow the practitioners and researcher(s) to work out exactly how the simulation will be delivered and iron out possible problems that are difficult to predict before an approach is tried out in a classroom. One approach would be to create a bank of videos of simulations of interactions previewing the type of speech genres that the placement will entail. These could be used as a prompt for discussion and for further role-play in the classroom with the experimental group.

With the approach refined on the basis of the pilot, the next step would be to arrange the experimental and control groups and carry out a baseline assessment for both groups. In this particular project, it would be beneficial to test both general oral skills and to carry out an interview or survey of the students'

levels of confidence and knowledge of the placement context they will be facing. The experiment would then run for the duration of the programme, say,
a university term, and the students would be retested. The second assessment
would be a repeat of the oral skills test and an opportunity for the students to
reflect on their levels of confidence and awareness of the skills needed for the
placement ahead of them. Ideally, the students would then be tracked through
their actual placements and their performance in the field compared to the
training they had received.

Stage 3: Analysis and Discussion

The results of the initial and final assessments and the reflections of the students on their confidence levels and their subsequent experiences in the actual
placements would provide rich data to evaluate the usefulness of simulations
and would provide the basis for further refinement of the curriculum. In this
approach the cycle of research into practice, and practice-informing research,
would become part of the focus of the project.

7.6 A Project on Speaking Assessment With Low Education Immigrant Test Takers

Quote 7.8 From (Simpson, 2006) 'Differing Expectations in the Assessment of the Speaking Skills of ESOL Learners'

This is a study of the assessment of the speaking skills of adult learners
of English for speakers of other languages (ESOL). It is prompted by a
concern that participants can have differing expectations of what nature
of speech event a speaking test actually is. This concern was identified
during the administration and analysis of assessments carried out as part
of a study into adult ESOL pedagogy in the UK. The paper employs
the notions of *knowledge schema* and *frame* in discourse to draw together
areas of interest in testing: whether the speaking assessment should be
viewed as an interview or as a conversation; divergent interpretations
of the test event by learners; and variation in interlocutor behaviour.
Implications for testing the speaking skills of adult ESOL learners are
discussed; these are pertinent at a time of large-scale high-stakes testing
of learners who are migrants to English speaking countries.

(Simpson, 2006: 40)

7.6.1   *Commentary and Ideas for Further Work*

This article reports part of a larger project on adult language and literacy teaching and testing for English for speakers of other languages (ESOL) in the UK—the Effective Practice Project—run by the National Research and Development Centre for adult literacy and numeracy. As such, it brings insights from a different perspective from the general English as a foreign language world and the applied linguistics world that many of the other studies in this chapter are dealing with. The students involved in ESOL classes may have very traumatic backgrounds and life histories if they are asylum seekers or refugees, and they may have minimal schooling in some cases. The testing of these learners may have particularly significant impact for them in terms of ability to remain in a country, as was highlighted at the end of Chapter 4. An example of the specific needs of these students is the fact that in adapting the test to the project the designers removed the question 'Why did you come to the UK?' The reason for this was that what would have been a neutral 'warm-up' question to the general English student would have had a very different significance for refugee ESOL student. Not only would the narrative involved in the answer have been potentially very emotive for the student, it would also have been asked at the point of entry to the UK in a very different interview context in the process of achieving entry to the country.

However, the insights gained by Simpson (2006) are valuable not only for this cohort but also for the wider implications they point to in terms of how expectations on the part of examiner and examinee affect oral communication under test conditions. The ESOL community from which the subjects were drawn provided a particularly clear data set on which to base conclusions about the effects of prior knowledge of what it is to be tested—the 'what kind of oral interaction am I in and how should I behave?' question—and the ability to 'perform' in these conditions.

From 400 possible oral interviews undertaken in the wider project, 23 were selected using the following criteria: learners were taking an examination at the higher of the two tested levels, and the test takers had little or no schooling. The reason for the former criterion being applied was that the lower level speaking test would only call for very basic factual responses from the examinee, and the researcher wished to have data in which longer and more complex information was being asked for. The reason to limit the number of years' schooling was to be able to investigate the reaction to being tested by learners with untrained expectations about the process in order to elicit 'nonschooled responses' or similar (Simpson, 2006: 47). Extracts from five interviews were used as the basis for the analysis in the current paper. The maximum number of years schooling of these students was four and the minimum zero.

In terms of analysis of the data selected by the criteria outlined here, a qualitative method based on conversation analysis was used. In contrast to the hypothesis-testing approach reported in Section 7.4 that also used CA methods, Simpson (2006) uses a much broader questioning approach. He selects sections of data that will help him illustrate the patterns that he sees as 'not atypical of the testing experience of ESOL learners in the effective practice project'. These are motivated by an overarching research question: 'What happens when learners with little or no experience of formal schooling carry out the speaking assessment?' (Simpson, 2006: 48). Through these examples he touches on four more specific aspects: whether the test taker regards the event as a test or a different kind of speech event; what might make a student say very little in the test (underelaboration); how speaker collaboration can help the test taker; how the examiner's stance towards the speech event may affect the test taker. The example of underelaboration is particularly clear and interesting. In the data illustrating this feature, the candidate provides single-syllable or no replies in the test but at the point when the test is over produces two extended turns. Simpson speculates whether the examinee had experienced situations where it was better to say as little as possible or to constrain replies to what she was certain was correct, and this is what led to the mismatch between her performance in the test and soon afterwards. The extract is salutary. Although not mentioned, presumably the lack of assessable material meant that the candidate would have failed the test. Seeing the large amount of material that could have been assessed and the clear motivation to speak that the candidate shows after the test provides a compelling indication of the need to ensure good preparation and practice testing for all candidates and particularly those from backgrounds similar to these ESOL students.

7.6.2 Potential Reader Project: Extension to Test Conclusions

There are several directions that could be followed up in relation to this project. First, as noted in the comments on methodology, the approach here uses illustrative material to make points about patterns that an expert in the field asserts are typical. The novice researcher may need to take a less 'open' approach, and so one project that would be of interest would be to replicate the basic data (speaking assessments with ESOL learners with minimal schooling) and apply a different method such as hypothesis testing and statistical analysis to look for correlations between instances of underelaboration to a variety of factors such as gender, years of schooling, age, and so on. A possible criticism of the current work is that the interactive behaviour ascribed to a naïveté about what it is to be in a test of speaking could be due to a number of other factors. A project that took one of the conclusions and worked on it in detail would therefore be interesting.

Stage 1: Preliminary Decisions

This project assumes that the researcher has access to ESOL learners of similar backgrounds to those described in Simpson (2006) and a comparison group with similarly low language ability but greater exposure to schooling. Decisions would be needed as to how to define the higher and the lower thresholds of schooling and some initial work done to ensure that the language levels were comparable. The investigation would also require some expertise in oral assessment or availability of standard oral assessments for the students to undertake.

Stage 2: Hypothesis Setting

According to Simpson (2006), ESOL candidates with very few years' schooling confuse an oral assessment interview with a conversation and do not know how to handle the interaction so that they perform the role of being examined appropriately. One of the features he points to as evidence of this is the under-elaboration of answers by candidates. A possible hypothesis therefore would be that ESOL learners with low levels of formal schooling ('Type 1') will produce shorter turns in response to examiner questions than ESOL learners with similar language levels in the target language to Type 1 but with adequate levels of formal schooling for their age ('Type 2').

Stage 3: Data Gathering

Students in the two categories would be given some preparatory classes, and then an oral assessment would be undertaken by both groups. Their interactions with the examiner during the test would be the basis for evaluating the strength of evidence for the hypothesis.

Stage 4: Analysis of Results and Discussion

A quantitative analysis would be made of the number and the length of turns by the two groups in response to examiner questions. Ideally, this would be carried out with a statistically significant sample and appropriate statistical techniques would be applied. This would allow some conclusions to be reached about the performance of the two groups that could be ascribed to the differences in schooling. Whether or not a significant difference was found between them, something of interest could be said. If, contrary to expectation, the two groups with similar language levels performed similarly, there would be less support for Simpson's link between levels of schooling and effects on candidates' performance in formal tests of speaking. If, on the other hand, the hypothesis was supported, there would be some grounds for suggesting that fair and appropriate assessments were not being achieved for some ESOL learners due to their incorrect understanding of what is expected in formal oral assessment, possibly based on a lack of schooling.

7.7   A Project Investigating the Relationship Between Gesture and Speech Processing Using fMRI Scanning Techniques

Quote 7.9   From (Straube et al., 2010) 'Social Cues, Mentalizing and the Neural Processing of Speech Accompanied by Gestures'

Body orientation and eye gaze influence how information is conveyed during face-to-face communication. However, the neural pathways underpinning the comprehension of social cues in everyday interaction are not known. In this study we investigated the influence of addressing vs. non-addressing body orientation on the neural processing of speech accompanied by gestures. . . . Our findings indicate that social cues influence the neural processing of speech–gesture utterances. Mentalizing (the process of inferring the mental state of another individual) could be responsible for these effects. In particular, socially relevant cues seem to activate regions of the anterior temporal lobes if abstract person-related content is communicated by speech and gesture. These new findings illustrate the complexity of interpersonal communication, as our data demonstrate that multisensory information pathways interact at both perceptual and semantic levels.

(Straube et al., 2010: 382)

7.7.1   *Commentary and Ideas for Further Work*

This paper presents work on speech communication that is at the cutting edge at the time of writing and is included for this reason. The technique used, fMRI scanning, is described on page 35 and is one that allows the researcher to see what parts of the brain are activated by different stimuli, in this case a combination of speech, stance, and gesture. This project shows that speakers' brains respond quite differently when someone speaks to them directly as opposed to standing as if speaking to someone else. They also respond differently when a speaker is describing an object with an illustrative gesture (such as 'The bowl in the kitchen is round' spoken in combination with a circular motion of the hands) or describing a human entity and using a commonly understood ('emblematic') gesture ('The actor did a good job in the play' in combination with a thumbs-up sign). These variables—stance and gaze, person- versus object-related message and descriptive versus culturally known gesture—were set up as four conditions to be combined with the gestures: Person-related +

Frontal stance, Person-related content + Lateral stance and ditto Object-related content. These were recorded as short video clips, and 30 of them in each condition were shown to 18 subjects. These were carefully chosen, as would be expected in the experimental paradigm being used, and were: all male, all right-handed, all native German speakers with no impairments to vision or hearing, had an average age of around 24 and between 20 and 30. The flow of blood to various parts of the brain was analysed and conclusions reached as to the differing effects of speech, content, stance, and gesture in the combinations outlined.

It is not assumed that classroom practitioners will wish to undertake this kind of neurolinguistic research directly or that they would have easy access to fMRI equipment if they wished to. However, it is included to suggest that our understanding of spoken communication may soon be very different and that this will have an impact on how the skill is regarded and is taught. As new insights such as those reported here are gained about the complex interplay between different modes and signals—speech, gesture, social cues—that need to be taken into consideration together when understanding speaking, our understanding of spoken communication will begin to change quite radically over the next few years. In particular, the idea that speaking can be treated as a simple linear process that is similar to writing but carried to the world on breath rather than paper or a screen will become untenable. The authors of the current study conclude: 'Our findings illustrate the complexity of natural communication, in which multiple channels of information interact at both the perceptual and semantic level' (Straube et al., 2010: 393). In terms of applications in teaching knowing that person-related information is processed quite differently from impersonal information, that believing a person is speaking to you affects how the brain is 'primed' to speak, and that understanding the subtle effects of gesture in relation to speech generally will all have clear relevance to both face-to-face classroom teaching and perhaps more importantly the ability to move the teaching of speaking online.

7.7.2 Potential Reader Project: Raising Awareness of Speaking as a Multisensory Skill

The findings reported in Straube et al. (2010) imply that many cues other than simply the stream of spoken sounds help us to communicate via speech. As noted elsewhere in this book, speaking is very often taught as if it is written language delivered through aural/oral channels. The cutting-edge work reported here suggests that our understanding of speaking may soon be very different. This project investigates the potential differences between listener comprehension of explanations with and without the benefit of visual cues.

Stage 1: Preliminary Decisions

This project could be based on the data gathered for the study on speech rates in presentations described in Section 7.3.2. The material could then be played to listeners via a sound recording only or via a video to include visual cues. A decision would need to be made as to whether particular sections of the presentation would be the focus, for example, where a student is explaining a technical term, or whether the whole presentation would be used. The benefit of using a particular functional category such as explanation or giving examples would be that some patterns of gaze, stance, and gesture could potentially be linked to the function. Another approach would be to begin from sections of talk where the speaker uses gesture to enhance meaning and extract these for the viewer/listener. Evaluating listener comprehension is a particularly tricky process, and thought would need to be given to the background knowledge of the listeners on a given topic and their current listening ability in the target language.

Stage 2: Experimental Phase

Two groups of listeners matched for age, language ability, and educational background would be played extracts from the presentations under two conditions: a) via video showing speaker plus gaze, stance, and gesture; and b) via a sound recording. The hypothesis would be that comprehension levels are higher under condition a). Ideally, there would be sufficient extracts for the listeners to be played a large enough set of samples for statistical analysis and for the same extracts to be played to different listeners to allow direct comparison by extract as well as general analysis. For each extract, the subjects would be required to indicate their level of comprehension. This could be a simple Likert scale (0 = could not comprehend; 5 = fully comprehend) or some other technique such as testing recall via a written reformulation or notes. The advantage of the former approach is that it does not depend on the subjects' written language ability, which may interfere with their capacity to explain clearly what they have really understood.

Stage 3: Analysis of Results

The hypothesis would be supported if there were higher levels of comprehension in listeners under condition a). Further analysis of any trends might show correlations between language function, gesture and other visual stimuli, and ease of comprehension.

Section IV

Resources and Further Information

8 Research Borders and Boundaries

This chapter will . . .

- provide indications of the relationship between research into speaking and other applied linguistics disciplines;
- situate work on spoken language in emerging trends in some other disciplines.

8.1 Introduction

As noted in many places in this book, there has been remarkably little work either in linguistics or in applied linguistics into speaking as a unified language faculty. Therefore, to a certain extent this book has needed to draw together work from different fields and at different levels within the skill of speaking to present a picture of research into speech. Any unified theory of speaking would need to both bring together and demarcate itself clearly from a number of interrelated academic disciplines, from pragmatics to corpus linguistics, from psycholinguistics to phonetics. All of these are well known and flourishing areas in linguistics, and each, along with a number of others, has something to say about speaking, even if they cannot provide a unified theory of spoken discourse in all contexts and domains.

We do not yet have such a theory, and the other parts of this book have, in part, been about why speaking has this ambiguous status in linguistics and applied linguistics. The growth of insights about the spoken form that are beginning to emerge from work in discourse analysis, conversation analysis, pragmatics, corpus linguistics, and neurolinguistics means that there is, however, a distinct pressure for more work on the topic and a need to make research findings usable by the more applied and pedagogically oriented sections of the linguistics community.

This chapter reviews some of the sister disciplines which are particularly pertinent to research into the faculty of speech and attempts to show how their insights could relate to a more holistic approach to research into speech. Initially this broadening of the scope of work on spoken data may seem to be unduly far reaching, making the study of spoken mode a study of global cultural and ethnographic issues, social issues, psychology, and biology, as well as the more traditional aspects of research into language, such as phonology, grammar, and syntax. However, I have been arguing throughout this book that there is a need to begin to tease out the differences between research into the language faculty and research into the faculty of speech. This can only be done by moving beyond conceptions of speech which are grounded in strongly text-based approaches to the study of language and which draw on emerging interdisciplinary insights.

Secondly, the broadening of the base of research into speech does not look as extreme as it might if it is compared with attitudes to research into the written mode. Work on literacy, particularly that in the field of critical linguistics, has long acknowledged the role of social and cultural factors in writing performance. It is perhaps only the conceptualisation of speech as 'simple' or natural and the primary form of language which has led to the mode being treated somewhat differently from the written form and, paradoxically, to the detriment of our understanding of the speech faculty.

8.2   Speaking and Ethnographic or Cross-Cultural Studies

At the broadest level, research into speech needs to be informed by the cultural expectations of speakers. Our understanding not only of conversational 'rules' and norms but also our interpretation of meaning or even individual words is coloured by our (generally unconscious) acceptance of certain fundamental cultural premises.

A better awareness of the potential differences between cultures in ways that affect language behaviour can also imbue research into speech with greater insight and sensitivity. For example, speech rate, intonation, interruption or self-correction, pauses, and attitudes to silence may all be areas that a researcher interested in spoken mode would investigate. While within one's own discourse and language community such aspects may have one interpretation, in a different one their implications and effects may be quite different—the silence that in one culture is uncomfortable or even rude is unproblematic, expected, or deferential in another. Awareness of such issues can provide insights for the researcher into speech, but, more importantly, can raise fundamental questions about the constructs we engage with in dealing with speech phenomena in the research process. Investigations carried out via actual speech data, particularly if quantitatively based, might attempt to answer research questions via inappropriate elements in the discourse if the broader cultural and ethnographic context is not properly understood. Work in the fields of the ethnography and pragmatics is clearly relevant to these broader questions about the relationship between spoken mode, conversational action, and social behaviour.

Current work in ethnography is interested in areas such as language and identity or ethnic affiliation; 'linguistic landscape studies'—work that maps the languages in a city, for instance, and includes 'nonstandard' data such as graffiti and billboards; or the effects of migration on language contact. Traditionally, ethnography began life as a scholarly activity with strong emphasis on spoken data and the careful transcription and meticulous 'outsider' understanding of language used by communities that were very different from that of the academic carrying out the study. In recent years there has been a reaction to the 'dominance' of spoken language as data in ethnography and also a greater understanding that ethnography has much to offer close to home in terms of understanding cultural norms and biases.

8.3   Speaking and Psycholinguistics

Psycholinguistic studies focus on the relationship between brain, language, and behaviour. The tendency has been for links to be investigated between psychological processes and speech behaviour at the level of planning and delivery rather than on wider psychological motivations to speech behaviour, for example, how idiolect is affected by emotional or experiential factors. Aspects of speech which the psycholinguist is interested in revolve around both practical topics such as the relationship between grammar, memory, and language processing and, at the more theoretical end of the spectrum, the different levels or hierarchies involved in language production and comprehension, or the links between brain and language acquisition.

In concrete terms, psycholinguistics is interested in a wide range of language phenomena—bi-lingualism and cognitive development, effects of brain damage, speech processing and word retrieval, and child language development, to name but a few—and the way that our minds and brains interact with the world and how we are affected by, or use, the phenomena being studied. Given the breadth of psycholinguistics (and the related techniques in neurolinguistics that have developed rapidly since the start of the twenty-first century—see next section) and its interest in the fundamentals of how language is structured and processed, there are considerable links between this discipline and an holistic understanding of the speech faculty.

At the time of writing, the types of study that psycholinguistics was carrying out related to, for instance, eye-tracking experiments to see how people process spoken sequences such as numbers, how people understand prior references in conversation and link old and new information together, or the effects of aging (other than hearing loss) on speech comprehension.

8.4   Speaking and Neurolinguistic Studies

Neurolinguistics differs from psycholinguistics in that the focus of research is primarily on the biological and neurological basis of language processing. As such, research into fundamental aspects of speech such as those outlined in Chapter 7 can be investigated within neurolinguistic frameworks. It is interesting to note how little either psycho- or neurolinguistics affects mainstream applied linguistics and language teaching, despite a long and reputable research tradition. There is, however, a strong link existing between this field and speech pathology/therapy.

At its most fundamental, neurolinguistics is pushing back the boundaries of our understanding of the language capacity. For instance, a debate in neuroscience is the existence, or the extent, of links between motoric signals (i.e. from the brain to a muscle to make it move) and our language facility. Unlike the universal grammar paradigm of Noam Chomsky, which has dominated linguistic thought for over half a century, these questions are being asked in the empirical tradition. Chomsky and the schools of linguistics that followed his traditions base their theories on assumptions and inferences (the human brain can understand infinite new sentences but has finite capacity; therefore, they infer an underlying 'hard wiring' or competence module). In contrast, neurolinguistic science often tests hypotheses experimentally through, for instance, measuring the activity in the brain and muscles when action-related nouns and verbs are heard.

8.5   Speaking and Corpus Linguistics

Until relatively recently the greatest part of corpus work in linguistics was based on written evidence, and overall the balance remains in favour of the written mode. This is due to the labour-intensive nature of preparing transcribed speech data in comparison with the relative ease, particularly in the age of electronic documentation and scanning, of capturing written material.

However, with a growing interest in speech data and the technological advances offered by powerful personal computers, mobile devices, cloud computing, and the Internet, a large number of projects based on spoken material is being created and, more importantly, being made generally available to researchers.

There is also a strong relationship developing between particular publishing houses and the creation of different corpora. (See e.g. Collins and the COBUILD Corpus (information at http://www.collins.co.uk/page/The+Collins+Corpus) or Longman and the British National Corpus, or Cambridge University Press (CUP) and the CANCODE (Cambridge and Nottingham Corpus of Discourse in English) project. At the time of writing, CUP and Lancaster University were developing a new Spoken British National Corpus continuing in this tradition of academics in leading linguistics departments collaborating with publishing houses in the field of corpus development.

Research into spoken corpora is throwing up many insights about the form, but from the perspective of a unified theory or approach to speech, work on corpus linguistics will always tend to isolate the samples of speech data from the original oral/aural channel in which they were produced and also from the overall context of the discourse. The development of multimedia corpora that is starting to emerge may begin to address this issue and is one of the most promising avenues for a model of the spoken form that does justice to its rich and complex resources for communicating meaning. Analysis of a corpus that can provide linked data on a number of factors at one time—gaze, gesture, prosody, syntax, and lexis—should provide a model that goes beyond the literate.

8.6 Speaking and New Technologies

A fast-moving area in recent years has been the development of new technologies that blur or alter the traditional boundaries between spoken and written mode. There are several strands to this, ranging from text-to-speech software, speech recognition, robotics, mobile computing, and telephony. The aim of much work is for users to be able to speak to a computer in much the same way as they would to another person and for the machine to be capable of carrying out the instruction. The major applications of human–machine speech are in automated call centres and Internet searching as well as applications in the military and aid for the physically less able. Uptake by the teaching community has tended to be slow, but in the first decade of the twenty-first century mobile phone providers were starting to offer English lessons via their handsets, and this was becoming particularly popular in markets where the demand for English teaching outstrips face-to-face teaching capacity, such as China. A review in 2014 (Golonka et al., 2014) suggested that pronunciation was the aspect of language learning that had the clearest evidence for improvement by means of new technologies via automatic voice-recognition software and related functions.

9   Research Resources

This chapter will . . .

- provide a selection of resources for the researcher;
- provide research process summaries in tabular form.

9.1   Journals and E-Journals

The following central journals in applied linguistics will all contain relevant material on the diverse aspects of spoken language, if not on spoken mode *per se*. It would be worthwhile adding these titles to any automatic alerting system and scanning the table of contents regularly for key words in relation to personal research interests in spoken language:

AILA Review
http://www.benjamins.com/cgi-bin/t_seriesview.cgi?series=AILA

Annual Review of Applied Linguistics
http://journals.cambridge.org/action/displayJournal?jid=APL

Applied Linguistics
http://applij.oxfordjournals.org/

Discourse & Communication
http://dcm.sagepub.com/

Discourse Studies
http://dis.sagepub.com/

ELT Journal
http://eltj.oxfordjournals.org/

Innovation in Language Learning
http://www.tandfonline.com/toc/rill20/current

Interaction Studies
https://benjamins.com/#catalog/journals/is/main

Intercultural Pragmatics
https://benjamins.com/#catalog/journals/ijcl/main

International Journal of Applied Linguistics
http://onlinelibrary.wiley.com/journal/10.1111/%28ISSN%291473-4192

International Journal of Corpus Linguistics
https://benjamins.com/#catalog/journals/ijcl/main

International Journal of Learner Corpus Research
https://www.benjamins.com/#catalog/journals/ijlcr/main

International Journal of the Sociology of Language
http://www.degruyter.com/view/j/ijsl

International Review of Applied Linguistics in Language Teaching (IRAL)
http://www.degruyter.com/view/j/iral

Journal of Applied Linguistics and Professional Practice
https://journals.equinoxpub.com/index.php/JALPP

Journal of Politeness Research: Language, Behaviour, Culture
http://www.degruyter.com/view/j/jplr

Journal of Pragmatics
http://www.journals.elsevier.com/journal-of-pragmatics/

Journal of Sociolinguistics
http://onlinelibrary.wiley.com/journal/10.1111/(ISSN)1467-9841

Language
https://muse.jhu.edu/journal/112

Language & Communication
http://www.journals.elsevier.com/language-and-communication/

Language Learning
http://www.tandfonline.com/toc/rllj20/current

Linguistics
http://www.linguistics-journal.com/

System
http://www.journals.elsevier.com/system/

TESOL Quarterly
http://www.tesol.org/read-and-publish/journals/tesol-quarterly

The Modern Language Journal
http://onlinelibrary.wiley.com/journal/10.1111/(ISSN)1540-4781

More specifically speech-oriented journals include:

Computer Speech and Language
http://www.journals.elsevier.com/computer-speech-and-language/

Dialogue and Discourse
http://www.dialogue-and-discourse.org/

Gesture
https://benjamins.com/#catalog/journals/gest/main

International Journal of Speech, Language & the Law
https://journals.equinoxpub.com/index.php/IJSLL

International Journal of Speech Technology
http://link.springer.com/journal/10772

Journal of Phonetics
http://www.journals.elsevier.com/journal-of-phonetics/

Journal of the International Phonetic Association
http://journals.cambridge.org/action/displayJournal?jid=IPA

Language and Speech
http://las.sagepub.com/

Phonology
http://journals.cambridge.org/action/displayJournal?jid=pho

Pragmatics
http://www.journals.elsevier.com/journal-of-pragmatics/

Research on Language & Social Interaction
http://www.tandfonline.com/toc/hrls20/current

Speech Communication
http://www.journals.elsevier.com/speech-communication/

Text & Talk
http://www.degruyter.com/view/j/text

Voice & Speech Review
https://www.vasta.org/voice-speech-review-1

9.2   Societies and Organisations

The special-interest groups of the UK English teachers association, the International Association of Teachers of English as a Foreign Language (IATEFL), on research generally, and on pronunciation, can be found at: *http://resig. weebly.com/* and *http://www.reading.ac.uk/epu/*

TESOL is a US-based association promoting English language teaching and research and can be found at: *http://www.tesol.org/*. The association has a special interest section on speaking and listening at: *http://www.sound sofenglish.org/*

Search terms: 'TESOL inc' and 'TESOL inc pronunciation'.

Other societies with links to spoken mode include those listed here. An Internet search containing the full title of the association should bring the reader to the current web presence.

American Dialect Society
http://www.americandialect.org/

Institute of Translation and Interpreting
http://www.iti.org.uk/

International Clinical Phonetics & Linguistics Association
http://www.icpla.org/SITE2007/index.php?ICPLA-HOME

International Phonetic Association
http://internationalphoneticassociation.org/

International Society of Phonetic Sciences
http://www.isphs.org/

Special Interest Group on Computational Morphology and Phonology (SIGMORPHON)
http://www.sigmorphon.org/

VUIDS—Voice User Interface Designers
https://groups.yahoo.com/neo/groups/vuids/info

9.3   Online Resources

The development of the Internet has meant that access to oral language data is becoming increasingly easy. As well as the corpora described in Section 9.4, sound archive material is available at the following sites, most of which provide downloadable sound files or can provide taped material for research purposes:

http://www.speechatsri.com/products/eduspeak.shtml
https://www.carnegiespeech.com/sales/index.php/vstore/csa
https://www.carnegiespeech.com/sales/index.php/vstore/nativeaccent
http://www.ets.org/Media/Tests/TOEFL/pdf/SampleQuestions.pdf

- The National Film and Sound Archive, Australia: *http://www.nfsa.gov.au/* (mainly relating to film and the arts but including interview material)

- The (British) National Sound Archive: *http://www.bl.uk/subjects/sound* (general and oral history material, including political history); and for material on British accents and dialects: *http://sounds.bl.uk/Accents-and-dialects*
- The Michigan State University voice library: *https://vvl.lib.msu.edu/* (including web access to samples of all US presidents' voices of the twentieth century)
- The BBC host and archive site on the evolution of the English language, which included downloadable examples of a cross-section of British voices: *http://www.bbc.co.uk/radio4/routesofenglish/index.shtml*
- The Stanford collection of Sound Recordings: *https://library.stanford.edu/ars*
- The Belfer Audio Archive at the University of Syracuse: *https://library.syr.edu/belfer/*
- A very varied and downloadable set of spoken English examples provided by: *http://alt-usage-english.org/*
- The US Library of Congress provides a sound archive reached through links from: *https://www.loc.gov/*
- A portal, i.e. a site at which other web resources and links on a variety of languages other than English are grouped, can be found at the LinguistList: *http://linguistlist.org/sp/GetWRListings.cfm?WRAbbrev=LangAnalysis*
- A site which incorporates sound clip and sound archive links into an EFL context including work on the differences between US and British English is: *http://eleaston.com/*

9.4   Speech Corpora

There are a growing number of access routes to spoken corpora on the web. For example, the ICAME website at *http://clu.uni.no/icame/* provides sample access to and also sells CD-ROM versions of the following corpora containing speech data:

- London Lund Corpus
- Lancaster/IBM Spoken English Corpus (SEC)
- Corpus of London Teenage Language (COLT)
- Wellington Spoken Corpus (New Zealand)
- The International Corpus of English–East African component

At Michael Barlow's Aethelstan site (*http://www.athel.com/cspa.html*) it is also possible to sample a corpus of professional and academic spoken interactions and buy related software; or find samples of more general spoken material at *http://www.natcorp.ox.ac.uk/* in the British National Corpus.

There many speech corpora that have been created to assist with research into speech recognition and other aspects of human-computer interaction (see, e.g. the 'Buckeye Speech Corpus', *http://vic.psy.ohio-state.edu/*).

The Centre for Spoken Language Understanding at the Oregon Graduate Institute of Science and Technology creates specialised corpora including children's speech and a variety of accents and languages: *https://www.ohsu.edu/xd/research/centers-institutes/center-for-spoken-language-understanding/*. The centre also provides a free 'toolkit' to work with these corpora.

A growing number of spoken corpora in a variety of languages are also readily available:

Chinese:
http://www.lancs.ac.uk/fass/projects/corpus/LCMC/

Russian:
http://www.ruscorpora.ru/ (includes a sub-corpus of spoken Russian from the 1930s to 2007)

Romance languages (Italian, French, Portuguese, Spanish):
http://lablita.dit.unifi.it/coralrom/index.html

Welsh:
https://www.bangor.ac.uk/canolfanbedwyr/ceg.php.en

As a hint when searching for resources online, the search term 'speech + corpus' is much more likely to bring up results in the speech recognition field than general corpus linguistics. In terms of searching for the latter, 'spoken + corpus' will be more effective, and 'spoken + corpus + [name of language]' should bring up a link to a corpus in almost any language that you name, although, again, many of these will be created for automatic speech recognition rather than broader applied linguistic analysis.

9.5   Speech Recognition and Text-to-Speech

A history of attempts to produce artificial speech can be found at:
http://www.ling.su.se/staff/hartmut/kemplne.htm

An example of a text-to-speech engine in seven languages is available at:
http://www.nextup.com/TextAloud/

A search on the term 'text to speech' will bring you to a large number of both commercial and free sites offering to produce spoken audio output from inputted text. Examples at the time of writing are:
http://www.voki.com/
http://www.oddcast.com/home/demos/tts/tts_example.php
http://www.cepstral.com/
http://hubpages.com/technology/text-speech-programs

9.6   Online Pronunciation and Intonation Resources

A site which provides examples of different accents of the British Isles is at:
http://www.phon.ox.ac.uk/files/apps/old_IViE/

A well-maintained site by Jennifer Smith links to a range of useful resources on intonation and phonetics:
http://www.unc.edu/~jlsmith/pht-url.html
Talking dictionaries are also common, such as the freely available:
http://www.howjsay.com/
http://www.fonetiks.org/
For the teacher and student alike there are a number of online discussion sites, networks and linked resources; for example:
https://www.linkedin.com/topic/teaching-pronunciation
https://www.englishclub.com/pronunciation/
http://www.bbc.co.uk/worldservice/learningenglish/grammar/pron/
A search on the terms 'pronunciation + video' will lead to a particularly rich set of resources demonstrating various aspects of pronunciation through online videos.

9.7   Miscellaneous Sites for the Applied Linguist With an Interest in Spoken Discourse

An excellent general website for the applied linguist is: *http://linguistlist.org/indexfd.cfm*
From this it is possible to search through, or join, various discussion groups; for instance, a group on discourse at: *http://linguistlist.org/lists/join-list.cfm?List=24* or language and culture: *http://linguistlist.org/lists/join-list.cfm?List=46*
There is an online bibliography of ethnolinguistics and conversation analysis and other resources at: *http://emcawiki.net/Main_Page*
Resources on speaking in a business context are to be found at:
http://www.cambridgesol.org/teach/bec/bec_higher/speaking/index.htm
General advice on teaching and learning speaking, as well as teaching resources, can be found at: *http://eleaston.com/speaking.html*
A highly useful site of tips, techniques, and news can be found at:
http://www.everythingesl.net/
A fun site with links to free games to generate talk can be found at:
http://www.englishbanana.com/

As a hint, when looking for resources online the results can be very diverse in this area and can also produce a very high number of returned pages. It is a good idea, therefore, to begin with two or three search terms in combination such as 'pronunciation + vocabulary + English' or 'pronunciation + intonation + questions'.

9.8   Moving Towards Your Own Project on Spoken Discourse

Figures 9.1 and 9.2 present some of the complexities of relationships between practitioners, research, and researchers in applied linguistics. Problems to think about at the outset are listed here.

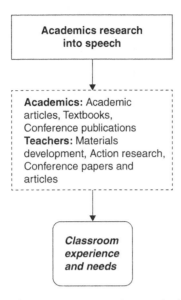

Figure 9.1 Information Exchanges Between Academe and Classrooms.

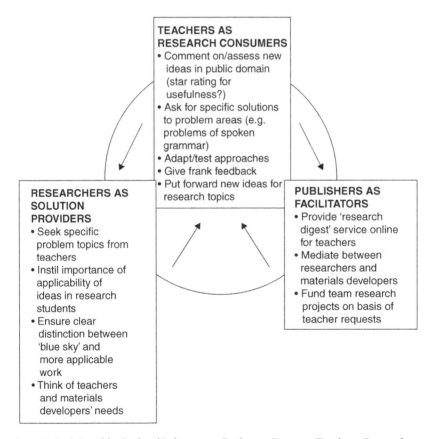

Figure 9.2 A Possible Cycle of Information Exchange Between Teachers, Researchers, and Publishers.

Global Problems for the Researcher Into Speech Data

1. Very few theories of speech *per se*.
2. Very few researchers have worked on speech in its own right within applied linguistics.
3. Within applied linguistic theory, 'speech' has often been conflated with 'language', and this can cause difficulties in trying to pin down the exact scope of a research project into the spoken form of language.

Further Issues for the Researcher Into Speech

Problem 1: What am I investigating?

>   Sounds?
>   Structures or forms?
>   Discourse?

Problem 2: What theoretical background can I use?

>   Theories of speech production?
>   Theories of speech processing?
>   Frameworks from discourse analysis or conversation analysis?

Problem 3: For language pedagogy, what is the target spoken form?

>   What dialect form shall I teach?
>   What model of correctness, if any, will I use?
>   What model of pragmatic or cultural behaviour will I use?

Problem 4: What are the most appropriate research methods to investigate speech?

>   Quantitative and/or experimental?
>   Qualitative and/or integrative?

9.9   Sources of Inspiration for Research

9.9.1 Personal Experience of the Profession

A research topic may grow from a problem, question, or challenge you meet in your working life. This could relate to your students' progress in their speaking abilities, the dynamics of interactions between them, confusion over who is allowed to speak at a given point, or their own questions to you about speaker dynamics or conversation.

You may find it helpful to keep a research questions notebook to hand at the early stages of a research project and jot down your queries and thoughts about these at the end of a working day. This will be a good source of practically oriented research questions, and looking back at the real-world questions which prompted you to begin can help with motivation as the research project develops.

An example of the kind of research which can grow from a problem experienced in a working context can be found in Tyler, Jeffries, and Davies (1988).

Quote 9.1   Tyler, Jeffries, and Davies on a problem arising in spoken academic discourse

Communication problems surrounding the spoken academic discourse of teachers who are non-native speakers of English are a growing concern at US universities. This paper presents partial results of an analysis of the videotaped teaching demonstrations of 18 Korean and Chinese graduate students at the University of Florida. The analysis was carried out within an integrative discourse framework, that is, one which considers the interrelatedness of various levels of linguistic organisation.

(Tyler, Jeffries and Davies, 1988: 101)

When it comes to presenting the research to a reader, these kinds of real-world difficulties give a sense of urgency and interest to the material and can help in particular with the introduction sections of the text.

9.9.2   *Developments in the Profession*

Inspiration for research topics can also be drawn from broader issues outside the classroom which are seen as influencing the profession as a whole.

A broad topic which you might want to pursue might be the changing role of the teacher in the communicative classroom and how this is reflected in teacher talk. In terms of teacher development you may wish to investigate how teacher trainers relate to novice teachers and conduct an ethnographic survey of their interactions. In general, these kinds of topics are most suited to experienced professional teachers who want to reflect on the skill of speaking within broader issues which they have seen alter their working lives (see also Quote 9.2).

Quote 9.2   Hoey on the teaching profession and spoken discourse

Why should a language teacher be concerned with the working of spoken discourse? Certainly not because the learner's syllabus needs to be augmented by explicit introduction to discourse analysis. . . . The real reason that language teachers should consider how discourses are organised is that it will help them to judge better the effectiveness of what they are doing. . . . If the teacher knows what a natural conversation involves, he or she will be in a better position to assess whether their learners are succeeding in developing the conversational skills that they need in order to be effective speakers of the target language.

(Hoey, 1991: 66)

9.9.3   *Social or Pragmatic Issues*

Topics for research can also arise from very general matters relating to the norms of conversation. In the early stages of a written introduction to a research paper it is quite common for researchers to relate their specific topic to a real-world issue of some kind which even the nonspecialist can understand, and then to use this as a lead into the specific, more academic, topic under consideration. Quote 9.3 gives an example of this approach.

Quote 9.3   Eisenstein and Bodman on cross-cultural norms of thanking

Most native speakers of English on a conscious level associate the expression of gratitude with the words 'thank you'; however, they are unaware of the underlying complex rules and the mutuality needed for expressing gratitude in a manner satisfying to both the giver and recipient.

(Eisenstein and Bodman, 1993: 64)

9.9.4   *Published Research and Theory*

A very common source of questions for the new researcher is existing work and theory. This is perhaps the most frequent technique by which an academic presents a topic as having relevance to fellow academics (see Quotes 9.4 and 9.5).

For the novice academic, providing clear links between previous work and your own also shows that you have carried out sufficient background research into your topic to be certain that what you are doing is not simply a repetition of the work of someone else. For this reason, unproven researchers may have to insert higher numbers of references in their literature review than a more seasoned academic.

Quotes 9.4 and 9.5 Two examples of researchers linking the inspiration for their work to previous studies

Another focus of our research has been on how Americans and Japanese perform such speech acts with status unequals. This question was asked because it is generally claimed that Japanese are very conscious of social status while Americans are relatively less status-conscious. Ide (1989) for example, argues . . . Similarly, Matsumoto (1989) argues . . .

(Takehashi and Beebe, 1993: 139)

Previous studies into non-native speaker interlanguage are dominated by a focus on the variation between correct vs. incorrect target language forms (. . . Ellis 1986 . . .;). We must distinguish between these studies of interlanguage *variation* and the study of target language *variability* in the discourse on non-native speakers, which is the topic of this paper.

(Haynes, 1992: 43)

Where the primary aim of research is to build on previous work, the researcher has to be particularly careful to show the novelty and interest of the work being presented. That is to say, if the object of the research is not to solve a real-world problem or to investigate the impacts of developments in the profession, then the value of the work has to be established in some other way. Traditionally in academic settings the appropriacy of a piece of research can be established by showing how it grows out of previous work in the field, and is fulfilling some need in relation to work done before. A good place to look for ideas for research topics is, therefore, in the discussion/conclusion sections of articles you read as background to your own work. Conventionally, academic writers will show that they are aware of the limitations of their present work by noting what further work could be carried out in the area, and this can help you to focus on a topic of your own.

9.10   Research Skills Summaries

This section gives a brief overview of some practical steps in research, the research process, and how to present findings clearly.

9.10.1   Research Questions

The most common way of shaping research is to found it on a single overarching question which summarises the main thrust of the project as a whole. Table 9.1 gives some examples of initial questions the reader might have after reading some of the articles presented in earlier chapters and which might grow into a new broad topic for further work.

Table 9.1 Broad Research Questions Growing Out of Previous Work

Article	*Potential further questions*
Liberman (1998)	Is there real evidence for the 'biological advantage of speech over writing/ reading' which Liberman takes as a premise?
Thompson and Couper-Kuhlen (2005)	How else could you investigate what speakers and listeners regard as a unit of talk? Could you apply their approach to L2 performance, and what would it tell you?
Morton (2009)	These findings were from the field of architecture and looked at student presentations. How do these differ from expert presentations by professional architects in authentic contexts? If they are very different, what does this tell us, and what are the implications for curriculum design?

9.10.2   The Cycle of Research

It is useful to remember that the process of research is cyclical. That is to say, until the final framework is set up and the research carried out, the experienced researcher will keep options open and add new knowledge to existing ideas in quite a fluid way until the steps needed start to 'gel'. Priorities and tasks will differ depending on what stage in the cycle the researcher is at, and good research is rarely a straightforward, unproblematic, linear process.

Table 9.2 The Cycle of Research

Research cycles	Earlier stages	Central stages	Final stages
Think (topic)	Define scope of project for yourself	Re-define scope and topic, redraft outline	Check and review scope of findings in relation to original aims
↓	↓	↓	↓
Find	Background readings; setting up relevant research questions; carrying out pilot studies	Carry out research activity to investigate topic, conducting surveys, and analysing data, detailed readings, and argument	Find final references, check references, complete bibliography
↓	↓	↓	↓
Think (audience)	Consider topic, outline, and scope in light of assessors of your work (supervisor—journal readership)	Draft chapters or sections aiming for consistency of style and taking into account readership—remember, no one will be as familiar with the detail of the work as you are	Review final draft of research text—will it make sense to a reader who has not experienced your research processes? Are there clear linking sections showing the logic and progression of your ideas? Write your introduction and abstract
↓	↓	↓	↓
Present	Present initial ideas	Present drafts to peer review, supervisor review, conferences/ seminars, etc.	Submit final draft (generally there will be a final cycle of comments and minor changes even after the submission)

9.10.3 Presenting and Commenting on Findings and Drawing Conclusions

Table 9.3 Examples of Data Commentary and Diverse Functions

Function of findings or data commentary sections in research texts	Examples from case-study articles in earlier chapters
To locate, or direct the reader to, detailed information	'Tables 2 and 3 summarise the frequency of these different question types by participant across the four role plays.' (Burns et al., 2008: 329)

(Continued)

Table 9.3 (Continued)

Function of findings or data commentary sections in research texts	Examples from case-study articles in earlier chapters
To direct the reader's attention to significant information (*not* simply repeating data without any evaluative language)	'As predicted, two partners together used fewer words in the workspace visible condition than in the workspace hidden condition. . . . Not surprisingly, directors used over four times as many words as builders.' (Clark and Krych, 2004: 67)
To begin to draw conclusions relating directly to the data	'These results indicate that there are distinct brain regions involved in the processing of specific pairings of actor orientation and speech-gesture content.' (Straube et al., 2010: 389)

9.10.4   Drawing conclusions

Table 9.4 Features of Conclusions

Contains new ideas/information?	✗
Contains repetition of main points of argument or of findings?	✓
Focuses on the best ideas you have had to 'sell' them to the reader?	✓
Gives a broad summary of all your points, whether stronger or weaker?	✗
Links back clearly to the original research questions?	✓
Gives sense of how far the research questions were answered?	✓
Hides any problems and limitations of the research process?	✗
Expresses the limitations of the research and possible further research?	✓
Gives a clear sense of finality to the research text?	✓

References

Aarts, B. and Meyer, C. (Eds) (1995). *The Verb in Contemporary English: Theory and Description*. Cambridge: Cambridge University Press.

Abercrombie, D. (1967). *Elements of General Phonetics*. Edinburgh: Edinburgh University Press.

Anderson, B. (2007). Pedagogical rules and their relationship to frequency in the input: Observational and empirical data from L2 French. *Applied Linguistics*. 28(2), 286–308.

Anthony, E. M. (1963). Approach, method, and technique. *ELT Journal*. XVII(2), 63–67.

Anttila, A. (2016). Phonological effects on syntactic variation. *Annual Review of Linguistics*. 2, 115–137.

Auer, P. (2009). On-line syntax: Thoughts on the temporality of spoken language. *Language Sciences*. 31, 1–13.

Bachman, L. F. (1990). *Fundamental Considerations in Language Testing*. Oxford: Oxford University Press.

Bachman. L. F. (2005). Building and supporting a case for test use. *Language Assessment Quarterly*. 2(1), 1–34.

Bakhtin, M. M. (1986). The problem of speech genres. (Trans.) McGee, V. W. In C. Emerson and M. Holquist (Eds), *Speech Genres and Other Late Essays*. Austin: University of Texas Press, pp. 62–102.

Baldwin, T., Beavers, J., Bender, E. M., Flickinger, D., Kim, A. and Oepen, S. (2005). Beauty and the Beast: What running a broad-coverage precision grammar over the BNC taught us about the grammar—and the corpus. In S. Kepser and M. Reis (Eds), *Linguistic Evidence: Empirical, Theoretical and Computational Perspectives (Studies in Generative Grammar)*. Berlin: Walter de Gruyter & Co., pp. 49–70.

Barbieri, F. and Eckhardt, S.E.B. (2007). Applying corpus-based findings to form-focused instruction: The case of reported speech. *Language Teaching Research*. 11(3), 319–346.

Bargiela-Chiappini, F., Nickerson, C. and Planken, B. (2007). *Business Discourse*. Basingstoke: Palgrave Macmillan.

Barron, A. (2005). Variational pragmatics in the foreign language classroom. *System*. 33(3), 519–536.

Beaucousin, V., Lacheret, A., Turbelin, M., Morel, M., Mazoyer, B. and Tzourio-Mazoyer, N. (2007). FMRI study of emotional speech comprehension. *Cerebral Cortex*. 17(2), 339–352.

Benson, P., Chik, A., Gao, X., Huang, J. and Wang, W. (2009). Qualitative research in language teaching and learning journals 1997–2006. *The Modern Language Journal.* 93(1), 79–90.

Berg, T. (1997). The modality-specificity of linguistic representations: Evidence from slips of the tongue and the pen. *Journal of Pragmatics.* 27(5), 671–697.

Berg, T. and Hassan, A. (1996). The unfolding of suprasegmental representations: A cross-linguistic perspective. *Journal of Linguistics.* 32, 291–324.

Bernstein, J., Van Moere, A. and Cheng, J. (2010, July). Validating automated speaking tests. *Language Testing.* 27(3), 355–377.

Biber, D. (1988). *Variation across Speech and Writing.* Cambridge: Cambridge University Press.

Biber, D. (2006). *University Language: A Corpus-Based Study of Spoken and Written Registers.* Amsterdam: John Benjamins.

Biber, D. and Barbieri, F. (2007). Lexical bundles in university spoken and written registers. *English for Specific Purposes.* 26, 263–286.

Biber, D. and Reppen, R. (2002). What does frequency have to do with grammar teaching? *Studies in Second Language Acquisition.* 24, 199–208.

Biber, D., Conrad, S., Reppen, R., Byrd, P. and Helt, M. (2002). Speaking and writing in the university: A multidimensional comparison. *TESOL Quarterly.* 36(1), 9–48.

Biber, D., Conrad, S. M., Reppen, R., Byrd, P., Helt, M., Clark, V., Cortes, V., Csomay, E. and Urzua, A. (2004). *Representing Language Use in the University: Analysis of the TOEFL 2000 Spoken and Written Academic Language Corpus.* Princeton, NJ: Educational Testing Service.

Biber, D., Johansson, S., Leech, G., Conrad, S. and Finegan, E. (1999). *Longman Grammar of Spoken and Written English.* Harlow: Longman.

Blake, C. (2009). Potential of text-based internet chats for improving oral fluency in a second language. *The Modern Language Journal.* 93(2), 227–240.

Boxer, D. and Cohen, A. D. (2004). *Studying Speaking to Inform Second Language Learning.* Clevedon: Multilingual Matters.

Boyd, M. P. and Markarian, W. C. (2015). Dialogic teaching and dialogic stance: Moving beyond interactional form. *Research in the Teaching of English.* 49(3), 272.

Brazil, D. (1994). *Pronunciation for Advanced Learners of English.* Cambridge: Cambridge University Press.

Brazil, D. (1995). *A Grammar of Speech.* Oxford: Oxford University Press.

Brown, A. and McNamara, T. (2004). 'The devil is in the detail': Researching gender issues in language assessment. *Tesol Quarterly.* 38(3), 524–538.

Brown, G. and Yule, G. (1983). *Teaching the Spoken Language: An Approach Based on the Analysis of Conversational English.* Cambridge: Cambridge University Press.

Brown, H. D. (1994). *Teaching by Principles: An Interactive Approach to Language Pedagogy.* Englewood Cliffs, NJ: Prentice Hall Regents.

Burns, A. and Joyce, H. (1997). *Focus on Speaking.* Sydney: National Center for English Language Teaching and Research, Macquarie University.

Burns, A. and Moore, S. (2008). Questioning in simulated accountant–client consultations: Exploring implications for ESP teaching. *English for Specific Purposes.* 27, 322–337.

Butler, F. A., Eignor, D., Jones, S., McNamara, T. and Suomi, B. K. (2000). TOEFL 2000 speaking framework: A working paper. *TOEFL Monograph Series 20.* Princeton, NJ: Educational Testing Service.

Bybee, J. (2006). From usage to grammar: The mind's response to repetition. *Language.* 82(4), 529–551.

Bygate, M., Norris, J. and Branden, K. (2015). Task-Based Language Teaching. *The Encyclopedia of Applied Linguistics*. 1–8.

Bygate, M., Skehan, P. and Swain, M. (2001). *Researching Pedagogic Tasks: Second Language Learning, Teaching, and Testing*. New York: Longman.

Canale, M. and Swain, M. (1980). Theoretical bases of communicative approaches to second language teaching and testing. *Applied Linguistics*. 1(1), 1–47.

Carlo, J. L. and Yoo, Y. (2007). 'How may I help you?' Politeness in computer-mediated and face-to-face library reference transactions. *Information and Organization*. 17, 193–231.

Carter, R. and McCarthy, M. (1995). Grammar and the spoken language. *Applied Linguistics*. 16(2), 141–158.

Carter, R. and McCarthy, M. (1997). *Exploring Spoken English*. Cambridge: Cambridge University Press.

Carter, R. and McCarthy, M. (2006). *The Cambridge Grammar of English*. Cambridge: Cambridge University Press.

Carter, R. and McCarthy, M. (forthcoming). Spoken grammar: Where are we and where are we going? *Applied Linguistics*, e-version pp. 1–21.

Carter, R., Hughes, R. and McCarthy, M. (2000). *Exploring Grammar in Context*. Cambridge: Cambridge University Press.

Chafe, W. and Danielewicz, J. (1987). Properties of spoken and written language. In R. Horowitz and S. J. Samuels (Eds), *Comprehending Oral and Written Language*. San Diego, CA: Academic Press, pp. 83–113.

Chai, X. J., Berken, J. A., Barbeau, E. B., Soles, J., Callahan, M., Chen, J. K. and Klein, D. (2016). Intrinsic functional connectivity in the adult brain and success in second-language learning. *The Journal of Neuroscience*. 36(3), 755–761.

Chapman, S. and Routledge, C. (Eds) (2009). *Key Ideas in Linguistics and the Philosophy of Language*. Edinburgh: Edinburgh University Press.

Cheng, W. and Tsui, A.B.M. (2009). 'Ahh ((laugh)) well there is no comparison between the two I think': How do Hong Kong Chinese and native speakers of English disagree with each other? *Journal of Pragmatics*. 41, 2365–2380.

Chiarcos, C., Nordhoff, S. and Hellmann, S. (2012). *Linked Data in Linguistics*. Heidelberg: Springer.

Choi, S. and Richards, K. (2016). Introduction to the special issue: Innovation in research methods in applied linguistics. *Applied Linguistics*. 37(1), 1–6.

Chomsky, N. (1965). *Aspects of the Theory of Syntax*. Cambridge, MA: MIT Press.

Clark, H. H. and Krych, M. A. (2004). Speaking while monitoring addressees for understanding. *Journal of Memory and Language*. 50, 62–81.

Clark, H. H. and Wasow, T. (1998). Repeating words in spontaneous speech. *Cognitive Psychology*. 37(3), 201–242.

Conrad, S. (2000). Will corpus linguistics revolutionize grammar teaching in the 21st century? *TESOL Quarterly*. 34(3), 548–560.

Cornbleet, S. and Carter, R. (2001). *The Language of Speech and Writing*. London: Routledge.

Couper-Kuhlen, E. and Selting, M. (2001). Introducing interactional linguistics. *Studies in interactional linguistics*. Amsterdam: Jonathan Benjamins.

Cullen, R. and I-Chun (Vicky) Kuo. (2007). Spoken grammar and ELT course materials: A missing link? *TESOL Quarterly*. 41(2), 361–386.

Cunningham, S. and Moor, P. (1992). *Everyday Listening and Speaking*. Oxford: Oxford University Press.

Curl, T. S. (2006). Offers of assistance: Constraints on syntactic design. *Journal of Pragmatics*. 38, 1257–1280.

Darling, A. L. (2005). Public presentations in mechanical engineering and the discourse of technology. *Communication Education*. 54(1), 20–33.

Dat, B. (2003). Materials for developing speaking skills. In B. Tomlinson (Ed), *Developing Materials for Language Teaching*. London: Continuum, pp. 375–393.

Davies, A. (2008). Textbook trends in teaching language testing. *Language Testing*. 25(3), 327–347.

Davletcharova, A., Sugathan, S., Abraham, B. and James, A. P. (2015). Detection and analysis of emotion from speech signals. *Procedia Computer Science*. 58, 91–96.

Degand, L. and Simon, A. C. (2009). Mapping prosody and syntax as discourse strategies: How Basic Discourse Units vary across genres. *Where Prosody Meets Pragmatics*. 8, 79.

De Knop, S. and Meunier, F. (2015). The 'learner corpus research, cognitive linguistics and second language acquisition' nexus: A SWOT analysis. *Corpus Linguistics and Linguistic Theory*. 11(1), 1–18.

Derwing, T. M. (2008). Curriculum issues in teaching pronunciation to second language learners. In J. G. Hansen Edwards and M. L. Zampini (Eds), *Phonology and Second Language Acquisition*. Amsterdam: John Benjamins, pp. 347–370.

Derwing, T. M. and Munro, M. J. (2015). *Pronunciation Fundamentals: Evidence-Based Perspectives for L2 Teaching and Research* (Vol. 42). Amsterdam: John Benjamins Publishing Company.

Dingemanse, M. and Enfield, N. J. (2015). Other-initiated repair across languages: Towards a typology of conversational structures. *Open Linguistics*. 1(1), 96–118.

Dörnyei, Z. (2007). *Research Methods in Applied Linguistics: Quantitative, Qualitative, and Mixed Methodologies*. Oxford: Oxford University Press.

Douglas, D. (1997). Testing speaking ability in academic contexts: Theoretical considerations. *TOEFL Monograph Series*. Princeton, NJ: Educational Testing Services.

Douglas, D. (2000). *Assessing Languages for Specific Purposes*. Cambridge: Cambridge University Press.

Douglas, D. (2004). Discourse domains: The cognitive context of speaking. In D. Boxer and A. D. Cohen (Eds), *Studying Speaking to Inform Second Language Learning*. Bristol: Multilingual Matters Ltd., pp. 25–44.

Drew, P. and Heritage, J. (1992). *Talk at Work*. Cambridge, England: Cambridge University Press.

Du Bois, J. W. (2014). Towards a dialogic syntax. *Cognitive Linguistics*. 25(3), 359–410.

Edwards, J. A. (2003). 17 The Transcription of Discourse. *The Handbook of Discourse Analysis*. 18, 321.

Eisenstein, M. and Bodman, J. (1993). Expressing gratitude in American English. In G. Kasper and S. Blum-Kulka (Eds), *Interlanguage Pragmatics*. New York: Oxford University Press, pp. 64–81.

Elder, C. and McNamara, T. (2015). The hunt for 'indigenous criteria' in assessing communication in the physiotherapy workplace. *Language Testing*. 33(2) 0265532215607398.

Ellis, A. W., Burani, C., Izura, C., Bromiley, A. and Venneri, A. (2006). Traces of vocabulary acquisition in the brain: Evidence from covert object naming. *Neuroimage*. 33(3), 958–968.

Ellis, R. (1986). *Understanding Second Language Acquisition*. Oxford: Oxford University Press.

Ellis, R., Basturkmen, H. and Loewen, S. (2002). Doing focus-on-form. *System*. 30, 419–432.

Ellis, R., Loewen, S. and Basturkmen, S. (1999). Focussing on form in the classroom (technical report). Institute of Language Teaching and Learning, University of Auckland.

Enfield, N. J. and Stivers, T. (Eds) (2007). *Person Reference in Interaction*. Cambridge: Cambridge University Press.

Eskildsen, S. W. (2012). L2 negation constructions at work. *Language Learning*. 62(2), 335–372.

ETS. (2014). *TOEFL Test ETS Independent Speaking Rubrics* https://www.ets.org/s/toefl/pdf/toefl_speaking_rubrics.pdf (accessed January 2016).

ETS. (2015). *TOEFL iBT® Test Questions* http://www.ets.org/Media/Tests/TOEFL/pdf/SampleQuestions.pdf (accessed January 2016).

ETS. (2016a). http://www.ets.org/toefl/ibt/scores/improve/

ETS. (2016b). http://www.ets.org/toefl/ibt/scores/improve/speaking_familiar_fair

Fitch, W. T., Hauser, M. D. and Chomsky, N. (2005). The evolution of the language faculty: Clarifications and implications. *Discussion/Cognition*. 97, 179–210.

Florez, M. C. (1999). *Improving Adult English Language Learners' Speaking Skills. Report for National Clearinghouse for ESL Literacy Education (NCLE)*. Washington, DC: National Clearinghouse for ESL Literacy Education.

Flowerdew, L. (2015). Corpus-based research and pedagogy in EAP: From lexis to genre. *Language Teaching*. 48(1), 99–116.

Folse, K. S. (2006). *The Art of Teaching Speaking*. Mahwah, NJ: Lawrence Erlbaum.

Foote, J. A., Holtby, A. K. and Derwing, T. M. (2011). Survey of the teaching of pronunciation in adult ESL programs in Canada, 2010. *TESL Canada Journal*. 29(1), 1–22.

Ford, C. E., Fox, B. A. and Thompson, S. A. (2002). Constituency and the grammar of turn increments. In Cecilia E. Ford, Barbara A. Fox and Sandra A. Thompson (Eds), *The Language of Turn and Sequence*. Oxford: Oxford University Press, pp. 14–38.

Fowler, C. A. (2008). The FLMP STMPed. *Psychonomic Bulletin & Review*. 15(2), 458–462.

Fox, B. A., Maschler, Y. and Uhmann, S. (2010). A cross-linguistic study of self-repair: Evidence from English, German, and Hebrew. *Journal of Pragmatics*. 42(9), 2487–2505.

French, P. and Local, J. (1983). Turn-competitive incomings. *Journal of Pragmatics*. 7, 17–38.

Fulcher, G. (2003). *Testing Second Language Speaking*. London: Pearson Longman.

Fulcher, G. (2015). Assessing second language speaking. *Language Teaching*. 48(2), 198–216.

Gammidge, M. (2004). *Speaking Extra*. Cambridge: Cambridge University Press.

Gan, Z., Davison, C. and Hamp-Lyons, L. (2009). Topic negotiation in peer group oral assessment situations: A conversation analytic approach. *Applied Linguistics*. 30(3), 315–334.

Gattegno, C. (1976). *The Common Sense of Teaching Foreign Languages*. New York: Educational Solutions.

Gimson, A. C. (1978). *A Practical Course of English Pronunciation*. London: Edward Arnold.

Ginther, A. (2012). *Assessment of Speaking: The Encyclopedia of Applied Linguistics*. Oxford: Wiley-Blackwell.

Golonka, E. M., Bowles, A. R., Frank, V. M., Richardson, D. L. and Freynik, S. (2014). Technologies for foreign language learning: A review of technology types and their effectiveness. *Computer Assisted Language Learning*. 27(1), 70–105.

Goodwin, C. (1981). *Conversational Organisation: Interaction between Speakers and Hearers*. New York: Academic Press.

Grabe, E. and Low, E. L. (2002). Durational variability in speech and the Rhythm Class Hypothesis. In C. Gussenhoven and N. Warner (Eds), *Papers in Laboratory Phonology 7*. Cambridge: Cambridge University Press, pp. 515–546.

Grice, P. H. (1975). Logic and conversation. In P. Cole and J. Morgan (Eds) *Syntax and Semantics*. 3: Speech acts. New York: Academic Press, pp. 41–58.

Grosjean, F. (1983). How long is the sentence? Prediction and prosody in the on-line processing of language. *Linguistics*. 21, 501–529.

Grosjean, F. and Hirt, C. (1996). Using prosody to predict the end of sentences in English and French: Normal and brain-damaged subjects. *Language and Cognitive Processes*. 11(1), 107–134.

Guchte, M., Braaksma, M., Rijlaarsdam, G. and Bimmel, P. (2015). Learning new grammatical structures in task-based language learning: The effects of recasts and prompts. *The Modern Language Journal*. 99(2), 246–262.

Gunn, B. (trans.) (1906). *The Instruction of Ptah-ho-tep and the Instruction of Kegemni: The Oldest Books in the World*. London: John Murray.

Gussenhoven, C. (2002). Intonation and interpretation: Phonetics and Phonology. *Speech Prosody 2002: Proceedings of the First International Conference on Speech Prosody*. Aix-en-Provence, ProSig and Université de Provence Laboratoire Parole et Langage, pp. 47–57.

Gussenhoven, C. (2004). *The Phonology of Tone and Intonation*. Cambridge: Cambridge University Press.

Hahn, L. D. (2004). Primary stress and intelligibility: Research to motivate the teaching of suprasegmentals. *TESOL Quarterly*. 38(2), 201–223.

Halliday, M.A.K. (1989). *Spoken and Written Language*. Oxford: Oxford University Press.

Hammerly, H. (1991). *Fluency and Accuracy: Towards Balance in Language Teaching and Learning*. Bristol, PA: Multilingual Matters Ltd.

Hamp-Lyons, L. (1997). Washback, impact and validity: Ethical concerns. *Language Testing*. 14, 295–303.

Hamp-Lyons, L. (2007). The impact of testing practices on teaching: Ideologies and alternatives. In J. Cummins and C. Davison (Eds), *International Handbook of English Language Teaching*. New York: Springer, pp. 487–504.

Hargreaves, R. and Fletcher, M. (1979). *Making Polite Noises*. London: Evans.

Hatch, E. (1992). *Discourse and Language Education*. Cambridge: Cambridge University Press.

Haynes, L. A. (1992). The development of speaking/writing variability in narratives of non-native English speakers. *Issues in Applied Linguistics*. 3(1), 43–67.

Heritage, J. and Maynard, D. W. (Eds) (2006). *Communication in Medical Care: Interaction between Primary Care Physicians and Patients*. Cambridge: Cambridge University Press.

Hewings, M. (2004). *Pronunciation Practice Activities Book and Audio CD Pack: A Resource Book for Teaching English Pronunciation*. Cambridge: Cambridge University Press.

Hincks, R. (2010). Speaking rate and information content in English lingua franca oral presentations. *English for Specific Purposes*. 29, 4–18.

Hirschberg, J. (2002). The pragmatics of intonational meaning. In B. Bel and I. Marlien (Eds), *Proceedings of the Speech Prosody 2002 Conference*. Aix-en-Provence, France, pp. 65–68.

Hoey, M. (1991). Some properties of spoken discourses. In R. Bowers and C. Brumfit (Eds), *Applied Linguistics and English Language Teaching*. Oxford: Modern English Publications in association with The British Council, pp. 65–84.

Holmes, J., Marsden, S. and Marra, M. (2013). Doing listenership: One aspect of sociopragmatic competence at work. *Pragmatics and Society*. 4(1), 26–53.

Howatt, A.P.R. (1985). *A History of English Language Teaching*. Oxford: Oxford University Press.

Howatt, A.P.R. and Widdowson, H. G. (2004). *History of English Language Teaching ELT* (2nd edn). Oxford: Oxford University Press.

Hu, G. and Lindemann, S. (2009). Stereotypes of Cantonese English, apparent native/non-native status, and their effect on non-native English speakers' perception. *Journal of Multilingual and Multicultural Development*. 30(3), 253–269.

Hughes, R. (1996). *English in Speech and Writing: Investigating Language and Literature*. London: Routledge.

Hughes, R. (2004). Testing the visible, literate biases in oral language testing. *Journal of Applied Linguistics*. 1(3), 295–309.

Hughes, R. (2010). Researching speaking. In B. Paltridge and A. Phakiti (Eds), *Continuum Companion to Research Methods in Applied Linguistics*. London: Continuum, pp. 283–299.

Hughes, R. (forthcoming) Navigation in a complex world: English as compass or map? In J.Kemp (Ed), *Proceedings of the 2015 BALEAP conference: EAP in a rapidly changing landscape: Issues, challenges and solutions*. Reading: Garnet Education.

Hughes, R. and Szczepek Reed, B. (2010). Learning about speech by experiment: Issues in the investigation of spontaneous talk within the experimental research paradigm. *Applied Linguistics*. 32(2), 197–214.

Hyland, K. (2015). *Teaching and Researching Writing* (3rd edn). Abingdon and New York: Routledge.

IELTS. (2015). Information for Candidates. http://www.ielts.org/pdf/IELTS%20Information-for-Candidates-March%202015.pdf

IELTS. (2016a). https://www.ielts.org/about-the-test/test-format-in-detail

IELTS. (2016b). http://www.ielts.org/~/media/pdfs/speaking-band-descriptors.ashx

Jefferson, G. (2004). Glossary of transcript symbols with an introduction. In G.H. Lerner (Ed), *Conversation Analysis: Studies from the First Generation*. Amsterdam/Philadelphia: John Benjamins, pp. 13–31.

Jenkins, J. (2000). *The Phonology of English as an International Language*. Oxford: Oxford University Press.

Jenkins, J. (2006). The spread of EIL: A testing time for testers. *ELT Journal*. 60(1), 42–50.

Johns, T. (1991). From printout to handout: Grammar and vocabulary learning in the context of data-driven learning. *English Language Research Journal*. 4, 27–45.

Johnson, M. and Tyler, A. (1998). Re-analysing the OPI: How much does it look like natural conversation? In R. Young and A. Weiyn He (Eds), *Talking and Testing: Discourse Approaches to the Assessment of Oral Proficiency*. Amsterdam and Philadelphia: John Benjamins Publishing Company, pp. 27–51.

Juzwik, M. M., Borsheim-Black, C., Caughlan, S. and Heintz, A. (2013). *Inspiring Dialogue: Talking to Learn in the English Classroom*. New York: Teachers College Press.

Kamp, H. and Reyle, U. (2013). *From Discourse to Logic: Introduction to Modeltheoretic Semantics of Natural Language, Formal Logic and Discourse Representation Theory* (Vol. 42). New York: Springer Science & Business Media.

Kaplan. (2009). *Kaplan IELTS 2009–2010 Edition*. New York: Kaplan Publishing.

Kasper, G. and Wagner, J. (2011). A conversation-analytic approach to second language acquisition. In D. Atkinson (Ed), *Alternative Approaches to Second Language Acquisition*. London and New York: Routledge, pp. 117–142.

Keller, E. and Warner, S. T. (1988). *Conversation Gambits*. Hove: Language Teaching Publications.

Kirkpatrick, A. (2011). English as an Asian lingua franca and the multilingual model of ELT. *Language Teaching*. 44(2), 212–224.

Klein, W. and Purdue, C. (Eds) (1992). *Utterance Structure: Developing Grammars Again*. Amsterdam and Philadelphia, PA: John Benjamins Publishing Co.

Knowles, G. (1990). The use of spoken and written corpora in the teaching of language and linguistics. *Literary and Linguistic Computing*. 5, 45–48.

Kormos, J. (2014). *Speech Production and Second Language Acquisition*. London: Routledge.

Kovelman, I., Norton, E. S., Christodoulou, J. A., Gaab, N., Lieberman, D. A., Triantafyllou, C., Wolf, M., Whitfield-Gabrieli, S. and Gabrieli, J. D. (2012). Brain basis of phonological awareness for spoken language in children and its disruption in dyslexia. *Cerebral Cortex*. 22(4), 754–764.

Krashen, S. D. (1981). *Second Language Acquisition and Second Language Learning*. Oxford: Pergamon.

Krashen, S. D. (1982). *Principles and Practice in Second Language Acquisition*. Oxford: Pergamon.

Krashen, S. D. (2008). Language education: Past present and future. *RELC Journal*. 39(2), 178–187.

Kunnan, A. J. (2012). Language assessment for immigration and citizenship. In G. Fulcher and F. Davidson (Eds), *The Routledge Handbook of Language Testing*. New York: Routledge, pp. 162–177.

Kunnan, A. J. (2013). *Companion to Language Assessment*. Hoboken, NJ: John Wiley.

Kvarnstrom, S. and Cedersund, E. (2006). Discursive patterns in multiprofessional healthcare teams: Nursing and health care management and policy. *Journal of Advanced Nursing*. 53(2), 244–252.

Ladd, R. (1996). *Intonational Phonology*. Cambridge: Cambridge University Press.

Lam, P. W. (2010). Discourse particles in corpus data and textbooks: The case of well. *Applied Linguistics*. 31(2), 260–281.

Larsen-Freeman, D. and Anderson, M. (2013). *Techniques and Principles in Language Teaching 3rd edition*. Oxford: Oxford University Press.

Lee, Yong-Won. (2006). Dependability of scores for a new ESL speaking assessment consisting of integrated and independent tasks. *Language Testing*. 23(2), 131–166.

Lennon, P. (1990). Investigating fluency in EFL: A quantitative approach. *Language Learning*. 40(3), 387–417.

Levelt, W. J. M. (1989). *Speaking: From Intention to Articulation*. Cambridge, MA and London, England: The MIT Press.

Lewis, M. (1982). *Partners 3: More Demanding Pair Work Practices*. Hove: Language Teaching Publications.

Liberman, A. M. (1997). How theories of speech affect research in reading and writing. In Benita A. Blachman (Ed), *Foundations of Reading Acquisition and Dyslexia: Implications for Early Intervention*. Mahwah, NJ: Lawrence Erlbaum Associates, pp. 3–19.

Liberman, A. M. (1998). When theories of speech meet the real world. *Journal of Psycholinguistic Research*. 27(2), 111–122.

Liberman, A. M. (1999). Seven Questions for a Theory of Speech. *Journal of Chinese Linguistics Monograph Series*. 13, 1–25.

Liberman, A. M. and Whalen, D. H. (2000). On the relation of speech to language. *Trends in Cognitive Sciences*. 4(5), 187–196.

Lindquist, H. and Mair, C. (2004). *Corpus Approaches to Grammaticalization in English*. Amsterdam: John Benjamins.

Lloyd James, A. (1940). *Speech Signals in Telephony*. London: Pitman and Sons.

Lotto, A. J., Hickok, G. S. and Holt, L. L. (2008). Reflections on mirror neurons and speech perception. *Trends in Cognitive Sciences*. 13(3), 110–113.

Lougheed, L. (2006). *Barron's How to Prepare for the IELTS*. U.S: Barrons Education Series Inc.

Low, E. L. (2014). *Pronunciation for English as an International Language: From Research to Practice*. London: Routledge.

Low, E. L. and Grabe, E. (1995). Prosodic patterns in Singapore English. In K. Elenius and P. Banderud (Eds), *Proceedings of the 13th International Congress for Phonetic Sciences*. Congress organisers at KTH and Stockholm University, pp. 636–639.

Lumley, T. and O'Sullivan, B. (2005). The effect of test-taker gender, audience and topic on task performance in tape-mediated assessment of speaking. *Language Testing*. 22(4), 415–437.

Luoma, S. (2004). *Assessing Speaking*. Cambridge: Cambridge University Press.

Lynch, T. and Anderson, K. (1992). *Study Speaking: A Course in Spoken English for Academic Purposes*. Cambridge: Cambridge University Press.

Maniwa, K., Jongman, A. and Wade, T. (2009). Acoustic characteristics of clearly spoken English fricatives. *Journal of the Acoustic Society of America*. 125(6), 3962–3973.

Marsi, E., Reynaert, M., Van Den Bosch, A., Daelemans, W. and Hoste, V. (2003, July). Learning to predict pitch accents and prosodic boundaries in Dutch. In *Proceedings of the 41st Annual Meeting on Association for Computational Linguistics-Volume 1*. Association for Computational Linguistics, pp. 489–496.

McCarthy, M. (1991). *Discourse Analysis for Language Teachers*. Cambridge: Cambridge University Press.

McCarthy, M. (1998). *Spoken Language and Applied Linguistics*. Cambridge: Cambridge University Press.

McCarthy, M. (2002). Good listenership made plain. In R. Reppen et al. (Eds), *Using Corpora to Explore Linguistic Variation*. Philadelphia/Amsterdam: John Benjamins Publishing, pp. 49–71.

McCrum, R. (2006). So, what's this Globish revolution? http://www.guardian.co.uk/theobserver/2006/dec/03/features.review37 (accessed 16 May 2009).

McLaughlin, B. (1987). *Theories of Second-Language Learning*. London: Edward Arnold.

McMurray, B., Samelson, V.M., Lee, S.H. and Tomblin, J.B. (2010). Individual differences in online spoken word recognition: Implications for SLI. *Cognitive Psychology*. 60(1), 1–39.

McNamara, T. (2001). Language assessment as social practice: Challenges for research. *Language Testing*. 18, 333–349.

McNamara, T. (2011). Managing learning: Authority and language assessment. *Language Teaching*. 44(4), 500–515.

McNamara, T. (2012). English as a lingua franca: The challenge for language testing. *Journal of English as a Lingua Franca*. 1(1), 199–202.

McNamara, T. and Ryan, K. (2011). Fairness versus justice in language testing: The place of English literacy in the Australian Citizenship Test. *Language Assessment Quarterly*. 8(2), 161–178.

Meeuwesen, L., Tromp, F., Schouten, B. C. and Harmsen, J.A.M. (2007). Cultural differences in managing information during medical interaction: How does the physician get a clue? *Patient Education and Counseling.* 67, 183–190.

Meroni, L. and Crain, S. (2003). *How Children Avoid Kindergarten Paths: Proceedings of 4th Tokyo Conference on Psycholinguistics.* Tokyo, Japan: Hitsuji Shobo.

Meyer, C. F. (1995). Coordination ellipsis in spoken and written American English. *Language Sciences.* 17, 241–269.

Mindt, D. (2002). What is a grammatical rule? In L. E. Breivik and A. Hasselgren (Eds), *From the COLT's Mouth . . . and Others: Language Corpora Studies in Honour of Anna-Brita Stenstrom.* Amsterdam: Editions Rodopi B.V., pp. 197–212.

Moore, C. (2007). The spread of grammaticalized forms: The case of be+supposed to. *Journal of English Linguistics.* 7(35), 117–131.

Morante, R. and Sporleder, C. (2012). Modality and negation: An introduction to the special issue. *Computational linguistics.* 38(2), 223–260.

Mori, J. (2007). Border crossings? Exploring the intersection of second language acquisition, conversation analysis, and foreign language pedagogy. *The Modern Language Journal.* 91(5), 849–862.

Morton, J. (2009). Genre and disciplinary competence: A case study of contextualisation in an academic speech genre. *English for Specific Purposes.* 28(4), 217–229.

Munro, M. J. and Derwing, T. M. (2011). The foundations of accent and intelligibility in pronunciation research. *Language Teaching.* 44(03), 316–327.

Murphy, B. (2012). Exploring response tokens in Irish English—a multidisciplinary approach: Integrating variational pragmatics, sociolinguistics and corpus linguistics. *International Journal of Corpus Linguistics.* 17(3), 325–348.

Mushin, I. and Gardner, R. (2009). Silence is talk: Conversational silence in Australian Aboriginal talk-in-interaction. *Journal of Pragmatics.* 41, 2033–2052.

Nariyama, S. (2004). Subject ellipsis in English. *Journal of Pragmatics.* 36(2), 237–264.

Nation, I.S.P. and Newton, J. (2008). *Teaching EFL/ESL Listening and Speaking.* London: Routledge.

Nelson, G. (1997). Cleft constructions in spoken and written English. *Journal of English Linguistics.* 25, 340–348.

Nelson, G. L., Mahmood, A. and Nichols, E. (1996). Arabic and English compliment responses: Potential for pragmatic failure. *Applied Linguistics.* 17(4), 411–432.

Nestor, M. and Vogel, I. (2007). *Prosodic Phonology.* The Hague: Mouton de Gruyter.

Nwosisi, C., Ferreira, A., Rosenberg, W. and Walsh, K. (2016). A study of the flipped classroom and its effectiveness in flipping thirty percent of the course content. *International Journal of Information and Education Technology.* 6(5), 348.

Ockey, G.J., Koyama, D., Setoguchi, E. and Sun, A. (2015). The extent to which TOEFL iBT speaking scores are associated with performance on oral language tasks and oral ability components for Japanese university students. *Language Testing.* 32(1), 39–62.

O'Connell, D.C. and Kowal, S. (2009). Transcription systems for spoken discourse. In S. D'Hondt, J. Östman, and J. Verschueren (Eds), *The Pragmatics of Interaction.* Amsterdam: John Benjamin's, pp. 240–254.

Ohala, J. J. (1983). Cross-language use of pitch: An ethological view. *Phonetica.* 40, 1–18.

Ohala, J. J. (1984). An ethological perspective on common cross-language utilization of F0 of voice. *Phonetica.* 41, 1–16.

Ohala, J. J. (1994). The frequency codes underlies the sound symbolic use of voice pitch. In L. Hinton, J. Nichols and J. J. Ohala (Eds), *Sound Symbolism.* Cambridge: Cambridge University Press, pp. 325–347.

Oller, J. W., Jr. (1983). Evidence for a general language proficiency factor: An expectancy grammar. In J. W. Oller, Jr. (Ed), *Issues in Language Testing Research*. Rowley, MA: Newbury House, pp. 3–10.

O'Malley, J. M. and Valdez Pierce, L. (1996). *Authentic Assessment for English Language Learners: Practical Approaches for Teachers*. New York: Addison Wesley.

Ono, T. and Thompson, S. A. (1995). What can conversation tell us about syntax? In Philip W. Davis (Ed), *Descriptive and Theoretical Modes in the Alternative Linguistics*. Amsterdam: John Benjamins, pp. 213–271.

O'Sullivan, B. (2000). Exploring gender and oral proficiency interview performance. *System*. 28, 1–14.

Özçalışkan, S. and Goldin-Meadow, S. (2005). Gesture is at the cutting edge of early language development. *Cognition*. 96(3), 101–113.

Paltridge, B. and Phakiti, A. (Eds) (2010). *Continuum Companion to Research Methods in Applied Linguistics*. New York/London: Continuum.

Partala, T. and Surakka, V. (2004). The effects of affective interventions in human–computer interaction. *Interacting with Computers*. 16(2), 95–309.

Pickering, L. (2006). Current research on intelligibility in English as a Lingua Franca. *Annual Review of Applied Linguistics*. 26, 219–233.

Pike, K. L. (1945). *The Intonation of American English*. Ann Arbor, Michigan: University of Michigan Publications.

Prabhu, N. S. (1987). *Second Language Pedagogy*. Oxford: Oxford University Press.

Prodromou, L. (2008). *English as a Lingua Franca: A Corpus Based Analysis*. London: Continuum.

Quintilian. (2006). *Institutes of Oratory*. L. Honeycutt, Ed. (J.S. Watson, Trans.). Retrieved Jan. 19, 2010, from http://honeyl.public.iastate.edu/quintilian/ (Original work published 1856)

Reed, M. and Levis, J. (2015). *The Handbook of English Pronunciation*. Hoboken, NJ: John Wiley & Sons.

Richards, J. C. and Rodgers, T. S. (2001). *Approaches and Methods in Language Teaching*. Cambridge: Cambridge University Press.

Riggenbach, H. (1998). Evaluating learner interactional skills: Conversation at the micro level. In R. Young and A. Weiyun He (Eds), *Talking and Testing: Discourse Approaches to the Assessment of Oral Proficiency*. Studies in Bilingualism, 14. Amsterdam and Philadelphia: John Benjamins Publishing Company, pp. 53–67.

Rigler, H., Farris-Trimble, A., Greiner, L., Walker, J., Tomblin, J. B. and McMurray, B. (2015). The slow developmental time course of real-time spoken word recognition. *Developmental Psychology*. 51(12), 1690.

Rignall, M. and Furneaux, C. (1997). *Speaking* (English for Academic Study series). Hemel Hempstead: Prentice Hall.

Rivers, W. M. and Temperley, M. S. (1978). *A Practical Guide to the Teaching of English as a Second or Foreign Language*. New York: Oxford University Press.

Robinson, P. (2011). Task-based language learning: A review of issues. *Language Learning*. 61(s1), 1–36.

Rost, M. (2015). *Teaching and Researching Listening*. Abingdon and New York: Routledge.

Rühlemann, C. (2006). Coming to terms with conversational grammar 'dislocation' and 'dysfluency'. *International Journal of Corpus Linguistics*. 11(4), 385–409.

Salter, C., Holland, R., Harvey, I. and Henwood, K. (2007, May 26). 'I haven't even phoned my doctor yet,' the advice giving role of the pharmacist during consultations for medication review with patients aged 80 or more: Qualitative discourse analysis. *British Medical Journal*. 334(7603), 1101.

Samuda, V. and Bygate, M. (2008). *Tasks in Second Language Learning*. Basingstoke: Palgrave.

Sarwark, S., Smith, J., MacCullam, R. and Cascallar, E. C. (1995). *A Study of Characteristics of the SPEAK Test*. RR94-47. Princeton, NJ: Educational Testing Service.

Schegloff, E. A. (1981). Discourse as an interactional achievement: Some uses of 'uh huh' and other things that come between sentences. In D. Tannen (Ed), *Analysing Discourse: Text and Talk*. Washington, DC: Georgetown University Press, pp. 71–93.

Schegloff, E. A. (1987). Recycled turn beginnings: A precise repair mechanism in conversation's turn-taking organisation. In G. Button and J. R. Lee (Eds), *Talk and Social Organisation*. Clevedon: Multilingual Matters, pp. 70–85.

Seidlhofer, B. (2001). Pronunciation. In R. Carter and D. Nunan (Eds), *The Cambridge Guide to Teaching English to Speakers of Other Languages*. Cambridge: Cambridge University Press, pp. 56–66.

Sheridan, T. (1781). *A Rhetorical Grammar of the English Language* (reprinted 1969). Menston, England: The Scholar Press.

Shin, D. H. (1989). Effect of formal vs. informal environments and Krashen's Monitor Model. Unpublished Master's thesis, University of Birmingham, Birmingham, West Midlands.

Shohamy, E. (2013). The discourse of language testing as a tool for shaping national, global, and transnational identities. *Language and Intercultural Communication*. 13(2), 225–236.

Shohamy, E. (2014). *The Power of Tests: A Critical Perspective on the Uses of Language Tests*. London: Routledge.

Sidnell, J. and Enfield, N. J. (2012). Language diversity and social action: A third locus of linguistic relativity. *Current Anthropology*. 53(3), 302–333.

Simpson, J. (2006). Differing expectations in the assessment of the speaking skills of ESOL learners. *Linguistics and Education*. 17, 40–55.

Sinclair, J. and Coulthard, M. (1975). *Towards an Analysis of Discourse: The English Used by Teachers and Pupils*. London: Oxford University Press.

Skehan, P. (2007). Language instruction through Tasks. In J. Cummins and C. Davison (Eds), *International Handbook of English Language Teaching*. New York: Springer, pp. 289–301.

Snedeker, J. and Trueswell, J. (2001). Unheeded cues: Prosody and syntactic ambiguity in mother-child communication. Paper presented at the 26th Boston University Conference on Language Development.

Snedeker, J. and Trueswell, J. (2004). The developing constraints on parsing decisions: The role of lexical biases and referential scenes in child and adult sentence processing. *Cognitive Psychology*. 49(3), 238–299.

Spada, N. M. (1987). Relationships between instructional differences and learning outcomes: A process-product study of communicative language teaching. *Applied Linguistics*. 8(2), 137–161.

Speer, S. J. and Ito, K. (2009). Prosody in first language acquisition—acquiring intonation as a tool to organize information in conversation. *Language and Linguistics Compass*. 3(1), 90–110.

Stenström, A-B. (1990). Lexical items peculiar to spoken discourse. In J. Svartvik (Ed), *The London-Lund Corpus of Spoken English: Description and Research*. Lund Studies in English 82. Lund: Lund University Press, pp. 137–176.

Stivers, T., Enfield, N. J., Brown, P., Englert, C. Hayashi, M., Heinemann, T., Hoymann, G., Rossano, F., de Ruiter, J. P., Yoon, K.-F. and Levinson, S. C. (2009).

Universals and cultural variation in turn-taking in conversation. *Proceedings of the National Academy of Sciences of the United States of America (PNAS)*. http://www.pnas.org/content/106/26/10587.full

Stivers, T., Enfield, N. J. and Levinson, S. C. (2010). Question-response sequences in conversation across ten languages: Special issue. *Journal of Pragmatics*. 42(10), 2615–2860.

Straube, B., Green, A., Jansenc, A., Chatterjeeb, A. and Kircherc, T. (2010). Social cues, mentalizing and the neural processing of speech accompanied by gestures. *Neuropsychologia*. 48, 382–393.

Svartvik, J. (Ed) (1990). *The London–Lund Corpus of Spoken English: Description and Research*. Lund Studies in English 82. Lund: Lund University Press.

Svartvik, J. (1991). What can real spoken data teach teachers of English? In J. E. Alatis (Ed), *Georgetown University Round Table on Languages and Linguistics 1991*. Washington, DC: Georgetown University Press, pp. 555–566.

Sweet, H. (1900). *The Practical Study of Languages: A Guide for Teachers and Learners*. New York: Henry Holt and Company.

Szczepek Reed, B. (2007). *Prosodic Orientation in English Conversation*. Basingstoke: Palgrave-Macmillan.

Szczepek Reed, B. and Persson, R. (2016). How speakers of different languages extend their turns: Word linking and glottalization in French and German. *Research on Language and Social Interaction*. 49(2), pp. 128–147.

Takehashi, T. and Beebe, L. M. (1993). Cross-linguistic influence in the speech act of correction. In G. Kasper and S. Blum-Kulka (Eds), *Interlanguage Pragmatics*. New York: Oxford University Press, pp. 138–157.

Tan, A. A. and Molfese D. L. (2009). ERP correlates of noun and verb processing in preschool-age children. *Biological Psychology*. 80(1), 46–51.

Taylor, L. (2006). The changing landscape of English: Implications for language assessment. *ELT Journal*. 60(1), 51–59.

ten Have, P. (2007). *Doing Conversation Analysis*. London: Sage Publications.

Thompson, S. A. and Couper-Kuhlen, E. (2005). The clause as a locus of grammar and interaction. *Discourse Studies*. 7(4/5), 481–505. [Reprinted in *Language and Linguistics*. 6(4), 807–837, 2005.]

Thornbury, S. and Slade, D. (2006). *Conversation: From Description to Pedagogy*. New York: Cambridge University Press.

Tong, F., Irby, B. J., Lara-Alecio, R., Yoon, M. and Mathes, P. G. (2010). Hispanic English learners' responses to longitudinal English instructional intervention and the effect of gender: A multilevel analysis. *The Elementary School Journal*. 110(4), 542–566.

Tribble, C. (2013). *Corpora in the Language-Teaching Classroom*. Malden, MA: Blackwell Publishing Ltd.

Tribble, C. and Jones, G. (1990). *Concordances in the Classroom: A Resource Book for Teachers*. Harlow: Longman.

Trinity College London Graded Examinations in Spoken English and Integrated Skills in English (Interview Component) Performance Descriptors. (2016). http://www.trinitycollege.com/site/?id=3109

Trinity College London Graded Examinations in Spoken English, Language Requirements. (2014, August). Grade 5, *Exam Information: Graded Examinations in Spoken English (GESE): Specifications, Guide for Teachers, Regulations*. London: Trinity College London, Sixth Impression, p. 27.

Tyler, A. E., Jeffries, A. A. and Davies, C. E. (1988). The effect of discourse structuring devices on listener perceptions of coherence in non-native university teacher's spoken discourse. *World Englishes*. 7(2), 101–110.

Underhill, N. (1987). *Testing Spoken Language: A Handbook of Oral Testing Techniques*. Cambridge: Cambridge University Press.

Uppstad, P. H. and Tønnessen, F. E. (2007). The notion of 'phonology' in dyslexia research: Cognitivism and beyond. *Dyslexia*. 13, 154–174.

Ur, P. (1996). *A Course in Language Teaching: Practice and Theory*. Cambridge: Cambridge University Press.

Usó-Juan, E. and Martínez-Flor, A. (Eds) (2006). *Current Trends in the Development and Teaching of the Four Language Skills*. Berlin: Mouton de Gruyter.

Vachek, J. (1945). Some remarks on writing and phonetic transcription. *Acta linguistica*. 5(1), 86–93.

Vachek, J. (1973). *Written Language: General Problems and Problems of English*. The Hague: Mouton.

Van Avermaet, P. Colpin, M, van Gorp, K., Bogaert, N. and van den Branden, K. (2007). The role of the teacher in task-based language teaching. In K. van den Branden (Ed), *Task-Based Language Education: From Theory to Practice*. Cambridge: Cambridge University Press, pp. 175–196.

Van den Branden, K. (2006). *Task-Based Language Education: From Theory to Practice*. Cambridge: Cambridge University Press.

Viney, P. and Viney, K. (1996). *Handshake: A Course in Communication*. Oxford: Oxford University Press.

Wallwork, A. (1997). *Discussions A–Z, Intermediate: A Resource Book of Speaking Activities*. Cambridge: Cambridge University Press.

Wallwork, A. (2013). *Discussions A-Z Intermediate Book and Audio CD: A Resource Book of Speaking Activities* (Cambridge Copy Collection). Cambridge: Cambridge University Press.

Walsh, S. (2006). Talking the talk of the TESOL classroom. *ELT Journal*. 60(2), 133–141.

Watanabe, M., Hirose, K., Den, Y. and Minematsu, N. (2008). Filled pauses as cues to the complexity of upcoming phrases for native and non-native listeners. *Speech Communication*. 50, 81–94.

Webber, P. (2005). Interactive features in medical conference monologue. *English for Specific Purposes*. 24(2), 157–181.

Web of Science (2016). *Web of Science*. http://webofknowledge.com

White, L. (1987). Against comprehensible input: The input hypothesis and the development of second-language competence. *Applied Linguistics*. 8(2), 95–110.

Widdowson, H. G. (1972). The teaching of English as communication. *ELT Journal*. 27(1), 15–19.

Widdowson, H. G. (1978). *Teaching Language as Communication*. Oxford: Oxford University Press.

Willingham, W. W. and Cole, N. S. (2013). *Gender and Fair Assessment*. London: Routledge.

Willis, D. and Willis, J. (2007). *Doing Task-Based Teaching*. Oxford: Oxford University Press.

Wolf, J. P. (2008). The effects of backchannels on fluency in L2 oral task production. *System*. 36(2), 279–294.

Wong, J. S., Pursel, B., Divinsky, A. and Jansen, B. J. (2015). An analysis of MOOC discussion forum interactions from the most active users. In *Social Computing, Behavioral-Cultural Modeling, and Prediction*. New York: Springer International Publishing, pp. 452–457.

Xi, X., Higgins, D., Zechner, K. and Williamson, D. M. (2008). Automated Scoring of Spontaneous Speech Using SpeechRaterSM v1.0. *ETS Research Report Series*. 2, i–102.

Yates, L., Dahm, M. R., Roger, P. and Cartmill, J. (2016). Developing rapport in interprofessional communication: Insights for international medical graduates. *English for Specific Purposes*. 42, 104–116.

Young, R. and Weiyun He, A. (1998). *Talking and Testing: Discourse Approaches to the Assessment of Oral Proficiency*. Studies in Bilingualism, 14. Amsterdam and Philadelphia: John Benjamins Publishing Company.

Yu, G. (2007). Students' voices in the evaluation of their written summaries: Empowerment and democracy for test takers? *Language Testing*. 24, 539–73.

Yu, G. (2010). Lexical diversity in writing and speaking task performances. *Applied Linguistics*. 31(2), 236–259.

Yungzhong, L. (1985). Writing versus speech in foreign language teaching. *Wai Guo Yu*. 3(37), 12–15.

Index

Aboriginal conversation 127
academics 9, 24–5, 45, 124, 199, 213;
  classroom 70; corpus linguistics 202–3;
  information exchange 211; language
  testing 103, 120; privileged insider
  approach 141–3; research paradigms
  27–8; teaching speaking 71–2, 79, 84,
  92; use of English in 151
accents 57, 58, 65; *vs* intelligibility 62;
  native speakers 76–7; pronunciation
  and 60–1; speech perception of
  77, 171
accountant-client consultations 185–6
accuracy 21; communicative approach
  60; fluency and 53, 59; grammatical
  53, 77, 112–14, 116; intelligibility
  over 45; language testing 93; speaking
  101, 107, 108, 118–19; spoken
  language classroom 83–4, 159, 164
adjectives 33, 111, 119
adverbs 33, 41, 119, 140
Aethelstan site 208
affect 34–5, 92
Anderson, K. 72, 73
applied linguistics 3, 11, 59, 62, 90,
  199; English as lingua franca 45;
  future research 174, 190; information
  exchanges 210–12; journals in 204–5;
  language education and 157–8, 160;
  language teaching 201; language
  testing 87; new directions in 150–3;
  psycholinguistics 34; researching
  speech 33, 42, 123–5, 128, 135,
  137, 142; resources for 209–10, 212;
  teaching speaking 73
arguments and counter-arguments
  18–19, 52, 69–70, 113
Aristotle 19
articulation 4, 34, 63, 131, 144, 152

Assessing Languages for Specific Purposes
  (Douglas) 102
assessment of speaking: automated
  online tests 91; debate about oral
  89–90; development of 87; direct
  and indirect testing 105–6; domains
  of speaking 90–1; end points of
  continuum of oral test types 105;
  measurement of performance 88;
  oral 88–9; project 88; *see also* oral
  assessment
attitudes: early, to speech 18–20; spoken
  form of language 17; spoken language
  50; stress data 30–4
audio-lingual approaches 21, 65,
  158, 159
Auer, Peter 43
aural channel 8–9, 13, 35, 83, 131,
  194, 202
Australia 36, 102, 120, 127–8, 207

Bachman, L. F. 103
backchannels 100, 145–7
Bakhtin, M. 102
bald-on-record strategies 182
Barlow, M. 208
Beebe, L. M. 215
behaviour 4–5, 140, 178; backchannel
  147; cross-cultural studies of 200;
  English speaking 182, 184, 189, 191;
  interactive 81, 128; psycholinguistics
  studies 201; psychology and speech 40;
  studying 132; verbal 150
behaviourism 14, 15
Biber, D. 10, 25, 33, 40, 41
Blake, C. 143–5
Bodman, J. 214
brain 4, 14, 153, 218; activity 35, 137–8;
  functional magnetic resonance

imaging (FMRI) 35; psycholinguistics
studies 201–2; research ideas 193–4
Brazil, D. 42
British Council: English language
teachers 73; MyClass materials 76
British National Corpus 42, 202, 208
Brumfit, C. 53
Burns, A. 185, 186, 187
business studies 38, 151
Butler, F. A. 98

Cambridge Advanced Grammar of English
(Carter and McCarthy) 7, 54
Cambridge ESOL *see* English as a
Second or Other Language (ESOL)
Cambridge University Press 202
Canada 60, 120
CANCODE (Cambridge and
Nottingham Corpus of Discourse in
English) 202
Cantonese speakers: English 171, 175
Carter, R. 7, 50, 56, 93, 152
Centre for Spoken Language
Understanding: Oregon Graduate
Institute of Science and
Technology 208–9
Chafe, W. 9
channel 8, 9, 13
chat rooms 13, 114–15, 163, 168, 184
Cheng, W. 181–4
child language development 11, 13–15,
31, 136–9, 160–2, 201
Chinese: English lessons 203; Hong
Kong (HKC) 181–2, 183; spoken
corpora 209
Chomsky, N. 13, 14, 22, 27, 31, 160, 202
Chomskyian linguistics 53
Chomskyian theory 162
Cicero 19
CLARIN project 42
Clark, H. H. 147–50
clauses 9, 16, 37, 38, 39, 41, 44, 102,
169, 176; grammar 32, 113, 119; quasi-
94; researching speech 139–41
closings: conversation 38
CLT *see* communicative language
teaching (CLT)
COBUILD Corpus 202
coherence 108–10; oral assessment
112–14, 115
colloquial speech 51, 58, 61
common core features 45, 64
Common European Framework B1 117

communication: channel of 8, 9;
negotiation between persons 97; role
in language teaching 159–70. 213
communicative approaches 11, 53, 65;
accuracy 60; competence in 5, 23,
53; early influence of 67; language
teaching 22, 23; speaking assessment
91; speaking in classrooms 158–60
communicative language teaching
(CLT): role of spoken interaction in
162–7; task-based language teaching
(TBLT) 164–5; teacher talking time
(TTT) 163
competence 5, 13–15; communicative
5, 23, 53; concept of 14, 27, 162;
development of 161; discourse 100;
English language 117; language faculty
14, 15; linguistic 97; neurolinguistics
202; strategic 100; term 13
compliments 6, 169
computational linguistics 28, 29
conclusions, drawing of 217–18
context 10, 13–14, 28, 33–4, 36, 43, 97,
99, 101–3
conversation 4–6, 10, 33, 116;
arguments and counter-arguments
69–70; art of polite 21; competence
in 100; exploration of intercultural
expectations 181–5; language choice in
9–10; mechanics of 38–9; micro skills
100; nontransferability of patterns
across cultures 168–9; preconceptions
about 92–5; in pub 68; questions about
83; research into 5, 179, 200; showing
interest in 66–7; starting and finishing
66–7; teaching English 24–5, 33;
teaching profession and 214
conversation analysis (CA) 4–5, 15, 94,
98, 123, 152, 173, 190; interactional
linguistics and 43–4; interpreting
interactive behavior 128; research
38–40, 199; researching speaking
126–9; resources for 210, 212; second
language acquisition and 129, 151;
social sciences 16; typical analysis of
140–1
Conversation Gambits (Keller and
Warner) 69–70
cooking rice 55–6
Corax of Syracuse 18
corpus/corpora, use of 17, 24; corpus
linguistics 24, 28–9, 35, 40–4, 102,
126, 142, 147, 151, 153, 173–7,

199, 202–3; in research 33, 36, 40–4; speech corpora 208–9; spoken grammar 50, 52, 58; spoken language in textbooks *vs* 173–8; studies of 102, 142; teaching speaking 73; video approach to speech processing 147–50, 153

counter-arguments: arguments and 69–70; oral test conditions 100–1

Couper-Kuhlen, E. 139–41, 216

critical discourse analysis 90

critical linguistics 26, 151, 200

cross-cultural studies 127, 153, 168–9, 200–1, 214

culture/cultural factors 4, 6, 17, 57, 67, 127; assessing speech 90, 146; backgrounds 187–8; communication 123; conversational patterns 168–9; conversations 40; discussions 52; expression of disagreement 181–5; kissing 54; norms 69, 77; speaking skills 83–4; teaching pronunciation 61–2; testing *vs* learning 121; writing performance 200

Cunningham, S. 70, 71

cycle of research 189, 211, 216–17

Danielewicz, J. 9

data 6, 14, 15, 17, 26–30; speech 7, 30–4

data commentary 217–18

Davies, A. 59

Davies, C. E. 213

delivery 5–6, 19–20, 89–90, 93, 108–10, 120, 143, 201

Demosthenes 19

De Oratore (Quintilian) 19

Derwing, T. M. 64

descriptive linguistics 25, 30, 52, 57

dialect 57–8, 97

didactic focus-on-form 164

direct methods 22–3, 158

disagreement, expression of 181–5

disciplinary socialisation 142

discourse analysis 4, 5, 15, 16; arguments and counter-arguments 69–70; competence in 53, 100–1; influence on teaching speaking 69; research in 199, 212; speaking skills 37–40; speech assessment 90; teaching profession and 59, 214

Discourse Analysis for Language Teachers (McCarthy) 39

Discourse and Language Education (Hatch) 39

discourse markers/particles 24, 39, 58, 173–7

Discussions A–Z (Wallwork) 51, 53

Douglas, D. 86, 90–1, 102, 103

drilling 159, 161

Du Bois, J. 43

dyslexia 35, 131

education 20–1

Educational Testing Services (ETS) 107; Internet-based TOEFL speaking test 107–10; TOEFL® iBT 111–12; user-friendly interface with public 110

Effort Code 134, 135

Egypt, ancient 18

eighteenth century 20–1

Eisenstein, M. 214

electroencephalography 137–8

electronic media 13, 126, 177, 184, 202

ELF *see* English as a lingua franca (ELF)

Elizabethan England 20

ellipsis 32, 41, 59, 102

Ellis, R. 164, 215

elocution 21

ELT (English language teaching) 23; adult books 58; communicative materials in classroom 67; professionalization of community 73; publishing 77, 85; staff 77

E-mail 6, 13

empiricism 14, 15, 26, 28, 30, 42, 132–3, 152, 202

English 32, 39, 139–40, 152; backchannel cues 146–7; Cantonese speakers 171, 175; globalization processes 151; Hong Kong 151, 174–5, 181–5; Native Speakers of (NSE) 181, 182–3; Queen's 96; Received Pronunciation (RE) 96; Singaporean 36; stress timed language 30; US American 152; world 90, 95, 151

English as a lingua franca (ELF) 44, 45, 62, 90, 95–6, 110, 151, 175; oral presentations 178; speech rate effects 178–81

English as an international language (EIL) 95

English as a Second or Other Language (ESOL) 106; further work 190–1; potential reader project 191–2; speaking skill assessment 189; University of Cambridge 96

English for Academic Purposes 71–3, 151

English for specific purposes (ESP) 71,
185–7
epistemology 124
error 16–17, 23, 44, 64, 91, 113–14,
148, 149
error correction 163–4
ESOL *see* English as a Second or Other
Language (ESOL)
ESP *see* English for specific purposes (ESP)
ethnography 26, 27, 127, 142, 159, 173,
200–1, 213
event-related potential (ERP) methods
137–8
Everyday Listening and Speaking
(Cunningham and Moor) 70, 71
experimental design: investigating oral
performance 145–7
experimental method: researching
speech 144
Exploring Spoken English (Carter and
McCarthy) 51, 52, 54

faculty of speech, of language 3, 6,
12–15, 17, 199–201
feedback 84, 145, 147, 163–5, 180
feminine: pitch and 133–4
fillers 40; conversation 81–2
Fletcher, M. 65, 66–7
Florez, M. C. 84
fluency: accuracy and 59; conversational
fillers 81–2; in delivery 108; group
approach to investigate improvement
143–5; impressions on 61; oral
assessment 112–13, 114, 116;
preconceptions of speech 94–5;
speech production 44; students
gaining 65, 67, 86
Fluency and Accuracy (Hammerly) 59
focus-on-form 163–4
Ford, C. E. 140
formulaic exchanges: conversation 38
framing 130, 174, 176
French 30, 54, 120
Frequency Code 134, 135
Fulcher, G. 87, 88, 94, 98–9
functional magnetic resonance imaging
(FMRI) 35, 153, 193–5

Gan, Z. 97
Gardner, R. 127, 128
gaze 38, 126, 137, 148, 193, 195, 203
genres of speaking 6, 44, 72, 91, 92; oral
assessment 101–4, 105; privileged
insider approach 141–2; professional

speaking 185–9; spoken and written
form 40–1
Germany 120, 152
gesture 17, 84, 137, 143, 147–50,
193–5, 203
Ginther, A. 88
Goodwin, C. 31
Graded Examination of Spoken English
(GESE) 117, 118–19, 120
grammar 4, 5, 15, 200, 201, 202;
assessing range and accuracy 113,
114; corpus-based approaches to 7,
28, 33, 40; describing of speech 32;
descriptively oriented models of 52;
grammatical range 112, 113, 114;
language choices 40–4; language
functions 119–20; researching speech
139–41; speech data about word
7; spoken 50, 52, 58; traditional/
pedagogic 20, 21, 32; translation
methods 21–2, 160
Grammar of Speech, A (Brazil) 42
grammaticalisation 41, 134
Greek 21
Greeks, ancient 18–19
Grice's Maxims of Cooperative
Conversation 135
Gunn, B. 18
Güssenhoven, C. 132–5

Halliday, M. 11, 102
Hammerly, H. 59, 60
Hamp-Lyons, Liz 89, 121
Handbook of English Pronunciation
(2015) 65
Hargreaves, R. 65, 66–7
Hatch, E. 39
Haynes, L. A. 215
hesitation strategies 82–3
high-stakes testing 89, 92, 106–21, 189
Hincks, R. 178–81
Hirschberg, J. 135
historical corpus linguistics 41
historical linguistics 29
historical perspectives 17–23
Hoey, M. 214
Hong Kong 151, 174–5, 181–5
Howatt, A. P. R. 21
human-machine speech 203
Hymes, D. 53

iBT/next generation TOEFL *see*
TOEFL (Test of English as a Foreign
Language)

idioms 6, 51, 58, 114, 116
immigration: language functions 119–20; speaking assessment of immigrant test takers 189–92; UK government testing 117–21
infants: understanding of speech 137–8
information overload 9
innate cognitive model of language 12, 14–15
innovation 11, 13
input hypothesis 160–2
inspiration for research topics 212–15
Institutio Oratoria (Quintilian) 19
Instruction of Ptah-ho-tep and the Instruction of Kegemni, The (Gunn) 18
Integrated Skills in English (ISE) 117, 118–19
intelligibility 6, 11, 44–5, 60, 62, 64–5, 170
interactional linguistics (IL) 42–4, 129, 140, 152–3
interactivity 13, 43, 171, 191; competence 91; language teaching 167–9; oral assessment 102, 104, 109; researching speech 141, 149–50; speaking skills 113, 116, 119–20, 128; teaching 78–83, testing 94, 96–100
intercultural pragmatics 40, 57, 123, 170, 182, 185
International Association of Teachers of English as a Foreign Language (IATEFL) 206–7
International English Language Testing System (IELTS) 76, 78–9, 89, 96, 107, 112–17
Internet 12–13, 76, 143–4, 202–3
intonation 5, 6, 17, 34, 76, 128; cementing theory of 134–5; in delivery 108–12; language and ethology 132–5; linguistic feature 38; online resources 209–10; research of 132–9, 200; teaching pronunciation 63, 84
Ito, K. 136–40

James, L. 30
Japan/Japanese 54, 61, 139, 140, 146–7, 215
Jeffries, A. A. 213
Johnson, M. 92–3
journals 12, 204–6

Kaplan 81, 82
Keller, E. 69, 70
kissing 54–5

Knowledge of Language and Life (KOLL) assessment 107; UK Border Agency 117–21
knowledge schema 189
Kormos, J. 34
Krashen, S. 23, 160–1, 162
Krych, M. A. 147–50

Lam, P. 173–6, 178
language 123, 201; affective aspects of 34; attitudes to spoken form of 17; awareness of 23, 52, 167; change 13, 42; functional magnetic resonance imaging (FMRI) and 35, 153; functions of 119–20; innate cognitive model of 14–15; innovation in 11, 13; levels of analysis 35–44; lingua franca 44, 45; of love-making 54–5; performance of learners 86–7; speaking 6–7; speech processing and demands 169, 170; speech *vs* 11–12; studies 13–24, 29–30
language acquisition: classroom management influencing 163–4; first 11–12, 136–9; role of spoken interaction in 160–2; second 11, 15, 23, 29; study of first, and prosody 136–9; *see also* second language acquisition (SLA)
language assessment: development of 87; nature of testing 87–8; spoken performances 86–7; testing 88–9; *see also* assessment of speaking
language faculty 12, 13, 14, 199
language teaching: communicative approaches 22, 23; eighteenth century and beyond 20–3; interactivity 167; natural or direct methods 22
Latin 21, 45
learning acquisition distinction 160–2
Lee, Y-W. 104
legal tasks and arguments 12–13, 20
Lennon, P. 61
levels of analysis 35–45
Lewis, M. 67, 68
lexical resource 112, 113, 114
lexicography 29
Liberman, A.M. 129–31, 132, 216
Liberman, I. 132
linearity of speech 43
lingua franca 44, 45; English as a 62, 90, 95
linguistics 11, 15, 26; attitudes in speech data 31; branches of 29; corpus 24,

28–9, 35, 41, 102, 151, 199, 202–3;
discipline of 87; interactional 43, 140,
152; rationalism and empiricism in
14; science of language 29–30; speech
and writing 12; usefulness of natural
speech 31
listener: backchannels 145–7; process of
understanding speech 31–2
listening 8, 12, 39, 57, 58, 70–1,
103, 104
logic 15, 20; philosophical 26
*Longman Grammar of Spoken and Written
English* (Biber) 24–5, 33
Lougheed, L. 81
love: language of 54
love-making: language of 54–5
Lynch, T. 72, 73

McCarthy, M. 7, 50, 56, 93, 152
Making Polite Noises (Hargreaves and
Fletcher) 65, 66–7
masculine: pitch and 133–4
matched-guise approach 171
materials development 65–83
medical discourse 125; conference
presentations 102; patient-practitioner
37–8, 102, 169, 185
memory 29, 201
Michigan Corpus of Spoken Academic
English (MICASE) 41
mobile phones 76
models and standards 52–65
Moor, P. 70, 71
Moore, S. 185, 186, 187
morphology 5, 29, 60
Morse code 30
Morton, J. 141–3, 216
motoric channel 8, 9, 13, 131
motor theory: of speech 131
multimodal approach: language view
148–9; research question 147–8
Munro, M. J. 64
Mushin, I. 127, 128

National Institute of Education in
Singapore 36
National Qualifications Framework,
UK 117
National Research and Development
Centre 190
Natural acquisition 20
natural approach 160–2
natural speech 24, 31, 50, 93, 100–1,
125, 152, 171, 174

neurolinguistics 4, 29, 170, 199, 201–2
news texts 33, 36
next-turn onset 139
nonempirical approach: research 28
notional-functional approach 65–7, 163
nouns 33, 202
null hypotheses 173, 183

Occupational English Test (OET) 102
Ohala, J. J. 132–5
Oller, J. 89
O'Malley, J. M. 97
online resources 207–8
openings: conversation 38
opinions: oral presentation of 93–4
oral approach 158
oral assessment: cultures of testing *vs*
learning 121; debate about 89–90;
direct and indirect testing 105–6;
end points of continuum of oral test
types 105; genres and skills 101–4;
high-stakes testing 106–7; IELTS
speaking test 112–17; interactive
speech with examiner 97–8; Internet-
based TOEFL speaking test 107–10;
language 88–9; three high-stakes
tests 106–21; TOEFL® iBT 111–12;
UK Border Agency Knowledge
of Language and Life 117–21; *see
also* IELTS (International English
Language Testing System); test
designers
oral channel 8, 9, 13, 131, 194, 202
oratory 19, 21
ornamentation, language 20

paradigms: definition of 27; research
26–30
Partners 3 (Lewis) 67, 68
patient-practitioner discourse 37–8, 102,
169, 185
pausing 13, 37–8, 40, 61, 83, 93, 110,
112, 114–15, 118, 127–8, 200
perception of speech 131, 171
performance 13–17, 23, 27, 145–7, 161;
see also assessment of speaking
personally-oriented nature of speech
170–1
philosophy: epistemology 124; of
language 17, 19, 29; logic 26; of
psychology 15
phoneme 63
phonemics 5
phones 63

phonetics 4–5, 29, 63, 83, 123, 131, 133, 135, 152, 159, 173, 199

phonology 7, 60, 64, 123; language functions 120; research 4, 5, 29, 44, 123, 130, 200

pitch: feminine and masculine 133–4

placement learning 187–9

Plato 19

politeness 6, 21, 65–7, 73, 183–4

position papers 129–32; first language acquisition and prosody 136–9; language and ethnology 132–5; qualitative principles of clause, grammar and interaction 139–41

potential reader project: extension by replication and qualitative phase 180–1; extension to classroom talk 175–8; extension to placement learning 187–9; replication and extension to online environment 183–5; speaking as multisensory skill 194–5

pragmatics 4, 5, 29, 123, 173, 199, 200; behaviour 57; historical 19; intercultural 170, 181–5; research 36, 40, 45; skills 6, 29, 78–83; teaching speaking 76; variational 151

presentation of research findings 217–18

privileged insider approach: researching speech 141–3

Production Code 134, 135

professional speaking genre 101–2, 185–9

project ideas: discourse particles in corpus data and textbooks 173–4; English for specific purposes (ESP) classroom 185–7; extension by replication and qualitative phase 180–1; extension to classroom talk 175–8; extension to placement learning 187–9; extension to test conclusions 191–2; gesture and speech processing using fMRI scanning 193–5; Hong Kong Chinese and native speakers of English 181, 182; intercultural expectations in conversation 181–5; neural processing of speech and gestures 193; professional speaking genre for classroom 185; replication and extension to online environment 183–5; speaking assessment of low education immigrant test takers 189–92; speech rate in English as

lingua franca presentations 178–81; spoken language in textbooks *vs* a corpus 173–8

pronunciation 4, 5, 6, 20, 42, 44, 77; accents and 60–1; accent *vs* intelligibility 62; assessment criteria 86, 101, 108–16, 119–20; empirical research 51, 152; models and standards 51, 59–65; online resources 203, 209–10; Quintilian on 20; received (RP) 96; social and cultural aspects of teaching 61–2, 64; speech production 44; teaching of 59–61, 63

prosody 5, 126, 141, 203; first language acquisition and 136–9; interface with syntax 42–4; research into 34, 35, 36; speech assessment 104

psycholinguistics 4, 5, 29, 34, 199, 201

psychology 15, 40, 200, 201

psychometric testing 89, 103

public speaking: ancient advice on 18

punctuation: correctness *vs* intelligibility 64

qualitative approaches 26, 123, 124, 125–8, 132, 139–43, 180–1, 184, 190–1

quantitative approaches 26, 123, 124, 125–8, 132, 143–50, 178–80, 181, 184, 192, 200

Queen's English 96

questioning 72–3, 131, 191; accountant-client consultations 185–7

Quintilian 19–20

rationalism 14, 15

real speech 49–65

real-time processing constraints 10, 84, 168, 169–70

received pronunciation (RP) 96

record keeping 12

redressive language 181–2

Reform Movement 21

register analysis 10, 41, 102

Renaissance 19, 20

repetition 40, 43, 61, 94, 102

research: analysing speaking skills 37–40; attitudes to speech data 30–4; classical paradigms in speaking 26–30; cycle of 216–17; drawing conclusions in 217–18; empirical *vs* nonempirical approaches 28; frameworks in study of speech 34–5; gap between output and teacher's knowledge base 59; language

choices 40–4; levels of analysis in language study 35–44; questions 216; *see also* project ideas
research borders and boundaries 199–200; corpus linguistics of 202–3; ethnographic or cross-cultural studies of 200–1; neurolinguistic studies of 201–2; new technologies for 203; psycholinguistic studies 201
Researching Pedagogic Tasks: Second Language Learning Teaching and Testing (Bygate) 165
researching speech: advantage of speech over writing 130–1; approaches 123–5; combining gesture, language and speech processing 147–50; contrasting approaches in 132–50; conversation analysis (CA) 126–9; disciplinary socialisation 142; epistemology 124; experimental design investigating oral performance 145–7; first language acquisition and prosody 136–9; group approach to fluency improvement 143–5; interpreting interactive behavior 128; introducing an experimental method 144; language and ethology 132–5; motor theory of speech 131; multimodal approach to research question 147–8; new directions in 150–3; qualitative principles of clause, grammar and interaction 139–41; qualitative privileged insider approach 141–3; quantitative and qualitative approaches to 125–9; rhetorical questions showing focus 127; theory-driven, positional and ideas-based approaches 129–31; young infants' understanding of speech 137–8
research resources: applied linguist with interest in spoken discourse 210; information exchanges 211; journals and e-journals 204–6; online 207–8; online pronunciation and intonation 209–10; project with spoken discourse 210–12; skills summaries 216–18; societies and organisations 206–7; sources of inspiration 212–15; speech corpora 208–9; speech recognition and text-to-speech 209
reservation: for counter-arguments 69–70
restarts 31
rhetoric 8, 17, 18–21, 69, 107, 142–3; rhetorical questions 127

Rhetoric (Aristotle) 19
rhythm 5, 1, 30, 63, 84, 108, 136
rice: activity of cooking 55; speakers and setting 55–6
Riggenbach, H. 94–5, 100
Rivers, W. M. 63
role-play 77, 185, 187–9
Romans 19–20
Ruhlemann, C. 152
Russian: spoken corpora 209; stress timed language 30

Santa Barbara Corpus of Spoken English 43
Saussure, Ferdinand de 27, 43
second language acquisition (SLA) 4, 6, 34, 50, 98, 141, 151, 153, 166; accent *vs* intelligibility 62; communicative approach to 23, 60; community of 129; fluency as goal in 11, 143–5; linguistics 29; natural approach for 162; pronunciation in 123; speaking rates for 178; studies of 13, 15, 22, 25, 165; theories of 11, 41–2, 162
Secure English Language Test (SELT) 117
Seidlhofer, B. 63, 64
self-repair/correction 10, 92, 94, 95, 100, 102, 147–8, 152
semantics 4, 28, 29
seminar skills 57, 72–3, 84, 110
Sheridan, T. 4
silence 18, 126–8, 200
Silent Way 163
Simpson, J. 189–92
simulations 185–9
Singaporean English 36
SiS (speech is special) 131
Skehan, P. 53
Skinner, B. F. 15
social interaction: speaking skills 37–40
sociolinguistics 5, 26, 29, 38, 123
sophistry 19
Sophists 18–19
Spada, N. 53
speaking 3, 4; core skills 4–5; digital technologies 24; everyday listening and 71; expressing an opinion 93–4; facets of 6–7; historical perspectives on 17; key word search 12; models and standards for teaching 49–65; research paradigms for researching 26–30; skill of 3–7, 37–40, 83–4, 103; *see also* assessment of speaking; research borders and boundaries

Speaking: From Intention to Articulation
(Levelt) 34
Speaking (Rignall and Furneaux) 72
speech: attitudes toward 10–13; corpora
24, 208–9; data 7, 30–4; early
attitudes to 18–20; experimental
design investigating 145–7; findings
counter to expectations 24–5;
language choices in 9–10; in language
studies 13–24; linearity of 43; nature
of *vs* writing 7–13; perception of 171;
problem of preconceptions about
94–5; processing of 169, 170; process
of understanding 31–2; production
of 8, 44, 147–50; psychology and 40;
research into 5, 34–5; social aspects
of 8; teaching 21; transferability
into writing 11; young infants'
understanding of 137–8; *see also*
researching speech; teaching speaking
speech recognition 44, 90, 109, 203,
208, 209
Speer, S. J. 136–40
Spoken British National Corpus 202
spoken language: conceptualisation of
clauses 139; models and standards of
49–65; rhythm in 30; *see also* teaching
speaking
stereotypes of speech perception 171
Straube, B. 193–4
stress timing 30
Study Speaking (Lynch and Anderson)
72–3
syllable timing 30
synchronous computer mediated
communication (SCMC) 145
syntax 4, 5, 29

Takehashi, T. 215
target language: issues in learning 57–8
task-based language teaching (TBLT)
164–5, 166
task-based learning materials: English
for academic purposes 71–2; seminar
skills 72–3
task-based syllabus: everyday listening
and speaking 71; teaching speaking 70
Tasks in Second Language Learning
(Samuda and Bygate) 165
Taylor, L. 96
Teaching and Researching Listening
(Rost) 8
Teaching and Researching Writing
(Hyland) 7

teaching speaking 5–6, 157; audio-
lingual and notional-functional
approaches 65; building skills 83–4;
classroom practice and research
167–71; current scene in materials
73–83; didactic focus-on-form 164;
early influence of communicative
approach 67; evolution of materials for
65–73; influence of discourse analytic
approaches 69; input hypothesis
160, 161, 162; interactive potential
of spoken form *vs* written 168;
interactivity 167; language pedagogy
157–8; learning *vs* acquisition
162; role in communicative
language teaching 162–7; role in
language acquisition 160–1; role
of communication 159; role of
teacher-student spoken interaction
166; speech production under real-
time processing 169, 170; spoken
discourse and deliverer 170–1; status
in classrooms 158–62; stereotypes and
speech perception 171; task-based
language teaching (TBLT) 164–5,
166; task-based learning materials
71–2; task-based syllabus approaches
70; thinking time 82–3; word cloud of
teacher challenges in 75; word cloud
of teacher enjoyment in 74
TEDtalks 76
Temperley, M. S. 63
TESOL (association promoting English
language teaching) 207
TESOL Quarterly (journal) 64–5
test designers: direct and indirect testing
105–6; formats and interactions
96–101; genres and skills 101–4;
integrated or discrete testing of skills
103–4; linking performance within
and outside the test 104–5; pairing
test takers 98–9; role and influence
of test methods 103; speaking as
challenge for 92–105; test formats
and task types 96; understanding
the construct 92–5; *see also* oral
assessment
Test of Spoken English 95
text analysis 16
text-to-speech 44, 203, 209
thinking time: hesitation strategies 82–3
Thompson, S. 139–41, 216
TOEFL (Test of English as a Foreign
Language) 78, 89; format and rating

process 108; independent speaking rubrics 109–10; negative features in oral discourse *vs* IELTS 115; online materials for practice 109; positive features in oral discourse *vs* IELTS 115–16; speaking rubrics 108; speaking test 96, 107–10, 112; TOEFL® iBT 111–12; user-friendly interface 110
Tønnessen, F. E. 132
total physical response (TPR) 22
transferability: speech into writing 11
transition-relevance point (TRP): conversation 38
Trinity College London 117; Graded Examinations in Spoken English and Integrated Skills in English 117, 118–19
Tsui, A. B. M. 181–4
turn-taking 34, 84, 100, 126, 145
Tyler, A. E. 213

UK Border Agency (UKBA): Knowledge of Language and Life 107, 117–21
Underhill, N. 87–8
United Kingdom: English as Second or Other Language (ESOL) 106; testing for immigration 117–21
University of Cambridge 96
University of Washington 94
university registers 10
Uppstad, P. H. 132
Ur, P. 60–1, 63

Utterance Structure: Developing Grammars Again (Klein and Purdue) 42

Vachek, J. 11
Van Avermaet, P. 166
Variation Across Speech and Writing (Biber) 40
video corpus approach: gesture, language and speech processing 147–50
Viney, K. 82–3
Viney, P. 82–3
vocabulary: language choices 40–4; spoken language 50

Wallwork, A. 51, 55
Warner, S. T. 69, 70
Widdowson, H. 23, 53, 159
Wolf, J. P. 146–7
word clouds 73, 74, 75, 77
World English (WE) 90, 95, 151
World Standard English (WSE) 95
writing: aspects of production 8; key word search 12; language choices in 9–10; nature of speech *vs* 7–13; social aspects of 8; transferability of speech into 11

young infants: understanding of speech 137–8
YouTube 76
Yungzhong, L. 50

Zeno of Elea 18